YALE UNIVERSITY PUBLICATIONS
IN ANTHROPOLOGY

NUMBER SEVENTY-FOUR

THE HAN INDIANS

A COMPILATION OF ETHNOGRAPHIC
AND HISTORICAL DATA ON THE
ALASKA–YUKON BOUNDARY AREA

CORNELIUS OSGOOD

NEW HAVEN
PUBLISHED BY THE
DEPARTMENT OF ANTHROPOLOGY
YALE UNIVERSITY

1971

EDITORIAL NOTE. The Yale University Publications in Anthropology embody the results of researches in the general field of anthropology which are directly conducted or otherwise sponsored by the University Department of Anthropology or by the Division of Anthropology in the Peabody Museum of Natural History. The issues, ranging in size from brief papers to extensive monographs, are numbered consecutively as independent contributions and appear at irregular intervals.

YALE UNIVERSITY PUBLICATIONS
IN ANTHROPOLOGY
NUMBER 74

THE HAN INDIANS

A COMPILATION OF ETHNOGRAPHIC
AND HISTORICAL DATA ON THE
ALASKA—YUKON BOUNDARY AREA

CORNELIUS OSGOOD

NEW HAVEN
PUBLISHED BY THE
DEPARTMENT OF ANTHROPOLOGY
YALE UNIVERSITY

1971

LIBRARY OF CONGRESS CATALOG CARD NUMBER: 76–156892

MICHAEL D. COE
Editor

ANNE F. WILDE
Assistant Editor

PRINTED IN THE UNITED STATES OF AMERICA

CONTENTS

iii

ILLUSTRATIONS

TEXT FIGURES

PLATES

ACKNOWLEDGMENTS

This monograph has been built upon a thirty-page paper published by Ferdinand Schmitter over sixty years ago, and it is timely to render tribute to those rare individuals who, without any professional obligation, provided irreplaceable ethnographic data. I do so here. I am also grateful to my colleague Richard Slobodin not only for placing an unpublished paper on the Han at my disposal, but also for reading my manuscript and giving it his approval. To another colleague, Catharine McClellan, I owe thanks for allowing me to read several unpublished manuscripts on Indian groups to the south of the Han as well as for her drawing several rare sources to my attention. Harry Hoijer and Michael Krauss helped me by answering questions, and the latter supplied a most useful statement. A third linguist, Paul Newman, advised me in adjusting the orthography for the press.

I also wish to state that there have been so many editorial changes in this manuscript, including the elimination of thirteen bibliographic items to which text references were not made (Campbell, Kirkby, McClellan, et al.) that the author must relinquish responsibility for conformation to the original copy submitted.

For aid in findings Han specimens and in obtaining photographs of them, I must thank William Sturtevant of the Smithsonian Institution, Washington, and Judy Thompson of the National Museum of Man, Ottawa. Two of the maps were drawn by Rosanne Rowen; the sketches are the work of Carl R. Wester. After the manuscript was submitted for publication, it was critically read by June Helm, who not only noted several corrections but suggested some appreciated emendations.

Publication of the manuscript has been made possible by a gift from William A. Castleton. A lesser amount of financial aid has come from the Department of Anthropology and the Peabody Museum of Yale Univeristy.

Finally I wish to express my appreciation and affection for Soo Sui-ling whose perfection as a typist is surpassed by the solace she provided as a wife during the inevitable anxieties and vexations that are involved in contriving a volume such as this one.

Cornelius Osgood

Yale University, 1971

Introduction

THE PRIMARY PURPOSE of this paper is to present the available ethnographic information on the culture of the Han Indians as it existed at approximately the time of first contact with Europeans or, let us say, during the middle of the nineteenth century. The Han are Athapaskan-speaking Indians who occupy the country bordering the Yukon River, including some of its tributaries, roughly between 64° and 65°30′ north latitude. The Alaska–Canada boundary line now divides their territory almost exactly in half (Fig. 1).

The sources of data on the culture of the Han merely by chance are more diverse than is usual. As with most Northern Athapaskan groups, their first contacts with Europeans resulted from the expanding fur trade. Two decades later, however, the Han country became significant to all officials concerned with determining the border between Canada and Russian America, and various surveying expeditions passed through it. Then, after a quarter of a century during which gold prospectors searched the country, in 1898 the Han suffered or enjoyed, depending upon a person's prejudice, one of the most concentrated invasions of white men into the north that history has recorded, for the Klondike, the very symbol of a gold rush, lies in the southern part of their territory. Finally, the twentieth century brought a few ethnographers into the area just as this northland merged into the united world of the automobile and the airplane.

No doubt it is partly on account of the unusual number and kinds of intrusions that we have relatively little data from anthropologists on the aboriginal life of the natives living on the banks of the upper Yukon River itself. The adjacent Kutchin nation to the north and northeast has been the source of several monographs embracing more or less of a general ethnographic reconstruction, but over 90 percent of the information pertains to hinterland tribes whose actual contacts with the great Yukon River were uncertain before the Hudson's Bay Company's trading posts were erected, and largely periodic thereafter. For various reasons including the obvious one, anthropologists have preferred to work first with Indians who are more removed from the distractions of the modern world with its fast-changing technology and customs.

If the lack of ethnographic data on the upper Yukon River tribes is one reason that leads me to present this summary, there are also others. Unquestionably, the variety of early commentators on the Han challenges a professional to interpret and to interrelate their observations, which are often of a casual nature or show an understandable lack of sophistication with respect to the people they encountered. Almost all of these sources are out of print and often not readily accessible. Therefore it is expected that the collation and reprinting of the older reports will prove a convenience to ethnographers and others concerned with these Indians.

1

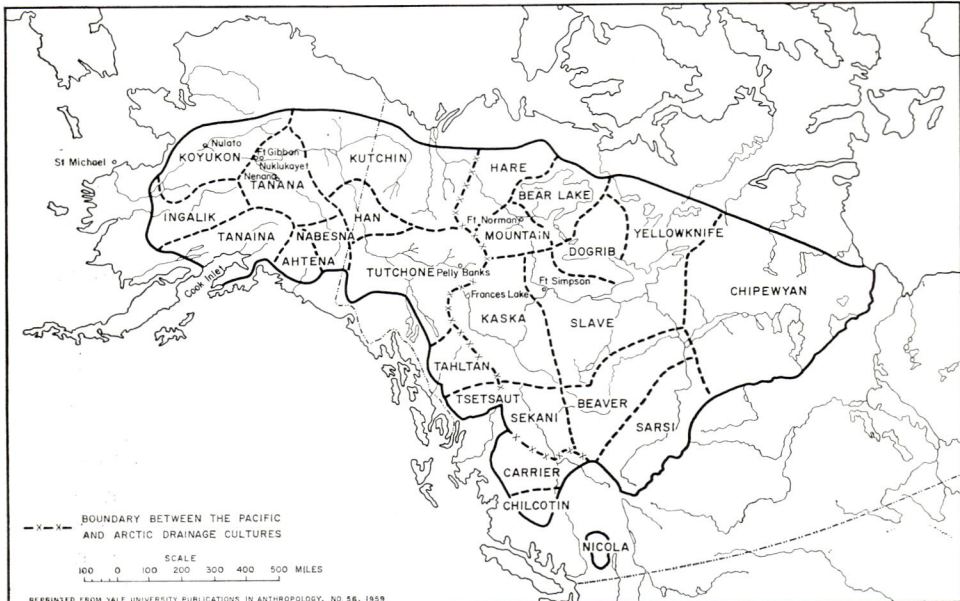

FIG. 1. Distribution of the Northern Athapaskan Indians.

It may be added that the best of the nineteenth-century information is inevitably based on observation, as verbal communication with most Athapaskans, save in the rare case, was a minimal affair. Before going further, let me state that in this paper the term Athapaskan will in all instances refer to the Northern division of those people, and not to the Pacific or Southwestern.

Secondly, there is the long-postponed opportunity to present the accessory notes on the Han which were accumulated in their territory when the writer was engaged in ethnographic field work on the Kutchin during the summer of 1932. Few though these may be, they provide the sinews with which to sew the pieces of the culture together.

Also, I have used the occasion to gather together the incidental information on culture change that inevitably rewarded the search for data on the aboriginal Han society. Recording this material by category and periods will not only raise some problems for special consideration at the end of this paper but should also assist those who in the future will be concerned with the acculturation of the Han.

Finally, I am very much aware that there remains a need to collect and collate the existing data on the aboriginal culture of at least one-third of the Athapaskan groups in Canada and Alaska. This must be done before effective studies can be undertaken for the area as a whole. Therefore, not least important is an effort to achieve a method of presentation which can serve as a model toward that end, although certainly one on which improvements can be made.

History

The survey of the available material may properly begin by considering the history of the Han country and the adjacent stretches of the Yukon River from which the contacts with civilization came. According to the record, Robert Campbell was the first European to reach the upper Yukon River when, on June 16, 1843, he drifted down to the mouth of the river he had earlier named the Pelly (Fig. 2). Since the beginning of the nineteenth century, the fur trade had been extended westward up the Liard River from the Mackenzie into British Columbia. Despite the difficulties of transportation over this route, Campbell had succeeded in erecting a Hudson's Bay Company post on Dease Lake in 1838, and then in 1840 discovered the upper reaches of the river that led him three years later to the Yukon. Once there, however, he encountered a short distance below the mouth of the Pelly what apparently were Tutchone Indians who warned him of others below them, claiming the latter were cannibals, whereupon Campbell and his companions turned back and retraced their route upstream (Campbell 1958: 66–71; Mathews 1968: 48–9).

The expansion of the English fur trade had also been extended to the delta of the Mackenzie River, John Bell having established Fort Macpherson near the mouth of the Peel River in 1840. Then in 1844 the latter crossed over to the Porcupine and descended it to the place where this river emptied into the Yukon. His intention, like Campbell's, was discovery, with an eye to extending the trading activities of the Hudson's Bay Company. There is no evidence and little likelihood that he met any of the Han on this initial journey, any more than Campbell had on his. Bell's route, however, was retraced by Alexander Murray who, during a year's residence between June 25, 1847, and June 5, 1848, established Fort Yukon on the right bank of the river of that name about three miles above the mouth of the Porcupine. During this period, Murray certainly did encounter many Han Indians who were attracted to the fort.

Without comprehending what Murray had accomplished, Campbell returned to the Yukon with nine men and on June 1, 1848, established Fort Selkirk on an island in the mouth of the Pelly (Campbell 1958: 81). After wintering three years at this post, he started downstream June 5, 1851, on a journey of exploration, naming the White and Stewart rivers as he passed them. He stopped at Han Indian camps along the way and from them learned that Murray's fort was on the same river. Proceeding thence, he was greeted by William Hardisty, who had been with him at Fort Selkirk in 1848. As Murray had just started up the Porcupine for Fort Macpherson, Campbell set out after a night's sleep to catch up with him, and having done so was associated with him in the journey as far as Fort Simpson, from which place he returned by his original route to Fort Selkirk on October 17 (Campbell 1958: 110–23; Mathews 1968: 50–8).

On May 14, 1852, Campbell (1958: 132–8) went down the river to Fort Yukon and up to La Pierre House again (Fig. 2), bringing back supplies on July 26. It is said that they included a cow, which, if true, and I find it quite incredible, must

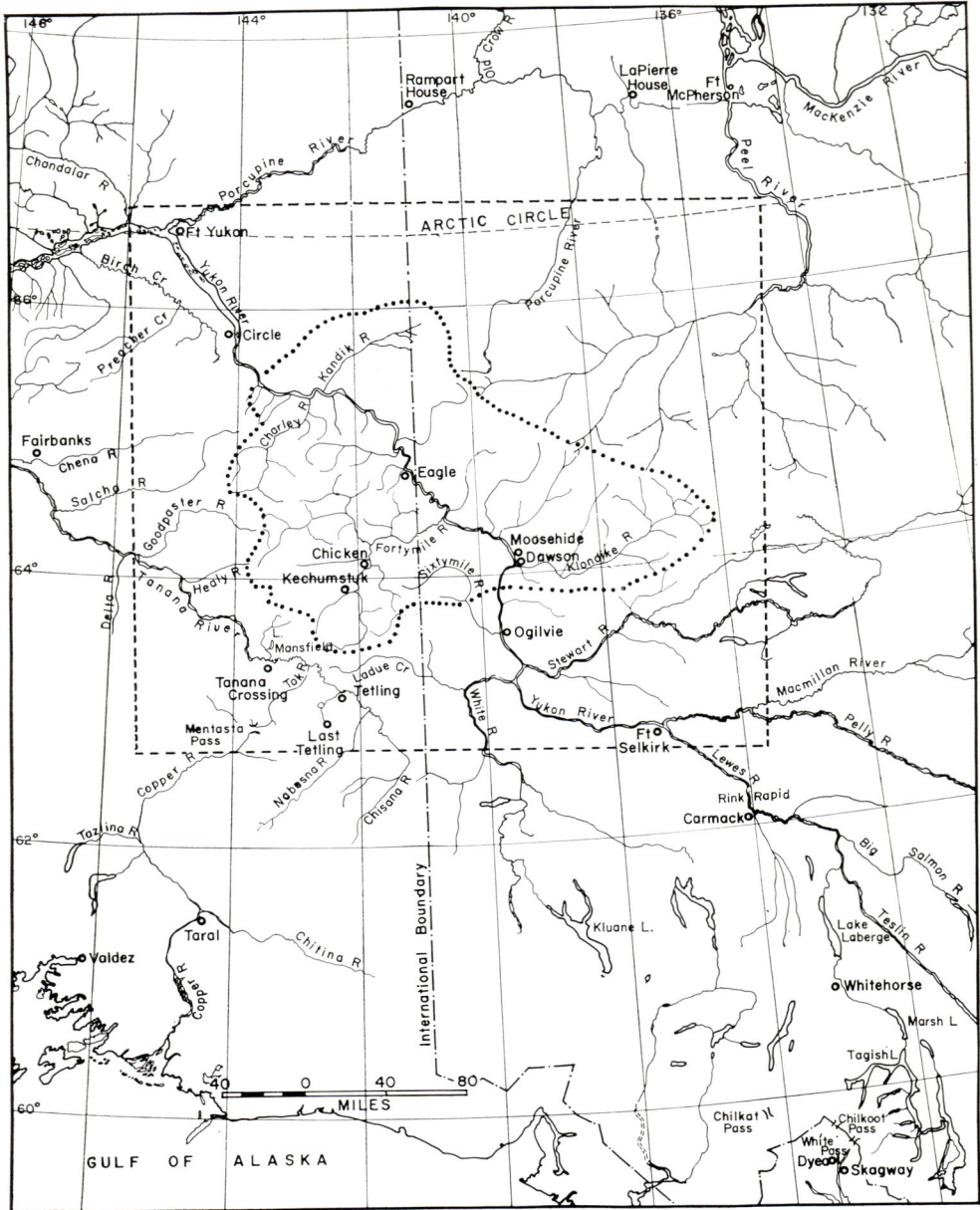

Fig. 2. Map of the Alaska–Yukon boundary area.

have been a surprise to the Indians along the way as well as to John Stewart and the other men who had been re-erecting buildings taken from the unstable island site to a more suitable one on the left bank of the Yukon below the mouth of the Pelly (Mathews 1968: 58).

Then on August 19, 1852, twenty-seven Chilkat Indians[1] arrived on five rafts and attacked the post, angered because of the interference with their trade. As it happened, most of Campbell's men were away and Campbell was fortunate to escape with his life. The Chilkat stole what they wanted and destroyed everything else, leaving the fort with no supplies for the winter. Campbell was thus forced to abandon it and he retreated up the Pelly with part of his men. The others he sent down the river to Fort Yukon with Stewart, who was just returning from a trip to that post, thus accounting for the seventh passage of Hudson's Bay men through Han territory by 1852, not counting that of the interpreter Antoine Hoole in October 1851 (Anon. 1916: 8; Campbell 1958: 110–23, 127–32, 138; Mathews 1968: 58–61). The site of Fort Selkirk remained abandoned for decades thereafter.

During at least part of the 1850s, William Hardisty was in charge of Fort Yukon as we have already learned, the year 1854, besides 1851, being specifically mentioned (Whymper 1868: 230). Strachan Jones was another early and significant figure among what must have been a series of Hudson's Bay Company men at the fort. While referring to this early period, I should add that Ivan Lukeen, a Russian Creole from St. Michael, had pushed up as far as Fort Yukon in the summer of 1863, thus proving that the Kvichpak and Yukon were one great river (Raymond 1900: 19–20). Lukeen repeated his trip in 1866 accompanied by Frank Ketchum and Michael Laberge, explorers for the Western Union Telegraph Company which since 1855 had been seeking a land route for a line connecting America with Europe. Then on March 11, 1867, Ketchum and Laberge alone left Nulato for Fort Yukon by dog team, arriving at the latter post on May 9 (Dall 1870a: 63, 277). When the river was free of ice, the two men went on by canoe as far as the site of Fort Selkirk, passing through Han territory again on their return to Fort Yukon which they reached on June 29 (Dall 1870a: 110). The information they obtained has come down to us only indirectly, however (Whymper 1868: 227). In August of that same summer of 1867, a miner named Michael Byrnes, also working for the Western Union Telegraph Company, climbed over the mountains from the Sitka area and arrived on the upper reaches of the Lewes River before he was recalled when the telegraph company suspended operations following the successful laying of the Atlantic cable. At that time, only the connecting links of the Yukon waterway above Selkirk had been left unexplored (Dall 1870a: 277; Schwatka 1885a: 117; Dawson 1889: 141B; Raymond 1900: 20).

The year of 1867 was one of great importance, and the sources for the history

[1] The raiding Indians have in various accounts been reported Chilkoot rather than Chilkat but McClellan's (1967: 72, 74) accounts seem to reinforce the evidence that the group were Chilkat who had come over the Chilkat Pass from Klukwan. It should be noted that the burning of the buildings took place at a later time, after the post was abandoned.

of Alaska expand from that date onward. On June 23, 1867, Frederick Whymper and William Dall reached Fort Yukon, having come up the river on a Western Union Telegraph Company expedition (Raymond 1900: 19). Both men wrote significant volumes on their observations (Whymper 1868; Dall 1870a). Neither man went above Fort Yukon on the journey, however, but both made comments on the Indians and on a few occasions at least, specifically mentioned the Han.

It is obvious that by the middle 1860s the Kutchin area was becoming relatively well known. Missionaries had come to Fort Yukon but, on the other hand, there had been as yet no European settlement in the actual territory of the Han. It is of course possible that other Europeans entered Han country between the last journey of Campbell's men in 1852 and that of Ketchum and Laberge in 1867 but, if they did, no record of their travels has been found.

Unquestionably, the factor of greatest significance for change in the third quarter of the nineteenth century was the purchase of the immense territory of Alaska from Russia by the United States, the act of formal possession taking place on October 18, 1867 (Wickersham 1927: 24). This transaction injected the tremendous force of the expanding American economy into the country.

The week before the transfer took place, the San Francisco firm of Hutchinson, Kohl, and Company purchased the entire Alaskan properties of the Russian-America Company for $350,000, and in September 1868 became incorporated as the Alaska Commercial Company (Ogilvie 1913: 64; Mathews 1968: 76–7). Realizing with reasonable certainty that Fort Yukon had been established in Russian territory which had since become American, an effort was made by the owners of the Alaska Commercial Company to have the United States determine the longitude of that post and allow them to take possession of it. Until this time, the Russians had established permanent trading posts as far up the Yukon River as Nulato, while the Hudson's Bay traders from Fort Yukon had gone down about 300 miles to Nuklukayet, which was located at the mouth of the Tanana (Raymond 1900: 20). The Russians had abandoned their trade immediately after the sale of Alaska, but the Hudson's Bay Company men kept on, aware that they could withdraw into Canada and still attract the Indian bands with which they had developed friendly relations.

To resolve the situation, in 1869 the Alaska Commercial Company had a stern-wheel steamer about fifty feet long constructed in California and transported on the deck of an Alaskan-bound brig to St. Michael (Fig. 3). In the party, besides employees of the Alaska Commercial Company, was Captain Charles Raymond of the Engineer Corps, U.S. Army, who had been instructed to proceed to Fort Yukon and take possession of the post if it proved, as expected, to be in American territory (Raymond 1900: 21).[2] The little *Yukon* did its job admirably, arriving

[2] William Ogilvie (1913: 69) states that the *Yukon* was built at St. Michael by a firm that was later sold to the Alaska Commercial Company. Whatever else may be the case, Raymond could hardly be mistaken about the stern-wheeler being carried on deck, since he accompanied it.

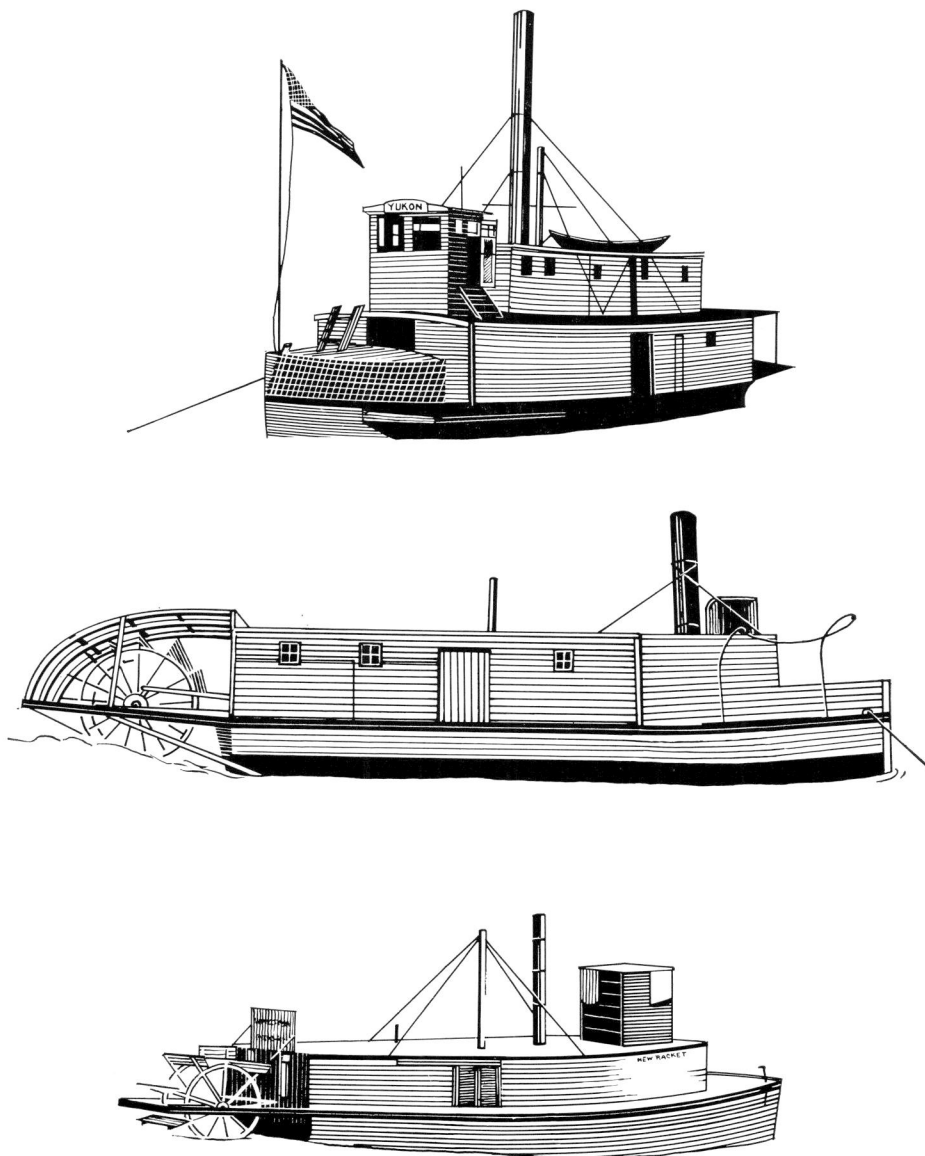

Fɪɢ. 3. Yukon River steamboats: *Yukon* (1869), *St. Michael* (1879), *New Racket* (1883) (after Schwatka 1900: 313, 314; Allen 1887: 89).

at the mouth of the Porcupine on July 31, 1869, a distance of over a thousand miles from St. Michael, in twenty-three days of actual traveling time including stops to take on fuel. Captain Raymond found John Wilson in charge of the Hudson's Bay post at Fort Yukon and, among other residents, the missionary William Bompas. With friendly cooperation, the longitude was duly established, and the post transferred to American hands on August 9. On the following day, the *Yukon* speeded off downstream, leaving Captain Raymond's party to complete their observations and follow in a crudely made skiff on August 28 (Raymond 1900: 23).

What is significant in this historical development insofar as the Han Indians are concerned is that this epochal run of the first Alaskan river steamer which, incidentally, scared most of the natives on the river below Fort Yukon, did not proceed above it, thereby leaving this aboriginal group still without a trading post in their own territory twenty years after the first European contact.

The situation was soon to change, however. About 1873, Moses Mercier, who was in charge of the old Hudson's Bay Company post at Fort Yukon that the Alaska Commercial Company had taken over, moved his establishment to a place he named Belle Isle, just offshore from the present town of Eagle on the left bank (always as one faces downstream) of the Yukon. The reason given for the removal was that the Hudson's Bay Company had adopted the leisurely method of trading that was preferred by the Indians, whereas Mercier wished to inaugurate a more American tempo of business.[3] If Ogilvie is correct, this was the first European settlement among the Han Indians, but a second soon followed.

In the summer of 1873, the first gold prospectors reached Fort Yukon, they having spent two years in their journey by way of the Mackenzie and the Porcupine rivers. One party was under the leadership of Arthur Harper and the other under Leroy McQuesten, the latter better known as Jack in the annals of the Yukon (Ogilvie 1913: 96; McQuesten 1952: 2; Mathews 1968: 86–8). McQuesten and his associates wintered about fifty miles down the Yukon, while Harper with his party went up the river. In the spring they regrouped and proceeded to St. Michael aboard Mercier's barge, a trip that took sixteen days. At St. Michael, four of the group, including McQuesten, and Alfred Mayo entered the employ of the Alaska Commercial Company, returning upriver on the steamer the same summer. Mayo was dropped off to run a post on the Yukon near the mouth of the Tanana, while McQuesten and a young Englishman named Frank Bonfield continued on to establish, sometime in August 1874, a trading post known as Fort Reliance on the right bank of the Yukon which, according to different authorities, was between seven and thirteen miles below present-day Dawson and the mouth

[3] Ogilvie, who supplies this information, is unfortunately not exact in giving the date. The order of presentation implies that the move occurred before 1874; elsewhere it is stated that Mercier was at Fort Yukon in 1873 (Ogilvie 1913: 64–5, 96). Frederick Schwatka (1885a: 259–60) mentions Belle Isle as a trading station about a mile or a little more below the Indian village but was under the impression that it was established in 1881 and abandoned in 1882. Schwatka lacked an interpreter and his dates seem improbable. Perhaps the post had been abandoned and then re-established for a year.

of the Klondike (Ogilvie 1913: 65, 97; McQuesten 1952: 5; Mathews 1968: 88–9). This we presume was the second trading post in Han Indian country.

In May of the next year, 1875, McQuesten and Bonfield went down to St. Michael, being joined by Harper and others on the way. There McQuesten, Harper, and Mayo accepted an offer of a franchise from the Alaska Commercial Company to trade on the river at Fort Yukon and above it. For three years thereafter, McQuesten remained at the latter post. Harper and Mayo ran Fort Reliance; in 1878, however, Reliance was abandoned because of the threatening attitude of the Indians, one of whom had been apprehended with tobacco stolen from the post. Later the same summer, despite these difficulties, McQuesten decided to reopen the store at Fort Reliance. The Indians, wanting the goods he brought, welcomed him, presenting compensation for the stolen tobacco (McQuesten 1952: 7; Mathews 1968: 90–4).

While the post had been left unoccupied, three Indian women died from eating arsenic in flour, both taken from the store. McQuesten (1952: 7) tells how he settled the matter:

"I told them that the poison was put in the store to destroy mice and it was out of the way of children and the old people ought to know better and [as for] the people that died it was their own fault for breaking into the store and taking things that didn't belong to them. There was one blind girl about sixteen years old that got poisoned—her father said she was a great deal of help to her mother and he had taken one of our dogs to replace the girl, but if I would pay for the girl he would return the dog. I told him I would think the matter over and let them know later on. Finally I told them the girl's Mother could keep the dog, so that settled the matter and that was the last I ever heard about the poison."

Concerning visits to the upper Yukon immediately above Han territory we have little information for the period between the explorations of Robert Campbell ending in 1852 and the well-described journey of Lieutenant Frederick Schwatka of the U.S. Army who in 1883 became the first man to record a descent of the entire length of the Yukon, which he accomplished as far as Nuklukayet on a raft (Schwatka 1885a: 311). George Holt, an employee of the Alaska Commercial Company, was later reported to have led in 1875 the first party across the Chilkoot (Dyea) Pass and into the Yukon Valley (Ogilvie 1913: 105); Dawson (1889: 179B) gives the date as 1878. Others soon followed, for the factor dominating the last quarter of the nineteenth century in the upper Yukon area was the search for gold. The impact was so strongly felt in the Han Indian country that this aspect of the historic contacts deserves special review. For the sake of avoiding confusion, before presenting that review I should point out that there were three well-known passes to the headwaters of the Yukon. East of the Chilkoot, or Dyea, Pass was the White Pass, later the route of the railroad. West of the Chilkoot Pass was the Chilkat Pass, the longest route of the three (Fig. 2).

As stated earlier, Harper and McQuesten seem to have been the first to come to the Yukon with the anticipation of finding gold that for geological reasons they had concluded was there (Ogilvie 1913: 87–8). Mayo, who came with McQuesten, should be mentioned with the other two as all three had exceptional contacts with the Indians since, after reaching the Yukon, they financed their prospecting by establishing posts for the Alaska Commercial Company and traded directly, or by franchise, for them (Ogilvie 1913: 67, 91; Mathews 1968: 90).

Actually, the availability of gold in the upper Yukon area had been obvious from the first European exploration. What was needed was the time and interest to search out the localities where it could be found in large quantities. Campbell knew there was gold around Fort Selkirk, and also the Reverend Robert McDonald who was stationed at Fort Yukon in 1862–63 had found gold, presumably on Birch Creek (Ogilvie 1913: 87; Mathews 1968: 123–4). The primary interests of these men were centered elsewhere, however.

The previously mentioned George Holt, who came over the Chilkoot Pass, has been recorded as the first man to send gold out of Alaska—two small nuggets obtained from a Tanana Indian (Ogilvie 1913: 105). Within a year or two afterward, groups of prospectors were coming into the country over the Chilkoot Pass from Dyea or up the river from St. Michael. By 1884, some of them were lucky enough to be panning a hundred dollars worth of gold a day on a sandbar about ninety miles up the Stewart River, and the next year, 1885, Richard Poplin and his party made the first great strike seven miles above them, the seasonal cleanup amounting to about $35,000 (Ogilvie 1913: 108–9; Mathews 1968: 103–5). In 1886, because of the gold strike, McQuesten and Harper abandoned Fort Reliance and established a trading post at the mouth of the Stewart River (Ogilvie 1913: 66; Mathews 1968: 106). Until after that date the concentration of mining remained some miles to the south of Han territory.

In 1886, however, a major strike was made in Han country on the Fortymile River, so-called because it was roughly forty miles below McQuesten's first trading post, Fort Reliance (Fig. 4). Again in consequence of the influx of prospectors, Harper and his partners opened a trading post the next year at the mouth of the Fortymile (Ogilvie 1913: 66–7; Mathews 1968: 108–10). It was in that year of 1887 that William Ogilvie, who was to become the historian of the gold rush, began his many years of service on the Yukon as surveyor and representative extraordinary of the Canadian government. Apparently, he left us little or no information on the Han Indians, however. R. G. McConnell (1891: 139D) arrived at Fortymile on August 9, 1888. He called it the headquarters for miners on the Yukon. Thirty or forty men were camped there, but ready to start at a moment's notice for any new strike because the persistent high water had limited the output of gold to scarcely $15,000.

It was that same year of 1888 that gold was found on Seventymile Creek, in this case seventy miles below Fortymile (cf. Stuck 1917: 76), and men with rockers in which to separate the gold made $50 a day (Adney 1900b: 457; for illustration of a rocker, see Kirk 1899: 159). Then, in 1895, gold was discovered on Mission Creek, near the mouth of which Eagle City was later established (Adney 1900b: 457).

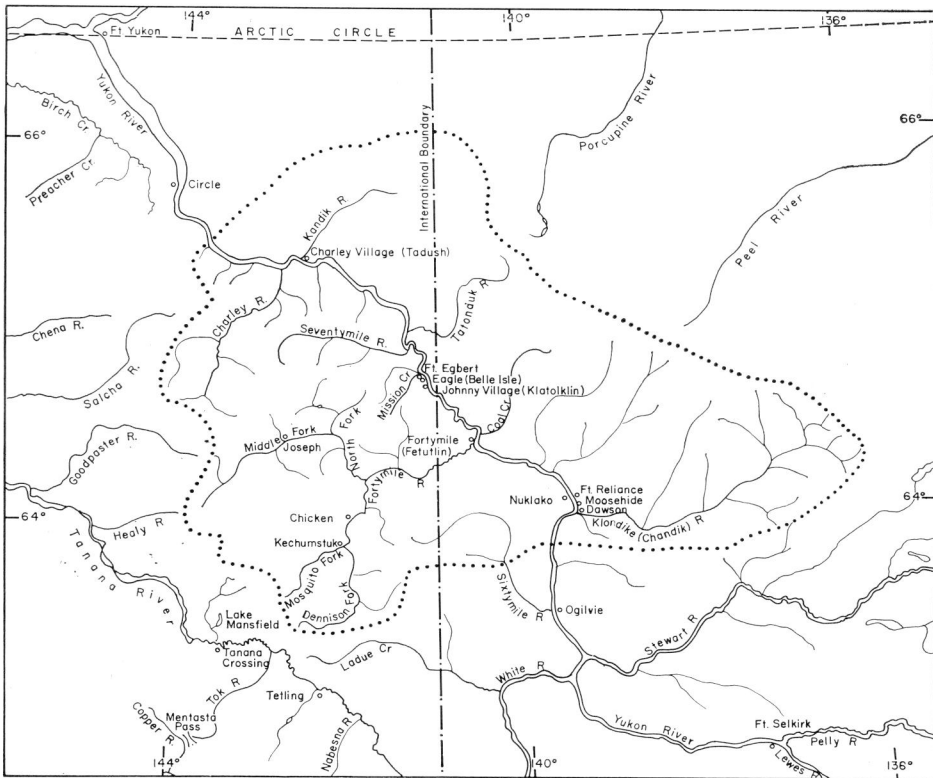

FIG. 4. Map of the Han territory.

In 1894, a trading post opposite the mouth of Sixtymile Creek (in this case sixty miles above Fort Reliance) had been named after Ogilvie by Arthur Harper who, in 1889, had disassociated himself from McQuesten and Mayo and re-established a post on the site of old Fort Selkirk. Ogilvie (1913: 67) says that Mc-Questen, in the same year of 1894, founded Circle City following the gold strike on Birch Creek. Adney (1900b: 457–8) tells us, however, that the original Circle City, some twelve miles above the present site, was founded about 1893 by eighty men from Fortymile who had been outfitted by McQuesten. The location was washed out by the spring floods and the camp was moved to a site seven miles below the beginning of the Yukon Flats, where ultimately there developed a set-tlement which straggled for two miles along the low left bank. All of this actually seems to have followed the discovery of gold on Birch Creek by two Indians who had been outfitted by McQuesten in 1893 to prospect in the Yukon Flats (Mathews 1968: 124).

In the winter of 1897–98, a town called Star City was laid out on the left bank of the Yukon perhaps three miles above the previously mentioned Seventymile

Creek which is thirty miles below Mission Creek (Eagle). When it flooded in the spring, a new town named Seventymile City was started two miles farther up the same bank. This camp had a population of two or three hundred for a short period. Apparently this is the place that was later known as Nation. Then, on May 28, 1898, twenty-eight miners drew numbered slips out of a hat for cabin sites in a settlement they named Eagle City, which was located on the left bank of the Yukon just north of the mouth of Mission Creek. About a thousand persons wintered there (Adney 1900b: 457). One can only imagine the effect of all this activity on the Indian village three miles above the new town.

As might be expected, with the rising population, commerce was also expanding. In 1879 the Western Trading and Fur Company, which was competing for the trade on the Yukon, introduced a second steamer on the river, the 75-foot *St. Michael* (McQuesten 1952: 8, 9; Mathews 1968: 95); Ogilvie (1913: 69) gives the date as 1871, but this seems to be a misprint. Then, in 1883, a third stern-wheeler with the onomatopoeic name of *New Racket* (Fig. 3), which had been built by a group of prospectors and later sold to the Alaska Commercial Company, arrived at Fortymile (Schwatka 1885a: 317). Both of these shallow-draft vessels were 70 to 80 feet long and carried most of the supplies upriver by towing four or five barges, each holding about ten tons. The round trip from St. Michael to the boundary took about a month, two-thirds of it upstream. The cargoes of the vessels soon proved insufficient to supply the demand for goods, and in 1889 the Alaska Commercial Company built the *Arctic*, which was 140 feet long with a 28-foot beam and drew 6 feet of water, a stern-wheeler almost twice as large as its three precursors. Then, as the gold miners increased in number, many more ships were constructed, with the same company building the *Hannah*, the *Sarah*, and the *Susie*, each no less than 220 feet 8 inches long with a beam of 42 feet and a draft of 6 feet 2 inches. These mammoths of the river had a speed in still water of seventeen miles per hour (Ogilvie 1913: 70–83, *passim*).

The culmination of the gold fever which led to the peak of population as well as this extraordinary commercial development was, as everyone knows, the discovery of fantastic amounts of the yellow metal on the side streams of the Klondike River. Robert Henderson made the original find on Bonanza Creek in the summer of 1896 and passed on the word to George Carmack and Two Tagish Indians who returned to the site and staked three claims on August 17 of that year. The panning was so rich that the most valuable claims were all taken up before Henderson learned that the great dream had come true (Ogilvie 1913: 120–34). The contrast in wealth may be demonstrated when one considers that the estimated value of all the gold recovered by all the miners on the upper Yukon in 1895 was about $400,000 (Ogilvie 1913: 113), while the estimate of the amount of gold from only the Klondike miners passing through Dawson in the winter season of 1897–98 has been placed at approximately $15,000,000 (Kirk 1899: 160) or, more accurately, for the years 1899 to 1905 inclusive, $104,806,624 (Anon. 1916: 38).

As to the population of the area, it has been recorded that between the Klondike strike of 1896 and September 1897, no fewer than 2,656 travelers had registered at Fort Selkirk, a figure which did not include the many who had not taken time to stop at that trading post. By that winter, an estimated throng of 5,000 had gathered in Dawson, and in the following one of 1898–99, the population was presumed to be between 20,000 and 30,000 (Kirk 1899: 81, 116). This seems to have been correct if one includes the gold-producing area of which Dawson was the magnetic center. More officially, Dawson had a population of 9,142 in 1901, a number which had dropped to 3,013 by 1911 (Gutsell 1953: 31–2). Since the Klondike was in Han territory, one can hardly conceive of what such an overwhelming encroachment meant to the Indians.

Mission activity among the Indians was also a correlate of the gold rush. The Church of England was the principal supplier of missionaries, and a brief summary of the men working in the area must begin with William Kirkby's visit to Fort Yukon between July 6 and 13, 1862, which, although brief, had the effect of bringing Robert McDonald to that post the following year for a long stay. Probably to McDonald must be attributed the so-called Christianizing of the Han. The roving Reverend William Bompas visited Fort Yukon in July 1869 and spent the following winter at Rampart House (Cody 1908: 55–7, 107–8). Then in 1881, the Reverend Vincent Sim went to Rampart House and, before he died in May 1885, he had traveled up the Yukon through Han country (Cody 1908: 229–30; Wesbrook 1969). A mission was finally established at Fortymile in 1887 by a churchman referred to as "poor Ellington," apparently because he shortly afterward went insane. The Diocese of the Mackenzie was divided in 1890, producing the Diocese of Selkirk (Yukon), with Bishop Bompas moving first to Rampart House where he wintered in 1891–92, and then to Fortymile (Buxton) where he arrived August 4, 1892, and, for the most part, remained until 1901, one year at Moosehide in 1899–1900 being the apparent exception (Cody 1908: 254, 258, 260; Archer 1929: 122, 130, 160–5).

In the twentieth century, the fury of prospecting gradually decreased and the ownership of the mines became consolidated in the hands of large companies. Like the winter's snow, the population melted away, leaving many of the early settlements as ghost towns. A few, and particularly Dawson, survived, but only the latter with a population running into the hundreds. Eagle, the other center of significance in Han Indian territory, dropped in population to a few score.

There was a period from 1899 to 1911 when an area downstream of Eagle, itself only ten miles within the United States territory (Colby 1941: 202–3), was occupied by a contingent of soldiers, a fact which must have had a special impact on the Han Indians. It should also be noted in this summary history of the area that the United States District Court was first located at Eagle before its removal to Fairbanks in 1904 (Colby 1941: 203).

In the second quarter of the nineteenth century, the Han territory had settled into relatively quiescent times with some mining continuing and an occasional old prospector living out his life on a trap line while furtively extending his search for gold, more perhaps from force of habit than any realistic hope that he would find what the thousands before him had missed. It was also at this period that the professional efforts directed toward the ethnographic reconstruction of the cultures of the aboriginal peoples of the United States and Canada—studies which had previously flourished in the more accessible parts of the continent—were at last extended to the distant interior of Canada and Alaska where the native population was sparse and dejected as a result of epidemics, and where the culture was materially and socially disintegrated by the gradually overwhelming influence of the fur trader and missionary. It was not a country for quick intellectual rewards, for the wealth of the culture, like the gold in the creeks, was no longer readily available.[4]

It was into this environment that the writer projected himself in 1932 on his fourth trip among the Northern Athapaskans. Limited to the summer season by teaching obligations, it was necessary to cross the continent by train and take a ship to Alaska to which place no air service was then available. Between late May and early September, such journeys greedily devoured one's time. In the company of my wife, a young woman who had already made two trips to Alaska, a departure was made from Whitehorse, Yukon Territory, on June 18, 1932, in a narrow Yukon boat purchased secondhand in that settlement for $40. To speed our progress, we had brought into the country a small outboard motor as well as camping equipment which we set up on the lower east shore of Lake Laberge the first night. The next day we stopped at a Tutchone Indian camp near the mouth of the Big Salmon River. Intent on reaching Kutchin Indians, we did not stay long, but sufficiently so to realize that finding efficient informants among them would have been difficult. Making only one or two other stops, and without meeting any Indians after leaving Big Salmon, we arrived in Dawson on June 22.

At Moosehide, a Han Indian settlement about three miles below Dawson, it proved profitable for us to remain until July 7. Following those two weeks, five days were spent at Eagle and a final three more at Nation. Thus we passed merely twenty-four days in Han territory, leaving it for the last time on July 15, 1932. It should be clearly stated, however, that for the most part while at Moosehide our ethnographic efforts were directed toward the recovery of data on the aboriginal culture of the Peel River group of the Kutchin, some of whom had moved permanently into the area during the period of the gold rush.

Twenty-nine years later, the ethnographer Richard Slobodin and his wife were in and about Dawson, Moosehide, and Eagle during the first two weeks of August and the first week of September, while in the following year, 1962, he returned to Dawson between August 11 and 16.[5] Although he, too, has been primarily con-

---

[4] One notes the contrast of successful ethnography among the Eskimo of the central arctic coast in the early twentieth century. Although also in a difficult area to reach, the difference resulted mainly because the research was on still-functioning aboriginal cultures rather than consisting of *ethnographic reconstruction*.

[5] Personal communication of September 2, 1969.

cerned with the Kutchin, his information on the Han made available to me in an unpublished paper constitutes one of the most important sources on the aboriginal life of the Han. Let us now consider these sources in more detail.

Sources

The first group of contributors to our knowledge of the Han are the early fur traders. Insofar as we are concerned with the certainty of customs being truly aboriginal, they are the most important. Unfortunately, none of these contributors was located specifically in Han territory during the first twenty-five years after direct and continuing contact with these Indians had been made. Murray, who in 1847 became the first to establish a more or less permanent trading post on the Yukon above the mouth of the Tanana River, was an energetic Scotsman with unusual artistic ability, and he has provided an illustrated journal of his experiences which, as might be expected, is more informative about the Kutchin than about the Han. Nevertheless, his comments on the Han should not be undervalued. What is regrettable is that he did not make clearer to what degree he was including the Han in his general statements about the Indians he met at Fort Yukon. Curiously, the largest group represented at that fort seems to have been the Han, but from this fact it does not follow that the Indians of whom he saw most were Han. Actually, when consulting Murray's work in preparing a monograph on the Kutchin (Osgood 1936a), I suffered the illusion that his important section on Indian culture (Murray 1910: 84–7) actually referred to the Han, whereas a more careful consideration has convinced me that basically he was referring to the Kutcha Kutchin in whose territory Fort Yukon was located. The fact seems to be that he lumped the two groups together with respect to their culture, merely recording such differences as distinguished the Han, and particularly their language. Under the circumstances, hardly more could be expected during that first year of his residence.

Campbell, who in 1851 was the first European of record to pass through the territory of the Han, left little or nothing of ethnographic significance. In his few paragraphs largely devoted to dress and boiling stones, he does not specifically locate the people. There is a slight element of stress on the Indians' never before having seen a white man (whereas by 1851 some of them certainly had). Campbell (1958: 96–7) states: "They were destitute of almost every article of civilized usage. The only arms they had were the bow and arrow; their substitute for axe & knife was a bone or stone." These sound like rhetorical statements and they contradict other evidence. After all, the statements come from his journal, not his diary, which suggests more generality.

Thanks to George Gibbs, significant reports on the ethnography of the Kutchin Indians were made by two Hudson's Bay Company traders, William Hardisty and Strachan Jones. Hardisty, who followed Murray in trading at Fort Yukon in the early 1850s, merely mentions the Han in his paper, but his contemporary, Jones, contributes several valuable comments on them in a companion paper. Clearly, the knowledge of the aboriginal culture of the Han during the all-important first thirty-five years of historic contact was minimal, and about this particular lack there is nothing one can do but report it.

During the period between 1883 and 1910, we are more fortunate, however. Often it is the early missionaries who recorded the best data about natives on whom the impact of civilization goes back more than a century, but this is not true in the case of the Han. Surely, a number of the missionaries at Fort Yukon knew these Indians, but we find specific evidence for only two visits to their country before the great gold strike on the Fortymile. It is said that the Reverend William Bompas traveled upriver from Fort Yukon as far as Fortymile, but I have not located any detailed account of his journey (Archer 1929: 121). The other missionary visit to Han territory was that undertaken by the Reverend V. C. Sim in the summer of 1883, and even his comments on Han culture are negligible (Wesbrook 1969: 40).

It is two officers in the U.S. Army and one journalist who come to our aid. Lieutenant Schwatka in 1883 specifically gathered information on the Indians of the Yukon River in the interest of the military establishment (Schwatka 1885a). Because he had interpreters who could talk to the Tutchone people whom he met first on his way downriver, he gives us more information on them than on the Han. Nevertheless, he must be credited with some of the best ethnographic data to be published on the latter Indians before 1900. Although without an adequate interpreter through whom he could communicate with the Han in their principal village near the present town of Eagle, he reported what he saw on his one-day visit, and what he saw was significant. Included in his report to the government, however, is a section on Alaskan natives which he says is due almost entirely to Dr. George Wilson, who accompanied him. Dr. Wilson apparently held a very low regard for the Han, and I have the same opinion of his reliability in writing about them.

Among the men of the great Klondike gold rush, one man is an outstanding contributor to our knowledge of the Han. He is Tappan Adney who, as well as writing a book on that stampede, contributed articles to the *Harper's New Monthly Magazine* (1900a) and to *Outing* (1902) which appear to be reliable accounts of Han Indian hunting parties in the late nineteenth century. He himself lived with the Indians for a brief period. As in the case of Schwatka, he depended largely for his report on what he saw, for the Indians do not seem to have known enough English for more than commonplace communications. Adney, however, illustrated his articles with drawings of ethnographic value. There are other writers of that period, such as Robert Kirk, who comment on the Indians, but none that I have found of comparable significance.

Among the men in the army, ethnographers were hardly to be expected at the beginning of the twentieth century, but one individual perhaps deserves the name. This was Captain Ferdinand Schmitter of the Medical Corps who, during his term of duty at Fort Egbert, adjacent to Eagle, recorded most of the data on the culture of the Han Indians that are available to us from the period of the first seventy-five years after continuing contact with Europeans had been established. The length of his stay is not clear, as he merely mentions that he was stationed at Fort Egbert in 1906, but from internal evidence one is led to believe that he was in residence for one year or more (Schmitter 1910: 1, 14–5). In 1906, the aboriginal culture must have been known to the Indians, and Schmitter probably had the services of the best interpreters the army could obtain. Furthermore, as a doctor, his counsel would have been in demand by the Indians and his consequent relationships with them must have been of great use in obtaining information, especially that which reflects his interest in the native medicine man and his practices. Surely without Schmitter's intelligent interest and recording of their culture, this late compilation of the available data would have suffered immeasurably, as soon will be seen.

Finally, we touch once again on the work of professional anthropologists. The writer has eighty-four typed sheets of paper four by six inches in size containing notes obtained in 1932. Of these, forty-six contain information from Walter Benjamin of Eagle, where the latter was born about 1882. His parents came from the same place and his mother was the sister of Chief Isaac of Eagle, who was later the leader of the Klondike band. Walter, incidentally, was one of the three Northern Athapaskans I have known of to stutter. Fifteen more slips (fully typed—but few are—they may contain 350 words) bear data from Angus Alexander, also of Eagle, who was born about 1872 on Charlie Creek, where he believes his parents were also born. An additional seven slips record information from Jonathan Wood, born about 1850, and six from Henry Harper, both of Moosehide.

Apart from the data from these Han informants, various comparative notes, mostly on food animals, were obtained from John Semple, a Peel River Kutchin born about 1888 who had settled at Moosehide. He was a better-than-average informant who spoke English fairly well, and his general knowledge of the Yukon River drainage, as well as that of the Peel, made him a useful informant in both areas with respect to the sources of food.

The data from Richard Slobodin's studies in the early 1960s are based on twenty-three double-spaced pages of typescript dated March 1963. His informants, all residents of Dawson at the time, were principally Charlie Isaac (b. 1912), Simon McLeod (b. 1883), his wife Mary McLeod (b. 1893), Chief John Jonas (b. 1877), Mrs. Lucy Wood (b. 1887), and Mrs. Ellen Taylor, all but the last being on the Bureau of Indian Affairs roll of Dawson Band No. 6 (Slobodin 1963a: 1–3). About his family, Charlie Isaac said, "My father had an older brother, Jonathan Wood, who lived in Eagle, and a younger brother, Walter Ben[jamin]. Jonathan Wood and Isaac were tall, slim dark men (as is Charlie Isaac) but Walter Ben was stout (indicating a paunch), with light complexion, pink cheeks, grey eyes, and big brown mustache. My father's father had two wives. Jonathan and Isaac were sons of the first wife and Walter of the second. Everyone thought Walter had some Russian in him from 'way back'." Isaac also said that in his youth he lived at Fortymile, but believed that "he was born farther west in

the Ketchumstock area, and that his father came from the upper Tanana region"
(Slobodin 1963a: 21).

On the basis of these statements several things are worth noting. First of all,
two of my 1932 informants, Jonathan Wood and Walter Benjamin, were uncles
of Slobodin's principal informant of 1962, Charlie Isaac. Second, the mobility of
the family is clearly indicated by its original home at Eagle in 1882 before the
disruption created by gold strikes. Third, if only by his implied age of about
thirty, Chief Isaac, the father of Charlie Isaac, must not be confused with the
chief of the same name encountered by Hudson Stuck northwest of Tanana
Crossing in 1910, since the latter is described as an old man (Stuck 1916: 260–3,
270–1; Slobodin 1963a: 18). Fourth, it is perhaps worth considering that since
the 1932 data are primarily from the northern group of Han at Eagle and only
secondarily from Moosehide, and although those of Slobodin are apparently entirely from a southern band resident in Dawson in 1961–62, the original source
of most of his information seems to have emanated from a northern Han band
by way of Charlie Isaac.

To the best of my memory, there were few if any Indians in Dawson in 1932,
whereas Slobodin reports that Moosehide was a moribund community of only
seven families in 1961, four of which were Han, two were Peel River Kutchin, and
one of mixed origins (Slobodin 1963a: 3).

It should be mentioned at this point that Catharine McClellan, who has undertaken extensive research on Athapaskan and Tlingit bands in the area interlock-
ing the uppermost of the Yukon tributaries with some of the streams that flow
into the Pacific Ocean, has placed at my disposal notes from Mary McLeod and
a few other Han Indians taken July 27 and 28, 1966, at Dawson. Since the data
comprise largely vocabulary and genealogy, I have not made use of them. I do
wish, however, to record my special gratitude to this colleague for her considerable
effort in making four unpublished manuscripts on neighboring Athapaskans avail-
ble.

Perhaps before going further, it may be of value to compare certain factors in-
fluencing the acquisition of data which appear in the more important sources on
the Han. For this purpose, we can divide the passage of time since 1847, when
Murray established Fort Yukon, into twenty-year periods.

From the first, 1847–67, we have the invaluable statements of Murray himself. These are essentially eyewitness accounts of the aboriginal culture. Although
the best of interpreters then available were almost certainly with him, verbal
communication between him and the Indians must have been extremely limited.
Some improvement in this respect may well have taken place by the next decade
or the time Jones added important details for the period. It is important to realize
that both men had experienced some years of contact with the Indians of the area.

In the second period, 1867–87, Schwatka is the only significant commentator
on the Han. The culture had probably changed little, but this traveler had no in-

terpreter worth the name and spent only a few days in the country. On the other hand, what he reported, he had seen.

By the third period, 1887–1907, great changes had begun to occur in the culture. Adney, who wrote in the middle of it, was interested in the Indians, but basically as a journalist, one might judge. He traveled with the Han briefly on a hunting trip during his winter in the country, 1897–98, and reported by word and drawing what he saw, but his verbal communication with them was limited.

Schmitter, almost ten years later, was in a locality with somewhat less impact from outsiders and consequently, despite the date, with probably no more significant change in the culture. His contacts with Indians, like his interests, were broader, and he no doubt gained immeasurably from having as good interpreters as the country could supply. One may regret, however, that it is not always possible to ascertain from his account whether he had seen what he reports of Han culture or had acquired his information secondhand.

Then, for the next period, 1907–27, we learn nothing about the Han.

Not until the fifth period, 1927–47, does the professional anthropologist appear on the scene, but only for three weeks as he was but secondarily interested in the Han. The old culture was no longer visible, and ethnographic reconstruction was the order of the day. Few Indians who spoke English even moderately well were available.

Near the end of the sixth period, 1947–67, a second anthropologist worked with Han informants during a period of a few weeks, and a third for a few days. Again the interest was a secondary one. If there was some compensation in the ability of informants to speak better English, it was offset in some degree by the greater disintegration of Indian culture. Indeed, in the last period, an interest in acculturation inevitably supplanted a primary concern for the aboriginal culture.

As a final comment on the sources, it must be pointed out as extraordinary that despite the long period of over a hundred years that they cover, there is a minimum of repetition from one account to another. Up until 1910 that situation can be explained by the fact that, first of all, the early writers saw little or nothing of each other and, secondly, the best of the papers on which one now depends were either unpublished (e.g., Murray, Schmitter) or not readily at hand (e.g., Jones, Adney). Although since that time the gatherers of information have been ethnologists who might be expected to have been aware of the data collected before their own field work, actually, because all were directing their primary interest toward neighboring groups, there is no evidence that any one of them had organized the earlier material on the Han before making their brief studies. Therefore, when the same data now appear more than once, it becomes significant confirmation, although it must be largely chance that even that kind of repetition proves so infrequent. It should also be stated that the data, from whatever source, have been kept intact and not expanded upon by the authority of greater knowledge unless the trait or custom seems unintelligble otherwise. Let us now go on to consider a collation and evaluation of the various morsels of information on the aboriginal culture of the Han that are available to us in 1970.

Identification and Location of the Han

Our first problem is to determine—with as much exactitude as this late date allows—just who were the Han and what was the extent of their territory. An obvious correlate of the procedure to be followed will be an examination of the early data respecting the subdivisions and villages of the people. That these matters will be concluded without questions remaining will be too much to expect, but we can hope that sufficient clarification will result to provide a satisfactory delineation of the cultural province to which our small aggregate of data belongs.

Although the pertinent sources have been reviewed afresh, it is not altogether disappointing to find that the composition of the result is not much more than an expansion of the statements published in 1934 in which I dealt with the distribution and synonymy of the Kutchin (Osgood 1934: 175–6). The early literature, which indeed, if taken collectively, pays more attention to distinguishing and locating the Indian tribes than to anything else, gives a clear majority support for designating at least four major groups in the Yukon River drainage east of the Alaskan boundary. These are from north to south: (1) the Kutchin, (2) the Han, (3) the Tutchone, and (4) the Tagish. These I shall comment upon individually, leaving the Han to the last (Fig. 1).

The Kutchin were a recognized unit to almost all the early fur traders and travelers, at least six of the eight or nine tribes being generally differentiated (Osgood 1934: 178). If it had not been for the publicity given Dall's use of that term with respect to numerous other Alaskan groups (Murray and Hardisty had previously begun the pattern of so-doing), much less confusion would probably have followed (Dall 1877: map). Clearly, the local residents did not fail to set off the Han from the true Kutchin as we shall see when we consider the former group.

The Tutchone, by which name I refer to a group of Indians whose central territory was the banks of the Yukon above the Klondike River to the area around the confluence of the Lewes and the Pelly, have always been a problem for Europeans in respect to their boundaries, and in some ways they continue to be. Parts of the valleys of the Stewart and White rivers were also their territory, and they apparently extended some distance up the Pelly as well as up the Lewes to the mouth of the Teslin. They have also been spoken of as the *Gens du fou*, a name primarily given the Han.

Murray in one place seems to include the Tutchone in his use of the term Gens du fou when he thus describes Indians coming from above the ramparts which one can reasonably think of as the area of Fort Selkirk (Murray 1910: 96–7). On the other hand, he may have meant merely the area above the lower end of the ramparts since elsewhere he clearly correlates the Gens du fou with the Han and distinguishes at least one other group above them certainly in Tutchone territory. He states: "On the banks of the Youcon below the Forks of the Lewis and Pelly are the 'Fathzei [Tathzei]—Kootchin' (People of the Ramparts) there are only about 20 men in this band, these with the others above mentioned trade with the Russians on the coast" (Murray 1910: 82). As elaborated later, Murray sometimes seems to refer to the people called Tutchone as the Middle Band, a term justified by one simply thinking of them as a group between the Han and the Tagish. In any event he knew little about them for he writes: "Having only seen three men who had been as far up as the *Pelly* [Lewes], I could get little knowledge respecting the tribes about the Lewis [Pelly] and Pelly [Lewes] and towards the Great Lake [Laberge or Teslin?]" (Murray 1910: 82). As indicated, Murray had transposed Pelly and Lewes, names given by Campbell that he may have first learned from Hardisty. Inevitably, the situation was confusing in 1848. After several readings of Murray's *Journal*, however, it seems clear that in almost every case this fur trader was thinking of the Han when he wrote Gens du fou.

This conclusion becomes reinforced by the fact that Hardisty in the 1850s not only distinguished the Han and Tutchone from the Kutchin but also from each other, in his case terming the Han as *Gens du fou* and the Tutchone as *Gens de bois*. He states specifically: "The first material change [above Fort Yukon] occurs among the 'Gens de Fou' or Hun-koo-chin, (river people.) These make use of a great many words in common with the 'Gens de Bois' [Tutchone]" (Hardisty 1872: 311).

Whymper (1868: 223) refers to the Tutchone as Tatanchok Kutchins, and also as Gens de bois, at the same time following the Hudson's Bay Company men in distinguishing them from the Han.

Raymond, who we may recall spent August 1869 at Fort Yukon, two years after Whymper's visit, clouds the issue by writing that year: "The principal tribes which have been accustomed to trade at this post [Fort Yukon] are the Kotcha Kotchins, (or lowlanders,) who live between [along?] the Porcupine and Youkon Rivers, near their junction; the Au [An?] Kotchins or Gens-de-fine [Han?], and the Tatanchaks, or Gens-de-wiz [Tutchone], who inhabit the upper Youkon, and the Porcupine, or Gens-de-ralt [rat] [Crow River Kutchin?], who live upon the banks of the Porcupine, or Rat River" (Raymond 1870: 593). Three years later in an article for the American Geographical Society, Raymond (1873: 178) proceeds to turn our clouds into rain by not repeating himself. "The principal tribes which have been accustomed to trade at this post [Fort Yukon] are the Kotcha-kutchins (or lowlanders), who live beyond [along?] the Yukon and Porcupine rivers, near their junction; the Ankutchins [Han] or *Gens de Bois* [?], and the Tatanchakutchins [Tutchone?], or *Gens de Foux* [?], who inhabit the upper Yukon; and the Porcupines, or *Gens de Rat*, who live upon the banks of the Porcupine or Rat river [Crow River Kutchin?]." I would gladly have eliminated Raymond's statements as unnecessary confusion, but my purpose is to present all the evidence, and I shall try to do so. Therefore a third account by him is added: "The principal tribes which have been accustomed to trade at this post [Fort Yukon] are the Kotcha-Kutchin (or 'Lowlanders'), who live between [along?] the Porcupine and

Yukon rivers, near their junction; the Hun-Kutchin [Han], or Gens de Bois [?],
and the Tutchone-Kutchin [Raymond admits to borrowing this name from Dall],
or Gens des Foux, who inhabit the Upper Yukon, and the Porcupines, or Gens de
Rat [Crow River Kutchin?], who live upon the banks of the Porcupine or Rat
River" (Raymond 1900: 38). We might almost regret that he did not try once
more.

Dall (1870a: 109), who received his information secondhand, introduces uncertainty again in one place where he mentions "the *Tutchóne Kutchin* (crow people), or Gens de Foux" as coming to Fort Yukon to trade from up the river beyond the Han. In a later paper he seems to rectify matters by saying that the
Tutchone "occupy the banks of the Yukon from the Deer River [the Klondike]
nearly to the site of Fort Selkirk and the watershed of the small streams flowing
into the Yukon from the north, especially on the Stewart River about Reid House;
the basin of the White River, heading in the glaciers of the St. Elias Alps; and
perhaps the Lewis [Lewes] River to some extent" (Dall 1877: 32). It is uncertain
how or where he obtained this latter information, although quite possibly it was
from Frank Ketchum. In any event, it is as reliable as any other.

Schwatka (1885a: 227–8) introduces a new note of confusion by speaking of
the Tutchone as Ayans. He writes: "These Indians called themselves the A-
yans—with an occasional leaning of the pronunciation toward I-yan; and this
village [Kah-tung, a few miles below Selkirk], so they said, contained the majority
of the tribe, although from their understanding of the question they may have
meant that it was the largest village of the tribe. Their country, as they claim it,
extends up the Pelly—the Indian name of which is *Ayan*—to the lakes, up the
Yukon from this point to the village of Kit-ah-gon [about fifteen miles above the
mouth of the Pelly], and down that stream [the Yukon] to near the mouth of the
White and Stewart Rivers, where they are succeeded by a tribe called the *Netch-
on-dees* or Na-chon-des—the Indian name of the Stewart River being Na-
chon-de." We might note here that Indians were infrequently encountered between
the village of Kit-ah-gon and Lake Laberge both in his day and in ours (Schwatka
1885a: 179–80).

The distinction Schwatka makes between the A-yans and the Na-chon-des tribe
is interestingly, if somewhat confusingly, followed by Dawson's division of the
upper Yukon people. George Dawson, who was in the Yukon Territory in 1887,
extends the term A-yans (Ai-ya-na, Ai-yan) to embrace seven groups including
two on the Tanana River and the Kutcha Kutchin of the Fort Yukon region
(Dawson 1889: 202B–3B). The first two of the seven groups are clearly in the
Tutchone area although he calls only one of them by that name, using the often
synonymous term Gens de bois for the other. He states specifically: "A tribe or
band named Klo-a-tsul-tshik (-otin?) range from Rink Rapid and its vicinity on
the Lewes to the head of the east branch of White River, where they go at the
salmon-fishing season. These people probably also range down the river as far as
the mouth of the Lewes, or further. They are the Gens des Bois or Wood Indians

of the fur-traders. It will be observed that their name does not terminate in the usual way, but of this no explanation could be obtained" (Dawson 1889: 202B). Then he goes on to say: "The To-tshik-o-tin are said to live about the mouth of Stewart River, and to extend up the Stewart as far as the Beaver River, meeting there the Es-pa-to-ti-na [Kaska] to whom they are or were hostile. The To-tshik-o-tin are no doubt the Tutchone-kutchin of Dall's map."

What seems to be clear from these data is that two bands, or tribes, have been distinguished in what we have chosen to describe as the Tutchone area. Schwatka's A-yans are Dawson's Klo-a-tsul-tshik, and Schwatka's Netch-on-dees are as clearly Dawson's To-tshik-o-tin, while Dall's Tutchóne certainly include the latter.

As far as the unity of these two groups is concerned, I have no doubt been prejudiced by Dall, and especially his map (Dall 1877). The early fur traders, however, in speaking of the Indians on the Yukon itself above the Kutchin as far as the junction of the Lewes and Pelly quite consistently distinguish no more than two groups. One is certainly the Han, thus leaving only one other to correspond to the Tutchone. Equally important for us, my Han informants spoke of but one other major Athapaskan group on the Yukon above them, and these centered at a village near the site of Fort Selkirk (Kah-tung?). Nevertheless, it is still possible on the evidence to contend there were two distinct groups equivalent to the Han within this area, while south of it the situation becomes even more confused.

I shall also briefly mention the Tagish Indians because they were discussed with my informants and present a special problem. They were not included among the groups presented in *The Distribution of the Northern Athapaskan Indians* (Osgood 1936b) because they are consistently reported as speaking a dialect of Tlingit, a North Pacific Coast language, although having a culture that was closer to the adjacent Athapaskan Indians (Dall 1877: 37; Dawson 1889: 192B, 203B).

Murray (1910: 82) says: "between the Pelly [Lewes] and the coast are a band called the 'Arlez (or Artez)-Kootchin' (Tough or Hard people) numbering about 100." The *Handbook of American Indians* (1910, *2:* 1028) lists the Artez as Ahtena, but from the location, it is much more likely that the Tagish are meant. Schwatka (1885a: 104) seems to extend the territory of the Tagish farther north when he writes: "the country of this tribe [Tagish], which stretches to the site of old Fort Selkirk at the mouth of the Pelly River." Under the name Chilkaht-kwan, Dall shows the Tagish territory as extending to the Lewes below Lake Laberge where they join his Tutchone (Dall 1877). Dawson states that the Tagish "occupy the greater part of the valley of the Lewes above the mouth of the Teslin-Too" (Tagish River) to the watershed of the Pacific coast (Dawson 1889: 192B, 203B). Schwatka (1885a: 104) says the Tagish (Chilkat Tahk-heesh) even extended to the site of old Fort Selkirk. If not to contradict himself, he probably meant the borders of Tutchone territory above Fort Selkirk. Then lastly, a Han informant said the Tagish—whom he referred to as "Whitehorse people"—were very different from the Tutchone, being related to the coast tribes.

We now come to the central problem, or the identification and distribution of the Han. Murray, as previously mentioned, distinguished the "Fathzei (Tathzei)-Kootchin," or People of the Ramparts, as living on the banks of the Yukon below the confluence of the Lewes and Pelly. Then he states: "Between them and the lands belonging to the natives of this place [Fort Yukon] are the 'Han-Kootchin' (People of the water) known as the *Gens du Fou*, this is the largest band of any here-about, there are in all 230 men. They are divided into four bands, the uppermost one is the 'Frawtsee (Trawtsee)-Kootchin' (People of the Forks) the Gens du fou inhabit a great extent of country, from the sources of Porcupine and Peels River to those of the River of the Mountain Men [Tanana River]; they often visit the Russians on the coast, but [also] frequently trade with intervening Indians. A few of them used to go to Peels River, last spring there were 16 men, and *here* in the summer and fall we saw a good many but what they brought was of little value" (Murray 1910: 82).

These somewhat unpunctuated lines written in 1848 probably constitute the earliest significant comment on the Han Indians. Three important points seem to be made. First, the Han are clearly distinguished as a unit; second, they are stated to have been divided into four bands; and third, their territory is fairly clearly delimited. Some additional comments may be added, however. As has been quite definitely established, the name he gives to these people is of Kutchin origin, *Han* meaning *water* in the latter language and *Kutchin, dwellers*. By using Kutchin terminology for non-Kutchin people—which was natural enough—he started the implication of their being Kutchin themselves, a confusing practice that was disseminated by Hardisty and Dall. Unfortunately, as has been noted earlier, he may also have used the term Gens du fou for Indians on the Yukon above the Han. Then he is casual in speaking of the Han as a *band* of Indians divided into four *bands*. Finally, he does not locate the "Frawtsee (Trawtsee)" with any decisiveness.

In a later place in his diary, Murray describes a party of Indians who came from above the Ramparts (which for the sake of consistency in his remarks must be the Han) as Gens du fou and again states that they were divided into four bands. Curiously, this party is reported to have heard from the middle band (and the latter from the upper band) that Robert Campbell was coming down the Pelly River—I say curiously because it is not simple to account for a middle band among four (Murray 1910: 96–7). Since we already know that Murray was not always precise in his use of the word band, it is possible that in this case his middle band is not one of the four Han bands, but actually the Tutchone. Elsewhere he seems to have used middle band in that sense when he says: "The Middle Band and People of the Butes [Tanana] speak the same" (Murray 1910: 83). He is not speaking of the Gens du fou since he deals with the latter language in the next paragraph on the following page. Let me conclude this commentary on Murray by expressing gratitude that under the circumstances he supplied as much information as he did.

Following Murray, Hardisty (1872: 311) likewise speaks of the Han as Gens du fou in distinguishing them from the Indians farther up the Yukon, but adds that they have many words in common with the latter. Gibbs, we might note, recorded that sixty Han hunters visited Fort Yukon in 1854, a fact apparently supplied by Hardisty (*Handbook* 1907, *1:* 531). Whymper (1869: 177) confirms that the use of Gens du fou for the Han was general in his time.

Dall (1877: 31), the compiler, creates a bit of purely gratuitous confusion when he indicates that the Han were the "Gens des Bois" of the Hudson's Bay Company men. Perhaps, just as Murray reversed the river names Pelly and Lewes, Dall has done the same with the Gens du fou and the Gens de bois. Furthermore, this reversal is shown when he states that the word *Han* means *wood* or *forest,* whereas *river* is the correct translation of this Kutchin word while *bois* is obviously wood (Petitot 1876: 318; Osgood 1934: 175[6]; Slobodin 1963a: 4). Dall (1877: 31) gives the range of the Han on the Yukon as extending from the Kotlo (Preacher Creek on Birch River) to the Deer (Klondike) River.

Schwatka (1885a: 249) is a poor informant on the identification of the Han since, as he clearly states, in going down the river he had no satisfactory interpreters after leaving the Tutchone area where he specifically notes a difference in language.

Two of Dawson's (1889: 202B) seven tribes grouped together as A-yans (Ai-ya-na, Ai-yan) are clearly in Han territory. These are the Tsit-o-klin-otin near the mouth of the Fortymile and the Ka-tshik-o-tin a short distance below them.

Schmitter (1910: 1), who has contributed important cultural data on the Han, seems to have had little interest in the boundaries of these people, simply concentrating his study on the natives at Eagle who, he unfortunately states, "are classified as the Vunta-Kutchin people of the Athapascan family" (*Handbook* 1910, *2:* 882), thereby needlessly confusing them with the Crow River Kutchin (Osgood 1934: 173; McKennan 1959: 23).

All the informants with whom I myself discussed the distribution of the Han affirmed the unity of the people on the Yukon from the Klondike down as far as the territory of the Kutcha-Kutchin below Charley Village, setting off as equivalents such groups as the Tutchone and the Kutchin.

Thirty years later, Slobodin (1963a: 3–4) states: "It is impossible to say whether, and to what extent, the people under consideration [natives at Dawson] had any sense of community beyond the local group in pre-contact or early post-contact times," but he later adds in the words of a son of Chief Isaac of the Klondike band: "We and the Eagle people are the only ones who speak our language. I've never heard of any others."

So much for the general information on the identification of the Han. We can now profit by a consideration of the data on the divisions among them, and

---

[6] This translation was also confirmed in 1932 by Edward Sapir, who made a special study of the Kutchin language.

particularly as shown by the distribution of their villages. Let us recall first that Murray (1910: 82) in one place clearly states in speaking of the Han: "They are divided into four bands." After Murray, another mention of four bands has not been found, but a compilation of data on Han villages indicates four distinct settlements which can now be considered in order from north to south (Fig. 4).

1) Charley Village (also known as Charlieville and Tadush) is said by Schwatka (1885a: 262) to have been located roughly opposite the mouth of the Kandik River on the left bank of the Yukon. We must note, however, that Hudson Stuck (1917: 82) insists that Schwatka was in error and that the village was just above the Kandik on the right bank of the Yukon in Schwatka's time, and that it remained there until 1914 when it was washed away and the few remaining natives moved to Circle.

I do not know what to make of this since Schwatka is so specific in locating the village on the left bank and, while so doing, comparing it with Johnny Village. On his map, curiously enough, Schwatka (1885a: 207) identifies "Charlies Village," but does not show its exact location in the manner that he distinguishes "John's Village." This seems to be a point in favor of Stuck. The *Geographic Dictionary* (Baker 1906: 170), which gives Charley Village as the accepted spelling, places it "at the mouth of Kandik river" which may again seem to support Stuck's assertion. I, incidentally, have adopted the spelling of Johnny Village, dropping the more common possessive form, in order to have it conform with Charley Village. One should also take note of the possible confusion between the Kandik River, called Charley Creek, and the Charley River (Willow Creek) that flows into the Yukon from the south a few miles below the Kandik.

Schwatka (1885a: 262) visited Charley Village in 1883 and reported that it contained six houses. He found Joseph Ladue there, an early prospector-trader and later founder of Dawson, who praised the character of the local Indians and is apparently responsible for the name *Tadush* by which he called the natives of Charley Village as well as those of Johnny Village, the next Han settlement above on the Yukon.

2) Johnny Village (three miles above Eagle) takes its name from that given the Indian chief, the native term for the settlement being Klat-ol-klin, according to Schwatka (1885a: 255). It is apparently the primary locale of Dawson's (1889: 202B) Ka-tshik-o-tin tribe. Hereafter, for convenience, I shall refer to the village as Eagle when speaking of the Indians of the area.

Schwatka (1885a: 262) pointed out that Johnny Village was the exact counterpart of Charley Village, even to the number of houses. It should be mentioned once again that Fort Egbert was established about three miles below Johnny Village in 1899 at the farther end of Eagle, of which it was an extension. Just below Eagle–Fort Egbert, the stream called Tatolinda by the Indians, and Mission Creek by the whites, flows into the Yukon.

It was from the Indians of Johnny Village that Schmitter's data on the Han were derived, as well as most of that recorded by Osgood. Schmitter (1910: 15) states: "The Eagle Indians themselves are called 'kkwi dyik' in their own tongue." In 1932, an Eagle informant said the natives of that village were called Өtahukli^n which referred to the eddy there (Osgood 1934: 176).[7] Two of Slobodin's informants at Dawson said the Eagle people were called eʒan kučin or eʒʸan kučin while one added that the Kutchin (Peel River?) called them ezʒin kučʔɪn and the Tutchone eʒana (Slobodin 1963a: 4). The last native term seems especially reminiscent of Dawson's (1889: 202B) Ai-ya-na.

Strangely, Schmitter (1910: 15) adopted the name Vuntakutchin for the people of Eagle despite the fact that he not only records their own name but states: "In the Porcupine [Kutchin] language they are called 'vun tte kwi chin,' which means 'the people of the Willow Creek,' since they came from what is now known as Charlie Creek, where willows abound and from which the creek was named by the natives." Referring to an Indian tribe by the name given them by neighbors is actually not uncommon, but it seldom results in the confusion that has occurred in this case. It is certainly noteworthy that Schmitter implies that the people of Johnny Village came from the vicinity of Charley Village.

3) Fortymile (Fetutlin) was located on the Yukon near the mouth of the Fortymile River. Dawson (1889: 202B) states: "Near the mouth of Forty-mile Creek are the Tsit-o-klin-otin." I have found little information on this group but there is evidence of sizable settlement before 1880 (Petrof 1900: 68).

4) Nuklako (Noo-klak-o, Nuclaco) was located on the left bank of the Yukon River about thirteen miles below the mouth of the Klondike (Fort Reliance was established across from Nuklako in 1874, but abandoned about 1883). The Indians there have been called *Takon* (*Handbook* 1910, *2:* 675). Schwatka (1885a: 246–7) reports receiving a protracted salute of muskets when he passed by without stopping in 1883, and speaks of the place as "a semi-permanent village."

Moosehide and Dawson, insofar as Indians are concerned, will here be treated as part of the Nuklako area since they are only ten and thirteen miles upstream respectively and are known from later settlements affected, if not brought about, by the gold rush. Tappan Adney may have been the first to write about the Dawson Indians specifically. He says their village was at the mouth of the Klondike River and that they were called Tro-chu-tin (Adney 1900a: 495). The village may well have been brought into being by the Klondike strike as I have found no mention of it earlier. At Moosehide in 1932, the name of the local Indians was recorded as tɣačik, meaning "mouth of the Klondike" (Osgood 1934: 176). The term was recorded thirty years later as tronʒiuk or trončik and translated by one native as "the people living at Water-Flowing-Through-Grass," while another said the term "had something to do with fish-traps" (Slobodin 1963a: 3).

Whether the existence of these four settlement areas is responsible for Murray's statement that there were four Han bands existing in 1848 is an open question. The constituency of Northern Athapaskan bands changes with time and probably

---

[7] The orthography of Kutchin words, when not quoted from the historic sources, has been adjusted to that adopted for Slobodin's transcriptions (cf. p. 27).

we shall never know more certainly what was the number during the period of
first European contact. It is interesting, however, that by the time the *Handbook
of American Indians* was published, *three* subdivisions of the Han are mentioned, the Katshikotin, Takon, and Tsitoklinotin (*Handbook* 1907, *1:* 531).
These names, as we have seen, correspond to the occupants of three of our four
villages—Johnny Village, Nuklako, and Fortymile—but leave out the residents
of Charley Village. This leads us to recall Schmitter's (1910: 15) intimation that
the Indians of Charley Village and Johnny Village were a single group.

The reduction continued, for in 1932 three Han informants—one at Moosehide
and two at Eagle—presented the consistent conception of the Han as being
divided into two bands, one centering around the mouth of the Klondike River
and the other around Eagle (Osgood 1934: 176; 1936b: 11). One informant at
Eagle tended to emphasize the difference between the two bands, while the other
asserted that they were certainly one nation or group.

Slobodin (1963a: 4) thirty years later pursued the matter further. Charlie Isaac
of Dawson, speaking of the Indians at Eagle, said, "We are the same people,"
and added significantly, "We were once one people, who camped in the summer
at various places between here and Charlie Creek. After the white man came,
and especially after the gold rush, we formed up into two villages. The [Inter-
national] boundary also helped to separate us. We couldn't help it." The evidence
speaks so clearly for itself that further comment does not seem needed.

Before concluding this discussion of the distribution of the Han, I must mention
the appearance of these Indians in the neighborhood of Kechumstuk on the upper
reaches of the Fortymile River. The question of their occupation of the area
in aboriginal times is so confused by the development of mining and telegraph
lines that I have relegated discussion of the problem to the section on the period
of culture changes, thus avoiding further complication in the introduction.

A Comment on the Country

Before going further, a brief description of the Yukon River country will enable
me to point out some of its features which seem especially pertinent to our
interest in the Han Indians. As should be generally realized, the Yukon is one
of the great rivers of the world. Its named length from the Bering Sea to the
junction of the Lewes and the Pelly is approximately 2,000 miles and, disregard-
ing terminology by including the Lewes to its ultimate source, it is several hundred
miles longer. Students, however, should be warned about distances between points
on the Yukon which are given in the literature. Surveyors may give those obtained
by sightings following the middle of the river, while those given from steamboat
routes, which follow the channel of heaviest current, can swing from bank to bank
and become greatly extended (cf. Stuck 1917: 17). For about half its length,
the Yukon flows northwesterly and then in the Yukon Flats area, after reaching
its most northerly point, turns at an angle of about 90° and flows southwesterly
until it makes a half loop before entering the sea.

There are two areas commonly spoken of as the ramparts of the Yukon. One begins almost 200 miles below Fort Yukon and extends southwesterly another 100 miles toward the mouth of the Tanana River; the other begins 7 miles above Eagle, or very close to the Alaska–Yukon boundary, and extends southwesterly roughly 340 miles to about the mouth of the Pelly. Between these two rampart regions spread the Yukon Flats where the great river for about 200 miles widens out into multiple channels over an area in some places 20 miles in breadth, thus forming innumerable islands. Some point on the lower ramparts is generally considered as the boundary between the lower Yukon region and the upper, although the latter is perhaps more often itself divided into the middle Yukon and the upper Yukon, the boundary again being set at some point on the upper ramparts, the latter constriction being not too sharply distinguished at its ends. It is obviously the middle Yukon, as here defined, with which I am primarily concerned.

Before considering the middle Yukon as a subarea, I should perhaps point out that the lower ramparts were something of a barrier. At least below them, the Yukon is as navigable a stream as one might ever expect to find, but to go up through the lower ramparts at certain stages of water creates a noticeable psychological, as well as physical, problem for those depending on primitive means of transport. This difficulty, although easily surmounted, was certainly a minor reason why the relationship between the two halves of the Yukon River was not properly comprehended until the middle of the nineteenth century. The lower ramparts with the high land behind them also undoubtedly marked off significant Athapaskan linguistic and cultural subareas.

The distinctions between the middle Yukon and upper Yukon, if any less obvious, are perhaps actually more real. Geologically, it would appear that the more impressive southern half of the upper ramparts results from the Yukon in its Cretaceous valley cutting through a belt of Mesozoic coast-range intrusives running east and west across the river above Dawson. Probably it has cultural significance that the middle Yukon was an unglaciated region, in contrast to the upper Yukon. The upper ramparts are also an area of discontinuous permafrost which means that excavations of a few feet, such as are needed for semi-subterranean houses and underground caches, can be more easily undertaken in well-chosen places. Even more important, it would seem, are the differences in flora. The higher land of the upper Yukon, which has been spoken of as a plateau, is significantly lacking in the birch, spruce, and paper-cottonwoods of a size and quality so useful to Indians. Finally, to a considerable degree, the food value of salmon decreases in the upper reaches of the Yukon drainage.

It is also easy to think of the middle Yukon as being divided into three segments of approximately equal length. The lowest on the river is the Yukon Flats, an area abundantly supplied with waterfowl and muskrats, and so many porcupines that the major river debouching into it was named after them (Schwatka 1885a: 293–4). The uppermost segment of the middle Yukon is also the more closed-in half of the upper ramparts, a stretch in which the river ice is said to melt in the spring rather than being washed out by the great flow of water that can result from such melting, as is the case in the central segment and all the Yukon below.

It is this central segment, and especially the lower portion, which might be preferred by any river Athapaskan if he had to choose a section of the Yukon for a permanent home. The riverbanks provide satisfactory sites for settlements, close to side streams which together with the Yukon contribute great quantities of fish, if not as many as in the lower Yukon. Timber of the desirable kinds is in good supply, and the accessibility of caribou grounds for fall hunting offers no great problem. What I am saying essentially is that the central segment of the middle Yukon was probably the best area for Indians in the surrounding quarter of a million square miles. As it happens, that central segment of the middle Yukon is practically identical with the territory occupied by the Han.

In concluding these brief comments on the Han country, I must admit that it is one of the coldest regions of the world, although the extremes of the winter months are offset by the warmness of the summer relative to some other regions. Fortunately, temperature records have been kept at Dawson (1,062 feet altitude) since the beginning of the twentieth century, and the monthly and annual normals of mean daily temperature in degrees Fahrenheit over a period of thirty years have been provided by Thompson (1962: 308–12) from whom I quote:

Jan.	−17.6	May	46.6	Sept.	43.5
Feb.	−11.1	June	56.9	Oct.	26.4
Mar.	5.7	July	59.8	Nov.	2.5
Apr.	29.4	Aug.	54.5	Dec.	−12.9

The annual normal for Dawson is 23.6°. A maximum temperature of 95° was recorded there on June 18, 1950, and there had been more than one such occurrence during the sixty-two years of record. The minimum temperature was −73° recorded February 3, 1947. Even somewhat lower temperatures have been recorded (the minimum is −81°) at higher places in the Yukon Territory but none so low in the Northwest Territories. As cold as it was for the Han, it probably was as cold, if not colder, in much of the surrounding territory because of the increase in altitude as one either moved up or away from the Yukon.

Language

The data that have been available for this study on the Han language are negligible. In 1932, Angus of Eagle said that the Indians of that place and the Dawson–Moosehide area could understand each other easily, thereby leaving the impression that there were dialectic differences between the two bands. Also, Mary McLeod of Dawson told Slobodin (1963a: 4) in 1962 when speaking of the Eagle people: "Their dialect is a little different from ours." [8]

Hardisty, who was unusually sensitive to the language problem, had already

---

[8] It must be noted that Charlie Isaac told Slobodin (1963a: 4): "My language is the same as that spoken at Eagle." Quite probably, I would think, since his father came from Eagle.

in the middle eighteenth century linked together the Kutchin of the Yukon Flats, Chandalar River, Black River, Crow River, Upper Porcupine River, and Peel River as speaking Loucheux (Kutchin) proper, adding "a slight difference of accent being all that is perceptible in their respective dialects" (Hardisty 1872: 311). What is important for us is that he noted that the Han language was different, continuing with the comment that the Han shared many words in common with the Gens de bois (Tutchone). Murray (1910: 84) himself says: "The 'Gens du fou' [Han] speak differently [with respect to the Kutchin]" and then goes on to say "the language is a mixture of the Loucheux [Kutchin] and Nawhawny [Tutchone? (cf. Honigmann 1954: 21)], and is nearly the same as is spoken at Frances Lake [Kaska], a number of the Gens du fou, those farthest north understand the Loucheux [Kutchin] well." His last instance, as I shall demonstrate later, refers to Han Indians who had learned Kutchin for purposes of trade.

More information is supplied by Schwatka (1885a: 249), who writes:

> Indianne, my Chilkat-Takh-heesh [Tagish] interpreter, got along very well among the latter tribe [as his mother was Tagish]. Among the Ayans [Tutchone?] were many who spoke Tahk-heesh [Tagish], with whom they traded, and here [on the Yukon after leaving Stewart River] we had but little trouble. Even lower down [in the Klondike area?] we managed to get along after a fashion, for one or two of the Ayan [Tutchone?] medicine-men who came as far as Fort Reliance [a few miles below the mouth of the Klondike?] with us, could occasionally be found, and they understood the lower languages pretty fairly, and although we struggled through four or five tongues [as from Han to Tutchone to Tagish to English] we could still make out that tea and tobacco were the leading topics of conversation everywhere. Beyond Fort Reliance, and after bidding adieu to our four Ayans [Tutchone?], we were almost at sea, but occasionally in the most roundabout way we managed to elicit information of a limited character.

These somewhat misleading suggestions of a closer linguistic relationship between the Han and Tutchone, and possibly with the Tanana and other neighboring groups to the west, south, and southeast have at least been intimated in several sources by such formulations as Dawson's (1889: 203B) grouping of the A-yans. A mention of this matter seems proper here, but speculation upon it will be reserved as a special problem to be treated when we deal with the period of culture change.

A final comment on the interaction of languages upon each other perhaps should be interpolated as a warning. Because of the motivation on the part of the Indians to trade European goods when first obtained, individuals of various tribes sojourned in the territories of others, a practice which probably had not been previously as common. The approach of the white man at first seemed to cause conflicts to arise, but later intertribal security was increased and alien Indians became accustomed to each other. In some cases, considerable numbers apparently learned the language of their neighbors. For instance, Murray (1910: 53) says:

"One band of the 'Gens-du-fou' have, of late years, had much intercourse with the Loucheux [Kutchin] Indians, and many of them speak the language." He says in another place that he brought the Peel River Indian named Vandeh to Fort Yukon as an interpreter for the Gens du fou, so we can assume that the knowledge of the adjacent language was not simply one-sided (pp. 51–2).

In 1932, the mixing of Han and Peel River Kutchin in the Dawson–Moosehide area was obvious, and it had apparently been going on at least since the gold rush days at the end of the nineteenth century. It follows that particular caution will be needed seventy years later in unraveling the linguistic relationships of the Han and Tutchone natives, not to mention the problems inevitably rising when the Indians of the middle Tanana River area are included.

Population

The data on the population of the Han at any period in the nineteenth century cannot be reduced to a satisfactory statement. The reports are too few, and they consist mostly of estimates taken at different periods with no certainty in every case whether only Han Indians are included. The information will be considered by village.

Charley Village. Reported to have a population of 48 in the census of 1880 (*Handbook* 1910, *2:* 668).

Eagle. Schmitter (1910: 1) reported the Indian village to contain about 200 inhabitants.

Fortymile. The population of Fetutlin for 1880 was given as 106 people by Petroff (1900: 68; *Handbook* 1907, *1:* 458).

Nuklako. The *Handbook* (1910, *2:* 96) makes the number 82, again following Petrof (1900: 68). Schwatka (1885a: 246–7), apparently relying on Leroy McQuesten, stated the population to consist of 75 to 80 permanent residents, although he estimates 150 people to have been at the village (including a large number of Tanana Indians) in 1883. The Reverend Vincent Sim, who visited the village during July of the same summer, said: "Many Indians were staying there [Fort Reliance] in ten houses each containing at least four families" (Wesbrook 1969: 43). That would mean 40 families or perhaps 200 people. Sim also mentions visitors, however, and perhaps more significantly, an epidemic (apparently diphtheria) which apparently had hit the upper Yukon in 1882 (Wesbrook 1969: 41).

From the above statements we derive a population figure for the Han of 430. Since some Indians were certainly not counted, a very tentative estimate of 500 for the last quarter of the nineteenth century can be proposed. What the population amounted to at the time of first European contact is another matter that cannot be resolved. I can reiterate that Murray (1910: 52) said about 1848 that the two nearest (of three? or of four?) bands of Gens du fou numbered upward of 100 men. Later (1910: 82) he asserted that Gens du fou was "the largest band of any hereabout, there are in all 230 men." These statements might be taken to mean that one-half to two-thirds of the population amounted to 500 individuals and the total somewhere around 1,000, but this is no more than a guess. There is little doubt, however, but that it was significantly higher than any of the later records show.

The Impact of European Contact

I once gave the date of direct European contact with the Han as about 1847 (at Fort Yukon), with settlement periodic from about 1875 at Fort Reliance (Osgood 1936b: 11). I would now rectify the last phrase to read "from about 1873 at Belle Isle near the present village of Eagle." Since rereading Murray several times, however, the question has been reopened in my mind as to whether any Russians reached the headwaters of the Yukon and possibly had contact with the Han before 1847. Burpee, who edited Murray's Journal, says: "In view of this evidence, it does not seem possible to accept Murray's statements, positive though they are, that the Russians had explored the Yukon, not only to the mouth of the Porcupine, but even to the headwaters of the Yukon, even before John Bell or Robert Campbell appeared on the scene." Then he seems to jeopardize his role as an impartial reviewer by adding, "In any event, Murray's evidence cannot be accepted as sufficiently conclusive to take from Campbell the honour of discovering and exploring the Yukon from its upper waters to the mouth of the Porcupine" (Murray 1910: 8). To me, the matter seems a question of the truth, not honor, and with great respect for Robert Campbell I am moved to consider the data again.

One thing seems worth noting; the men who write journals and books are usually preceded by adventurous and often uneducated men who do not. This applies to regions where the motives for exploration are commonplace and certainly to the area of the fur trade in Canada and Alaska, some notable exceptions simply illuminating the rule. It is also significant for Alaska that the Russians had a declining interest in the area during the last twenty-five years of their control, and the activities of their traders in the interior of the country seem to have gone largely unrecorded. Certainly the Indians who met Murray at Fort Yukon knew of the Russians and had been trading with them directly or indirectly for years. A Russian trading post had been established at Nulato, about 500 miles below Fort Yukon in 1839, and probably some exploration was made above that place in the years following. At least in June 1843 the remarkable traveler Lavrentiy Zagoskin with a number of men spent the rest of the month pulling up the Yukon in a six-oared boat before they turned back. It had been their intention to reach British Territory, and this was the year before Robert Bell crossed over from the Mackenzie country (Osgood 1940: 39; Chernenko et al. 1967: 17, 157–9). Clearly, the Indians of the middle Yukon area knew of these activities and some direct contact with them may have been made (cf. Murray 1910: 7–8 n).

It is not the Russians who were established in the lower Yukon who really concern us, however. Murray mentions the Russians in his Journal in about ten different places of which more than half refer to locations in the Yukon River drainage *above* him. For example, he writes: "We lived on good terms with the natives and feared nothing, except to see two boat loads of Russians heave around the point on a nocturnal visit from the Gens-du-fou," while four pages later, again speaking of a large party of Gens du fou that had arrived, he speaks of their Russian trade pipes and says he had a long talk with them in the evening about that trade and that they reported the killing of some Russians who would not give the Indians what they wanted. Murray even interpolates the statement that he had heard previously of that attack (1910: 56, 59–61). A dozen pages later (p. 73) he states with unmistakable clarity: "The Russians have also been on the head waters of this great river [the Yukon], not so far down as the forks of the Lewis [Lewes] and Pelly but below the 'Great Lake' [Lake Laberge?] the place I have marked as shown by the Gens du fou, but I am not aware that they come there regularly." One may contend that the Great Lake shown on Murray's map is Teslin Lake as does Burpee (Murray 1910: 76 n), or some other near the head-waters of the Pelly, but that changes matters little.

Twice again Murray reports (p. 97) on the Russians having contact with the Indians on the upper Yukon and in one case he specifies various details. He writes:

> These Indians [Gens du fou] have been trading some furs with the Russians last winter, going there principally for a supply of snuff and tobacco. These Indians are very fond of snuff and generally carry it with them. The distance from this to one of the Russian Forts is not great, and ten of the Russians with a party of Indians started to come here in winter to see who and where we were, but returned on account of the severity of cold. They have discovered another and nearer route to the Youcon by descending a river which joins this in the Gens du fou country (above this) and they are coming with a large party of these Indians this summer. The Indians have been telling us all about their Fort, their trade and their goods, etc., etc. Amongst other things which they were bringing accross the new portage was a *cannon* one of which they always carry on each boat in 'these parts'. If all this be true we shall yet see the Russians. I had hopes that from below they would scarcely reach us, but since they descend the river it is most probable they will be here.

It is impossible for an ethnographer to disregard these statements by Murray. The Han and Tutchone had certainly been trading with the Russians, but exactly where the contacts were made and whether through intermediaries is open to debate. Of course, under the name of Russians, we must include Russian Creoles, in keeping with the recognition of the offspring of mixed marriages elsewhere in the annals of the north. The difficulty was certainly not the challenge of crossing the coastal ranges along the Pacific shore. Thousands of tenderfoot Americans managed that in the nineteenth century. Also we know that the Russians had entered the interior through the difficult Copper River Valley as early as 1843, and that Rufus Sebrebriannikov wintered at the Russian post or roadhouse at Taral just below the mouth of the Chitina in 1847, and in the following year explored the Tazlina River, returning to continue up the Copper River where, in some undetermined spot, he and his companions were murdered, interestingly enough not for plunder but because of an involvement with a daughter of one of the chiefs (Allen 1887: 19–22; Tompkins 1945: 203; Gsovski 1950: 69–70). The real problem was whether the Tlingit and Ahtena ever allowed either Russians, or Russian Creoles, to pass through their country to meet any interior Indians or the latter to do so to meet Russians.

As was stated, I have been moved to consider the evidence again. After having done so in connection with this study, I can only say I have not found any positive evidence that men with Russian blood reached the headwaters of either the Yukon or the Tanana in the first half of the nineteenth century, but I think, because of the Tlingit and Ahtena control of the passes, that they probably did not. In any event, since no written record has been found, the question has become more academic than ethnographical.

The Record of Han Culture

The method of presenting the data on Han culture will be to proceed according to traditional categories although in approximately the reverse of what may be the commonest order—in each case presenting the earlier information on a specific aspect first, and then indicating, but not repeating, later confirming reports. At the end of each section of culture, opinions about the cultural data, or pertinent comments on their recording, will be added.

No gestures will be made toward a comparative study of Athapaskan culture, itself a tremendous undertaking if properly carried out, and one not to be confused with the presentation of original data. References to the culture of other Athapaskan groups will occasionally be given in the sections entitled *Commentary*, however, in the following special circumstances: (1) to support the appearance of an unusual trait (e.g., polyandry); (2) to explain the recording of opinion on an oddity (e.g., circumcision); and (3) to clarify a cultural concept (e.g., eninglani).

Since the stated purpose of this paper is to present the aboriginal culture of the Han, and since the record of contact with informants is spread over a period of 115 years, the special problem arises of how to be certain how much of the data is applicable. I have chosen neither to disregard this problem nor to slip by it with a casual mention of its existence. On the other hand, as this paper makes no pretensions of being a study of acculturation, I shall not honor the data in this respect with more critical attention than can be quickly applied. The guide lines will be as follows. When there is no clear evidence of a complex or trait having been introduced by direct European contact, it will be included as aboriginal in the sense of its having existed in Han culture before contact. Also, when a particular trait has been obviously introduced but only appears as an accessory element in an aboriginal complex, it also will be included and with a comment only when deemed necessary.

Occasionally there is also a question whether data can be properly attributed to the Han at any period, as for example when there is a question of utilizing data attributed to the Gens du fou, or, in a few cases, when the description of a culture element is presented in a source which seems to be applicable over a larger area and thereby to include the Han. I can only state that I am conscious of such difficulties and feel able to be relatively unbiased when faced with decisions; in any event the citations will show the sources of the data for further consideration when desired.

Finally, whatever data manifestly record material, behavior, or ideas that represent historic changes in the culture of the Han will be presented in a summary section entitled THE PERIOD OF CULTURE CHANGE.

Religion

Murray (1910: 87) in his peculiarly punctuated English states, presumably speaking of the Indians that he knew at Fort Yukon, "They have like all other tribes their good and evil spirits, which they seldom trouble except in cases of sickness or war, the evil spirit is the one generally invoked, they being most afraid of it; according to their account the spirit works mighty wonders betimes." Schmitter (1910: 2) associates these spirits with dreams, saying: "The native believes in a rather concrete existence of dream life, and he sees spirits as if they were real creatures." What is more, these spirits are generally identified with animals. Schmitter goes on to say: "Only the medicine-man [shaman] has access to this dream life and he alone can transfer animals from real to dream life and vice versa. One might assume from the tricks of the medicine-man that he is an impostor, but he is really sincere and believes in himself, although he has the faculty of believing what he must know 'isn't so.' "

In the field of religion, it was this role of the shaman that primarily impressed the commentators from the time of Murray down to the most recent among them. Schmitter, the doctor, was particularly attracted by this aspect of the culture and he mentions specifically the functions of the shaman, his sources of power, his methods of curing, and the procedure of learning the profession. He says of the shaman (1910: 17): "his aid is sought for more purposes than healing the sick, and he can perform to defeat the enemy, to overcome famine, or to make a prospective hunting trip successful. When a man is sick he calls in this Indian doctor, who sings to drive away the disease. Each medicine-man has his own way of singing, though the general form is a chant like those used in dances, in which words are sometimes used, but generally meaningless syllables. The medicine-man goes to sleep and dreams songs, and what he hears in the dream he repeats as an incantation over the sick one."

Conflicts between shamans of different bands or tribes was first mentioned in the area by Murray (1910: 87), and Schmitter (1910: 19) provides data on a specific case when he writes: "Last winter one of the Indians had severe tuberculosis, bronchitis, and pleurisy, for which I treated him, unaware that he was a medicine-man, and during the spring he recovered. He has since confided to me that his illness was caused by a bad medicine-man from 'Tanana', who sent the quill of a large eagle feather that entered into him and caused his sickness. He insisted that he extracted this quill in the presence of several witnesses, thus defeating with his magic the machinations of his enemy and curing himself. On of the witnesses assures me that this actually happened."

Shamans are clearly divided into two types, good shamans and bad ones, and the latter are naturally feared. Both derive their power, or "medicine," from animal spirits. "Whenever a sick man dies the bad medicine-man takes back the evil spirit, and these spirits, which he sees only in the form of animals in his dreams or when he sings, are kept for future use. It is believed that a stronger medicine-man can kill a weaker one's animal, thus stripping the latter of his power, who thus becomes like anyone else and liable to destruction by the stronger one" (Schmitter 1910: 18–9).

The shaman actually could derive his power from any animal that he saw in his dreams, and Schmitter specifically mentions the weasel (ermine), the marten, and the wolf, but such power was also obtainable from inanimate objects, both close and far. Furthermore, the shaman might possess amulets or, more properly, fetishes, correlated with specific sources of power. For example, the species of animal from which power was derived in a dream might be killed in real life and treated as follows: "The skull and claws are sometimes removed from the skins, but generally are left on. Formerly they were ornamented about the neck and mouth with porcupine quills, but more recently with beads. Although a skin is still most popular, there are many other fetiches in use. A beaver's tooth, wound with beads and suspended on a string, is a useful fetich, and is made to disappear and reappear at the convenience of the medicine-man. Small bones are decorated and used in the same manner. A great many medicine-men dig a certain kind of root from the ground which they carry about in their pockets. It appears to be alive and at times grows larger or smaller. Some medicine men employ the sun, moon, or stars in their songs instead of an animal, while others call upon the trees, birds, brush, or any convenient object" (Schmitter 1910: 18).

One of the most unusual references to a source of shamanistic power is given by Slobodin (1963a: 19–20) in the words of Charlie Isaac. The shaman "might be walking in the mountains and he would see a certain flower. Blue flames coming from this flower. You and I couldn't see the blue flames, but he could. He would pick some and keep it, and use it later for power. He could use it to hurt or kill people, too. He would make something from the flower or whatever it was and shoot it, send it a long distance, and it would hit his enemy, say in the chest, and that man would start to get sore, and then infection, pus, flesh get rotten. Then he would probably die."

As to the procedure of learning the shamanistic profession, Schmitter (1910: 19) states: "If a man wants to become skillful in magic healing he goes to sleep in the same blanket with a medicine-man. When they are asleep and dreaming, he is taught the medicine by his instructor. The medicine-man, however, is disinclined to teach others, because he is apt to lose his power and since a stronger one could [then] kill him. A bad medicine-man likes to kill, but a good medicine-man always wants to cure, and it is said the good are apt to live longer."

I shall deal with more of the shaman's activities in the report on medical practices. From my own notes of 1932, I have only a few points to add, although first affirming the specific notion that a shaman's power comes from his association with animals and other objects specifically introduced through dreams. It is also significant to state that shamans may be of either male or female sex. In my attempt to find out if there was anything distinctive in the appearance of shamans, it was said that when practicing, a shaman tied his hair into a bunch on top of his head and

THE RECORD OF HAN CULTURE

stuck in an eagle feather. No masks were used but a shaman might beat out a rhythm when he sang by hitting one stick with another.

Apart from shamans, my informants were well aware of the concept of the Nakani, or Bad Indian. No details of the belief were recorded, as it seemed to conform to that given by the Peel River Kutchin (Osgood 1936a: 154; also cf. 157, 160). Walter at Eagle gave the Han name for this well-known superhuman personage as na aι.

Finally, although the informants were not disposed to talk about monsters, one did mention the "fire man" (dιn ʒι e o k̓ʊn), who lives in a house built of white clay and stones. In the house is a small table with a big hole behind it. The "fire-man" is seen in dreams.

Commentary. The data are so limited on Han religion that I am moved to speculate why this is so. Three factors immediately come to mind after almost half a century of interest in the Athapaskans. First, there has always been the problem of communication. To discuss religion comprehensively and objectively requires exceptional knowledge and sensitivity, while to find an Athapaskan-speaker and an Indo-European speaker with the necessary ability and rapport to do it together is a miracle that seldom occurs. Probably few good informants on religion ever were available among Northern Athapaskans, and under the impact of acculturation, that few probably diminished in number. Recognition should be given the work of J. Alden Mason, who in 1913 was almost the first professional anthropologist to work among the Northern Athapaskans. Surprisingly, he captured much of the essence of Athapaskan religion in less than 2,000 words while studying the Slave (Mason 1946). Certainly, his statements became more comprehensible as information was intermittently added in a dozen more monographs. For the writer, a satisfying comprehension of Athapaskan religion was a slow and confusing process which consisted in breaking a trail first in one direction and then in another, only to become lost and have to struggle back to some known point before setting out once again. An appreciation of shamans came relatively easily, but a real sense of the animatistic world of the Athapaskans and the true comprehension of magical songs came late (cf. Osgood 1959: 120 ff, 167 ff). As far as religion is concerned, if one were aware of all that has been written on that subject with respect to the Northern Athapaskans, it would be difficult not to find the Han data greatly illuminated by that on the Ingalik. Indeed, so much so for this writer that he may have lost some of his objectivity.

Social Organization

That there were clans (or sibs) among the Han in aboriginal times there can be little doubt, for clans have been mentioned in the earliest descriptions of neighboring Alaskan tribes, the most significant of the reports coming from the Kutchin to the north (Hardisty et al. in Osgood 1936a: 128–9). In 1932 the clan system was no longer functioning and it was with difficulty that information on the subject could be obtained. Fortunately, while I was staying at Moosehide, a Peel River Kutchin Indian named John Semple was able to supply clan names not only for his own people but parallel ones for the Han. This man, born about 1888 on the Peel River, where his parents were born before him, had lived in the Klondike area since the period immediately following the gold rush at the end of the previous century. According to him, there were three exogamous, matrilineal clans among the Han for which he gave the following names and comment:

nats ι	proud people
ιts ya	people who act funny
ta nǯι γa tsa	middle people

The correlation with Hardisty's terms recorded at Fort Yukon was immediately obvious, and he was asked about the association of light or dark color with the clans as indicated by the early fur trader (Hardisty 1872: 315). He replied that he had never head of anything apart from what he said. Perhaps reacting to the disappointment that he sensed, he added the the terms wolf and crow (or raven) which are sometimes associated with the clans (or moieties) "belonged to the Whitehorse Indians (Tagish?)" and not to the tribes on the Yukon. Later, at Eagle, this information was in general corroborated by Angus but with a different name for one of the clans, as follows:

na tsιn
čι čel
tan ǯι γa tsιl

Walter, also of Eagle, concurred independently except that he said ta ndu a tsιl for the third clan. What was more interesting, Walter stated that the three clans were divided into two moieties with the na tsιn clan alone representing one of them. Later, Angus gave the čι čel clan as the one standing alone, but when the two informants were brought together and shown the conflict, Angus revised his opinion in favor of Walter, who claimed he was only corroborating Angus in the first place. Walter used the term e gσn ya interchangeably for ta ndu a tsιl, and I noted later that whereas he and his mother were e gσn ya, his father was a čι čel, as, incidentally, was Angus. Thus we end up with no satisfying certainty as to how the clans were combined into moieties.

It might seem that further clarification could have been gained, but even this little was the result of long conversations in which the ethnographer had to be careful not to suggest answers. Walter did say that na tsιn does not mean "proud people," and that John Semple was probably only describing the attitude of the members of that clan. He added that the na tsιn were sometimes referred to as "crow." Angus stated that ta ndu a tsιl could be translated as "middle people." Neither man had anything to say as to the origin of the clans, but they knew that parallel clans existed among the Kutchin. Walter asserted that the members of the na tsιn clan (and moiety) could be distinguished by the fact that they wore feathers on the right side of the head while members of the opposite moiety wore their feathers in the center of the front part of the head or in the center at the back part. He also made clear that the moieties were not only exogamous but functioned reciprocally in the giving of potlatches which normally followed a death. He was even more certain that what was really important about the clans was that they created a potential bond with individuals of other bands which provided security when visiting. A member of one clan would seek out a fellow member with assurance that he would be well received.

Thirty years after these conversations with Angus and Walter, Slobodin (1963a: 13) pursued the subject with Charlie Isaac of Dawson who told him that the Han had three matrilineal exogamous clans (or sibs?). Charlie said: "There was nɑ tsɑɩ . . . tsɑɩ means 'red paint,' and nɑ tsɑɩ were kind of higher people. I am a nɑ tsɑɩ because my mother was one. You were supposed to marry into the other side . . . . There were the kɛ kut?ɩn, that means 'low' . . . Oh, I remember, the other side was ɑ gon dʸɑ; I don't know what that means." At another point in the interview, Charlie said that nɑ tsɑɩ was one tribe and eʒan was another.

There is an obvious correlation between nɑ tsɑɩ and nɑ tsɩn, while the relationship of ɑ gon dʸɑ and e gʊn yɑ is equally close. Also there is an association of superiority and inferiority with the clans, an attitude not reported by earlier Han informants, but one frequently attributed to the Kutchin (Osgood, 1936a: 107, 122–3, 128; McKennan 1965: 60–1).

Han informants in 1932 clearly rejected the notion of distinct classes of people, while at the same time recognizing the paramount roles of rich men and shamans in aboriginal times, an attitude widely spread among Athapaskans. Angus said there were no slaves among the Han, and Walter said he also had never heard of them among his people, although he was aware of the concept and had been told about slaves among the Chilkat of the North Pacific Coast. It should be recognized, however, that the capture of women was greatly desired as a means of increasing children in the family, but Angus, who discussed the matter, clearly rejected the notion that such women were slaves. Furthermore, both men refused to set off chiefs as a class, claiming they were rich men who became leaders of specific groups of Indians. Admittedly, they had other men working for them, but to Walter, such individuals were "friends."

Before going further in our consideration of chieftainship, I should record what Schmitter has to say on this subject. "Under their primitive form of government the chief (ha-kkih) had despotic authority. He detailed hunting parties and dictated their duties, and when game was brought into camp he assumed charge of it, apportioning it out to whom he pleased. The chief of the Moosehide Indians near Dawson shows much of the pristine dignity and authority of his rank, and whenever he buys anything in Dawson he does not carry it home, but sends an Indian after it. He shows his genteel extraction by always wearing a pair of fancy decorated gauntlets when he goes on a several days' visit to Eagle during warm weather." In the next paragraph, he adds, "At one time a chief from farther down the river came here [Eagle] and assumed to be chief, but he was never generally recognized as such and ended his career when he hid from the village and the police" (Schmitter 1910: 11). In another place Schmitter also mentions that chiefs have special features on their ceremonial dress, a matter which will be set forth in the section on arts and amusements.

However despotic some chiefs might be, Schmitter (p. 11) himself indicates the periodic existence of a council with considerable power when he states: "During the absence of a chief, or when he is incapacitated, a patriarchal form of government exists, and all important measures are decided by the old men after holding the 'big talk.' Public opinion is very strong and each individual has great respect for the opinion of the community concerning his personal actions. For several years the chief of the Eagle Indians did not attend to public affairs on account of age and feebleness; hence the functions were carried on by the old men."

Angus spoke of councils which he called yɛ tɣɛ čɪn. He said that all the people of the community came together irrespective of age or sex in order to decide important questions and to elect chiefs. The decisions were made only by adult men of about 25 years of age or over. There was much talk and then a count of the affirmations to a proposal by the breaking off of a piece of stick for each man's agreement. When the question was the matter of organizing a raiding party, however, "they did not count sticks—count talk."

Furthermore, according to Angus, in aboriginal times a chief was elected by the council. Admittedly, the major qualification was wealth, but intelligence was also a factor. Inevitably, the son of a chief was often a likely candidate, but if he was not highly regarded he would not be accepted. Angus referred to a chief as a dɑ bʊl nɪ θɑ or "warm mouth," which is an Athapaskan way of designating a person with a strong temper. He said that a chief was appointed at the time of the potlatch given following the death of a chief. The chief then elected might be of either moiety, but a second chief was also chosen, and the latter was usually of the opposite moiety. This second chief was called a ze ke which means "bow and arrow," not because he was a war leader, but because of a weapon that a mythical chief clutched to his breast when his son died. One of the functions of a chief was to kill good-for-nothing men of the community who stole continually. Walter corroborated the method of electing chiefs by talking in the council, but stated that each clan had a chief. He was not too certain about clans and moieties in the first place. He was, however, sure that no woman was elected as chief.

Efforts in 1932 to evoke evidence of the strong partnership relationships characteristic of many Athapaskan groups failed. Walter had heard of them among the Kutchin but did not know of them among the Han. He did mention a hunting partnership called sɛ lʊk, however. Such a relationship lasted only for one hunting expedition, which might be only one day. The men joined each other only on the basis of hunting skill plus compatibility, and they were not necessarily of the same clan.

A feeling of individual ownership of material property was not strong, according to Walter. It was the moiety relationship that counted. It was "no shame" to take a canoe of a member of one's own moiety, but it would be to take one belonging to a member of the opposite moiety. There were no marks of ownership on such objects as everyone knew who the owners were without any mark. If one borrowed a canoe of a fellow moiety member and wrecked it, there was "no pay, no fight," but if it belonged to a man of another moiety, then the value would have to be repaid or there would be a fight.

According to Angus, the property of a deceased person was inherited by the children of the same sex. If the deceased were rich and he had an accumulation of goods, these were used for the inevitable potlatch which would follow when sufficient preparations had been made.

On the position of women, Murray (1910: 86) has commented significantly, although it must be admitted that he was speaking generally of the Indians visiting Fort Yukon in 1847–48. He writes: "The women do all the drudgery in winter, collect fire wood, haul the sleighs along with the dogs, bring snow for water, etc., but the men always cook, and the women are not allowed to eat until their husbands are satisfied. They treat their wives generally with kindness, but are very jealous of them." A sentence later, he adds, "The women do little in summer except drying the fish or meat [actually a tremendous undertaking], the men alone paddle the canoes, the women go as passengers, I have even seen the men carry them from the canoes to where the ground was dry for fear of having their feet wet."

Walter said that when killings occurred within the Han tribe, the chiefs of the clans met together and discussed the matter. In his words: "talk good—no trouble; talk bad—trouble." Amplification brought out the fact that a killing could only really be settled by the payment of a blood price; if it were not paid, revenge ensued until an even number was killed "on each side." Sometimes a chief or rich man paid the wergild for his clansman. Murder within a clan was a more personal matter with varying consequences.

In an attempt to find out something about joking relationships in 1932, I discussed the Peel River behavior—which had been recorded a short time before—with Walter. His negation of this aspect of culture among the Han was given some reinforcement by his knowledge of its existence among the Kutchin (cf. Osgood, 1936a: 115–6). As far as Walter knew, among the Han a person could joke with anyone who was a friend.

Recognizing the difficulty of recording kinship terms from informants, I made no attempt to do so in 1932. Slobodin's (1963a: 11–3) data will therefore be quoted in entirety:

"My information on [kinship terminology] is particularly unsatisfactory. I had hoped to extend and clarify it in further interviews with Charlie Isaac. The relationship term is given in the first person singular possessive: "my grandfather," etc.":

	Informant*		
	J. Jonas	M. McLeod	C. Isaac
GrFa		cι tsαι	
GrMo		cι tson	
Fa	ctα	stα	ct æ
Mo	cana^n	cn^{y}a^n	cn^{y}a^n
FaBr	ct'αι†		soʔι
FaSi	sθo^n		
MoBr	ceʔεʔ		soʔι, ctαι
MoSi	cα kαι		
ElBr		con dαι	con dαι
YgBr		cə ču	cə ču
ElSi	catι		cat^{y}ε
YgSi	ct^{y}u		cto
MoSiDa	cd^{y}u		
"Cousin"		cα k̇αι	
So	cιʒιʔ	cι ʒα	
Da	cιʒα tsut		
BrSo	cʒe		
SiSo	cə hαr		
SiDa	cə hαr		
Grandchild	cə ču	cəču	
Husband		cιka^n	
Wife	cιʔεʔ	ctε^{n}ʒα	
HuBr		cεxεl	

* A few notes on Slobodin's orthography will be helpful (the values are all approximate; no attempt is made here to indicate an exact phonetic specification).

α	as in German *Mann*	ð	as *th* in *this*
æ	as in *cat*	c	as *sh* in *wish*
e	as in *hate*	ʒ	as *z* in *azure*
ε	as in *met*	x	as *ch* in German *ach*
ι	as in *hit*	γ	as Greek *gamma*
o	as in *coat*	č	as *ch* in *chill*
ɔ	as in German *Gott*	ǯ	as *j* in *jam*
u	as in *boot*	ʔ	glottal stop
ʊ	as in *foot*	^{y}	(raised) indicates palatalization
ə	as in *cut*	^{n}	(raised) indicates nasalization
θ	as *th* in *thin*		

† In a personal communication of August 21, 1970, Slobodin writes: "This raises a problem in relation to John Jonas' information since he undoubtedly gave ct'αι, presumably not significantly different than ctαι, for FaBr. I cannot really resolve this except to surmise that in some Han usage, FaBr and MoBr were called by the same term, a situation which may be due to the small number of speakers using and acting in terms of the kinship structure in recent decades. You may recall, as a comparison, that although you [Osgood], McKennan, Sapir (and I, also) obtained at least four different terms for FaBr/MoBr and for FaSi/MoSi, John Fredson gave you [Osgood] one term for uncle and one for aunt. In 1961 I found some Fort Yukon people who did the same."

"Charlie Isaac said that the mother's brother who is called ctaι is 'like a second Dad'; other mother's brothers, he stated, are classified with father's brothers as so?ι.

"Mary McLeod lumped all cousins together, but it was not clear whether they were really so classified, or that her memory on the subject was vague.

"Analysis is interdicted by the incompleteness of the list and lack of textual material to make possible a phonemic collation of the terms given. It is probable that the terminology for primary relatives is bifurcate collateral, as with the Kutchin, but even this is not certain. The type of cousin terminology cannot be determined: but see below, pp. 50–1.

"There is evidence in the list for the recognition of relative age among siblings, found in other Athapaskan kinship systems. No information was obtained, however, on what Murdock calls "the criterion of speaker's sex," also found in other Athapaskan kinship systems.

"Charlie Isaac's statement that the MoBr, or rather, a particular MoBr, is 'like a second Dad' is suggestive of, e.g., matrilocality, cross-cousin marriage."

Commentary. The frustrations of ethnographic reconstruction are exemplified by the attempts to clarify the social organization of the Han. Schmitter has little or nothing to contribute in the matter, and there is no reason to think that the question of a society being divided into clans or moieties could have occurred to him. At any time in the twentieth century it was not a subject about which it was easy to gain information. In 1932, I was particularly interested in this aspect of the culture, for I was not only cognizant of the clans reported among the adjacent Kutchin by Hardisty and Kirby (Kirkby), as previously mentioned, but I had become involved with questions about moieties from my work among the Tanaina during the previous year (Osgood 1937: 128–31, 159). Moiety organization, however, was never established for the Kutchin (Osgood 1936a: 107, 122–3, 128–9; McKennan 1965: 60–1). It is significant, however, that I did not know at that time of the completely independent, slightly earlier record of moieties (phratries) among the neighboring Nabesna, or Upper Tanana, Indians (McKennan 1959: 123–7). In any event, the information obtained from the Han was negligible.

As might be expected, thirty years later Slobodin was no more successful. The possibility should be recognized in this matter that, despite efforts to the contrary, I may have suggested the dual organization, and that my informants' awareness of that system among adjacent Indians triggered responses born of their own uncertainty. I do not think this is the case but it may be. I looked for supporting data from other aspects of culture, but when found and elaborated upon, the dangers of doing so became obvious again. Unfortunately, the problems special to ethnographic reconstruction will only be fully understood by the field worker who has depended upon informants having suffered such cultural disruptions as have the Han.

Chieftainship was undoubtedly influenced and reinforced by the Hudson's Bay Company factors who found that supporting a strong official by giving him a fancy uniform and other emoluments served their purposes, but the aboriginal pattern

seems to shine through the frosted window of the contact period. Certainly chieftainship antedates Murray, the first trader to reside in the area, as he himself records (Murray 1910: 46, 48, 49). The same is true of the councils (Jones 1872: 324).
The data on a second chief bear comment, and there was the temptation to speak of
him as a hunting chief, for such a role was in the ethnographer's mind (Osgood 1932:
74). Again we have the example of a case in which previous knowledge justifies following a lead but inhibits pressing the flow of information beyond its normal course.

To rediscover the statement in my 1932 notes that one of the functions of a chief
was to kill good-for-nothing men was particularly interesting, since it meant very
little when recorded. It became more significant while I was working among the
Ingalik where the concept of eninglani is important, and to which the interested
person may be referred (Osgood 1959: 61–5). It is also perhaps worth suggesting
that the seemingly light emphasis on partnership relationships may be a complement
of the Indians' heavy dependence on clan or moiety members when visiting.

The Life Cycle

Angus said that when a woman was going to give birth, the shelter was specially
warmed. Two sets of crossed poles were set up in the form of an X with a horizontal pole between them from which the woman supported herself at the armpits.
Two other women assisted, raising her stomach slightly. Walter stated that a husband did not stay in the shelter when his wife was giving birth, if he were a young
man, but if middle-aged or older, he might do so.

Slobodin's (1963a: 15) informant confirmed the position at birth and his account is somewhat more detailed, no doubt because it came from a female informant, Mary McLeod. "When an expectant mother entered her labour, two
vertical stakes were set up in her lodging, with a crosspiece padded with moose-
skin tied at a height such that the woman could suspend herself on it in a squatting
position by hanging her arms over it. Preferably, clean sand was spread under her,
and new caribou skins laid over this. She was attended by an older woman experienced in midwifery. Some of the midwives were skilled; they were able to save
the mother, and sometimes the child, by turning the foetus in the womb, etc., or to
save the mother by removing a stillborn foetus. However, quite a few women died
in childbirth. The newborn child was washed and wrapped by the midwife."

Angus went on to say that the baby was washed in warm water and then always
dressed in rabbit skins. He was more detailed in his description of the treatment of
the umbilical cord which he said should be cut with a white stone (quartz?) knife
eight inches from the navel. Any other length of the cord would prevent the child
from reaching maturity. Both the placenta and the attached cord were wrapped in
a piece of skin and usually cached in the top of a tree, but sometimes they were
buried under a bank of dirt. If simply discarded, the baby would not live long.
The eight-inch cord which remained attached to the child was tied up with sinew,
the binding being changed every day. When the cord dropped off, spruce gum and
charcoal were applied as a salve to the navel.

Slobodin's (1963a: 15) informant added to her previous data, "The placenta was thrown away, but the umbilical cord put into a sack and saved. If the child became a shaman, he or she usually used the cord as part of the medicine bundle. Sometimes a shaman bequeathed his cord to a younger shaman to whom he had given instruction."

Schmitter (1910: 14) informs us that the Han believed in reincarnation, a fact which is not surprising as this view is shared by neighboring tribes (Osgood 1936a: 140, 146; McKennan 1959: 160). He writes: "It is an old tradition that when persons die they go into a woman and are born again as a baby. The man is born again as a male and the woman as a female. They have no notion of transmigration into animals, believing that when an animal dies it is not born again as a man is."

Walter said that if a woman dreams about a dead person and then has a baby, it probably contains the soul of the person dreamed about. Such a child is called na·dlⁿ, or "born again." Walter attested to believing in reincarnation himself. Neither Walter nor Angus had ever heard of Athapaskans being circumcised, a custom reported among some Mackenzie drainage Athapaskans, apparently erroneously, by an early missionary (cf. Osgood 1932: 76).

Angus claimed that infanticide was common in aboriginal days. A girl might simply find the child too much trouble. Sometimes men killed women for this. As for twins, Angus knew of two sets. Men liked them but women did not because of the physical demands on the mother. A wet nurse was sometimes employed, and often one child was given away.

Some Han babies cried a good deal. Adney (1900a: 506) speaks of one as a fearful nuisance. "He was crying about a third of the time. Not a regular cry, but a nasal, monotonous drone, punctuated at intervals by three or four inward catches of breath. He would keep this up for perhaps half an hour without the slightest diminution, until humored or petted. Often Billy's boy would imitate him, with the result only of increasing and prolonging the distressful performance. I rarely saw a child punished, and never one whipped."

Schmitter (1910: 13) says, "These Indians are quite strong in tradition, and no household event is passed over without ceremonious observances that usually take the form of 'banquets,' given by the person immediately interested. Thus, at the birth of a child the father celebrates the event by giving a dinner to the entire tribe." Walter confirmed this, giving the time as at least two weeks after the birth, pointing out that the parents wanted to be sure that the baby would live before giving the feast.

"Individuals were given names from incidents of their infancy," states Schmitter (1910: 15). According to Walter, a name might be given a child by anyone, irrespective of his clan affiliation, and that it usually embodied a joke on the parent of the same sex. John Jonas told Slobodin (1963a: 15) that a child might be named by anyone, but that this was done most often by a shaman. He added that new names were taken or bestowed at important events during one's lifetime.

Walter affirmed the practice of teknonymy, making it clear that a parent was called by the name of the oldest *living* child, regardless of its sex.

No information was found on the adoption of young children except that referred to in the case of twins and Schmitter's (1910: 11–12) simple statement that "sometimes children are adopted into a family." He adds more unusual data in the same paragraph, however, when he tells us: "Joseph, the chief at Ketchumstock, has two boys which, it is said, were taken from Tanana [Indians] when they were infants, and, strange to say, such kidnapping appears not to be considered a serious offense."

Murray (1910: 86) writes, speaking generally of the Indians, including the Han, who traded at Fort Yukon, "The young children are not bandaged in moss bags or Indian cradles common with other tribes, but placed in a kind of seat made of birch bark, with back and sides resembling an arm chair, and in front like a Spanish saddle. In this, the women carry their children by a strap around the shoulders in the usual manner. The child's legs hang on each side, encased in boots, the feet are confined to prevent them from growing, they have all short and unshapely feet, but this with them is considered handsome."

Undoubtedly, if this description did not fit the Han, who we should remember were the largest single group trading at Fort Yukon, Murray would have said so, as he noted their peculiarities in that same general section of his journal. Furthermore, two Han informants at Moosehide in 1932 definitely corroborated the use of the birch-bark cradle chair.

Charlie Isaac told Slobodin (1963a: 16):

> The boys and young men were trained. Endurance, agility, speed, and surefootedness were very important—important not only to the man but sometimes to the whole tribe. A young man should not eat fish skin, especially the skin of the king salmon, because it is slippery, and people thought it would make him slip when chasing caribou. They should also not eat unborn calf (of moose, caribou, or sheep) because it made them heavy and made them get old soon. They must not sleep with their legs stretched out, but always with their legs bent. If someone in the lodge noticed a boy sleeping with legs straight, they would take a little stick and hit his legs hard, until he curled them up. If he slept stiff-legged, he would be stiff-legged on snowshoes. When you are running on snowshoes, especially in deep snow and uphill, you have to be able to step high and bring your knees up in a good pace. Our people were very good runners, famous for it. They beat the Loucheux [Kutchin] in races.

The Han usually celebrated the event when a boy killed his first big game. Schmitter (1910: 13) states: "A similar banquet [to that after the birth of a child] is given when the oldest boy kills his first bit of game, thereby attaining his majority and proving himself a hunter. It is incident to the custom on this occasion for the youth to present a bird to the head man of the tribe, while his father also makes the chief a present in token of his esteem and pleasure at his son's accomplishment." Walter made the significant addition that in the case of a rich man, he might give a feast for each of his sons on their first killing of game, but that when a father was poor, he did not do it at all.

The rigorous taboos on girls at the period of their first menstruation is one of the more impressive traits of Athapaskan culture. Schmitter (1910: 13–4) writes: "Corresponding to the feast in honor of the boy's maturity, a similar celebration is held when a girl arrives at the age of puberty. Everybody in the community is informed, and the girl's father gives a dinner in honor of the event. The girl then goes about a mile from home, where she lives in isolation for a year under the care of a relative of her fiancé. She does not eat fresh meat during this year, and if she breaks the rule it is supposed to make the game few in number and hard to get during the ensuing year. As a punishment, in case she violates this tradition, she is compelled to stay away for another year and wear a peculiarly fashioned cap in the form of a cape which extends to her knees. This is to prevent her seeing any men, though she may talk to them. She may raise her cap only to do sewing or other work in her tent." Then he adds: "A neighboring tribe has a custom of not allowing the girls to drink from anything but a special ceremonial drinking cup made of woven roots. This is not allowed to touch her lips; she drinks by making a gutter of the palm of her hand, through which she pours the water into her mouth." The neighboring tribe was the Yukon Flats (Kutcha) Kutchin (cf. Osgood 1936a: 150), but what is important is the implication that the use of the woven basketry cup did not serve this purpose among the Han.

Walter said that the girl was isolated from one to two miles away from the village, but as the year went by, the shelter was moved closer to it. This shelter consisted of a small hemispherical construction with a foundation of about ten spruce poles bent and dried at the lighter ends. Over this was thrown a two-piece cover of caribou skins tanned with the hair on for winter use and without for summer. The girl's mother prepared and brought her food which included no fresh meat or fish. Dried salmon eggs were the mainstay of the menu, but she could eat other dried foods as well as all berries except cranberries. Soup made from the viscera of the caribou was also an important dish. The girl drank it from a small spoon.

When outside the shelter, the girl wore a special hood that prevented her from looking anywhere except at the ground in front of her, and she was not allowed to walk in an established trail. Angus contributed additional information. He reported that if circumstances in the winter required the group to travel, the girl would be guided by a suitor holding one end of a six-foot pole with the girl on the other end behind him, she blinded by her hood. The man would break trail for her with his snowshoes. The reason for such effort in making a separate trail was that anyone walking in the trail of a menstruating woman would get sore legs. At the end of her isolation, the girl was dressed in new clothes and her old ones burned. Angus commented that the girl's face was white after her long lack of fresh food.

Mary McLeod thirty years later gave Slobodin (1963a: 15–6) corroboration of the following details. The shelter was about a mile away from the rest of the people; the girl was fed by her mother and forbidden fresh food. The point was added that the girl was not supposed to sit or be with her legs outstretched, and that the house was so small that she could not anyway. Also, her hood was said to be made of moose skin.

According to Angus, at her monthly periods following menarche, the isolation and deprivations of the girl were not so severe. She was allowed to remain in the shelter with her family but had to remain at a distance of about six feet from any man.

The betrothal of girls by their parents during their first few years of life has been reported among neighboring Athapaskans (Osgood 1936a: 142–3, 148, 151; McKennan 1965: 56), and consequently it is not strange to find Schmitter (1910: 13) doing so for the Han. He tells us: "An interesting old custom was that of the arrangement of marriages during the infancy of the children. The question was settled by the parents, who met in consultation and made the arrangements for the prospective marriage, choosing for the girl a boy usually about three years older. Between the ages of 10 and 15 the boy left home to live with the girl's parents, although they were not married until the boy was able to hunt and work. The boy became a part of his wife's family and never returned to his own.

"Marriage usually took place between the ages of 16 and 20, but sometimes as late as 25 years of age. Although the agreement had been made by the parents of the intended bride and groom, yet their own desires were considered before the actual marriage took place, and they were not forced to marry unless they felt they were suited for each other."

Slobodin (1963a: 14) adds a very pertinent point when he writes: "Charlie Isaac was very definite that the preferred marriage was between a man and his MoBrDa, or a girl and her FaSiSo." He goes on to quote Charlie: "In the old days a boy or girl was told whom to marry. Usually it was arranged by the mothers. A boy's mother likes him to marry a girl of one of her brothers, so the marriage they liked best was for a boy to marry his mother's brother's daughter. My mother had three brothers, and if this was the old days I would have first choice of one of their girls. I can't marry my father's brother's daughter. That's the way my father married. He was around Fortymile then, and his Dad and Mom talked it over with one of her brothers and wife, and my Dad's mother's brother called him up to the Klondike here to marry that girl. My Dad and mother had nothing to say about it." Slobodin goes on to comment: "If Charlie Isaac's statement about preferred cross-cousin marriage is correct, it is probable that, unlike the eastern Kutchin, the Han do distinguish between parallel and cross-cousins. The marriage preference described by Charlie Isaac, especially when coupled with initial matrilocality, would certainly put a particular MoBr in the position of 'a second Dad'; in fact, a father-in-law." In further corroboration, Slobodin (p. 15) adds: "A MoBr of Ellen Taylor, and a younger brother of hers, both of whom were married within the last twenty years [after 1940] and whose marriages, she said, were more or less by individual choice in the Western fashion, did marry their matrilateral cross-cousins."

Neither Angus nor Walter confirmed the importance of either child betrothal or a preference for cross-cousin marriage, but they were not asked to. The former said that girls lived more or less loosely with respect to sexual relationships until they were about twenty years old. He insisted that most of them were interested in nothing more than men; in fact they were "crazy after men." If a girl became pregnant and bore a child, she would tell by whom, and he would have to marry her. On the other hand, when a boy wanted to marry a girl, he went to live with her family and worked for her father for a year or more. All of Slobodin's (1963a: 14) informants on marriage likewise said that "matrilocality was preferred for the first few years of marriage." When the young couple had acquired sufficient experience to become economically independent, according to Walter, they moved apart from the girl's family and constructed a shelter of their own. Nonetheless, the young man helped his father-in-law occasionally. Clans were strictly exogamous. Walter never heard of a man hanging his inner pants on a tree limb when he wanted to marry, an oddity reported among both the Peel River and Crow River Kutchin (Osgood 1936a: 143, 148).

One informant at Eagle in 1932 said that the Han engaged in sexual intercourse in any of three positions. One position was with the couple on their sides, another with the female lying stretched out on her back, and the third in the same general position with the woman's knees drawn up and spread apart. Another informant said that when a wife knew she was pregnant, she told her husband who, in turn, told the woman who was a "best friend."

It seems important before going further to quote Schmitter's (1910: 11) brief statement: "They occasionally marry into other tribes."

Murray (1910: 86), writing in 1848 about the Indians at Fort Yukon—and apparently including the Han—tells us: "The principal men of the nation have two and three wives each, one old leader here has five, while others who have few beads (and beads are their riches) to decorate the women, remain bachelors, but a good fighter though a poor man can always have a wife." Walter gave the expected report that chiefs were polygynous, while most men were limited to a single wife. Angus seemed to regard polygyny as common, making the remark that one "can't help it if two girls love you." According to him, if a man had two wives, one slept on each side of the husband. Before going on it should perhaps be recalled that the father of the informants Jonathan Wood and Walter Benjamin seems to have been polygynous.

Walter also explicitly noted that some women had two husbands, which brings to mind occasional cases of polyandry among the Kutchin (Osgood 1936a: 143, 148).

About death, Schmitter (1910: 14) reports: "When a chief, 'Ha-kkih,' died, men were hired to burn his body, and what was left of bones and ashes were placed in a wooden receptacle hewn from a tree trunk and hung about ten feet high in a tree." Angus said that long ago cremation was the only method for disposal of the dead. Walter's data are general confirmation of Schmitter's for he stated that the ordinary disposal of the dead was by burning on a cremation pyre, after which the remains were collected and put into a hollowed-out box of wood, sometimes painted, which was put up on a post. He added the significant information, however, that this work was carried out by men of the opposite moiety to that of the deceased. The clothes of the dead person were burned at the same time, and some of his possessions. Angus supplied a point by stating that personal belongings were burned, but not the house.

Of special interest is the fact that Walter said that chiefs were sometimes interred in two halves of a hollowed-out log, which was then bound together with skin or willow lines and put up on a platform such as is made for a cache. He added that this method of disposal required a great deal more work and hence was only suitable for chiefs.

Nabesna (Upper Tanana) informants, interestingly enough, denying deposition on platforms for themselves, reported it in use at Kechumstuk in Han territory (McKennan 1959: 147). Angus, with unusual clairvoyance, placed the introduction of burial in a log at about 300 years ago, but claimed to know nothing of its origin. Two Han informants at Moosehide in 1932 said they knew of burial in split-log coffins, but Jonathan, born about 1850, while hearing of cremation, admitted that he had never actually seen it undertaken.

According to Schmitter (1910: 14): "The men who burned the body ate no fresh meat for a year, because, according to the law, if those who worked for a dead man should eat fresh meat within a year they would die. They could eat dried meat, but if there was none dried they must wait until some was made." Walter also reported that those engaged in the disposal of the dead ate no fresh fish or meat, and that they lived apart for about six months, attributing this behavior to fear of dire consequences should they not.

Schmitter (p. 6) also tells of the abandonment of the old, and presumably of their bodies, a situation which under aboriginal conditions must have sometimes been inevitable. He writes: "A few years ago some government packers were traveling from Fort Egbert to Tanana Crossing, and on their way they passed a camp which the Indians had just deserted, leaving behind a sick old woman and a crying baby, but no attention was paid to them, as it was supposed the Indians would return to get the woman and child. The packers on their return trip a few weeks later found the old woman and child dead, evidently left by the Indians to starve."

Walter said people danced after a death as an act of mourning before the disposal of the body took place, but he did not know of any self-abuse under the same circumstances.

Schmitter (1910: 13) recorded that, "On the death of a wife or husband, it was not customary for the survivor to remarry for several years, since the relatives of the deceased might think the survivor was glad of the other's death."

Commentary. This is a relatively satisfactory outline of the Han life cycle, given the potential for reconstructing Athapaskan culture, and consequently only a few comments will be made. It is probable that Schmitter's statement that the girl at menarche wore a hood as punishment for violating the taboos pertinent to her first menstruation is an error, since the hood is one of the traits most consistently associated with any girl's isolation at that time. The reference to the location of the menstrual hut at a distance involving a mile by at least three informants spread over a fifty-year period is striking, but probably no more than a convenience of language to indicate a considerable distance. The mile, of course, is not an Athapaskan unit of measurement, and Indians, like others, can be extremely inexact in its use. Perhaps, before leaving the subject of menarche, it might be recorded that the strictness of controls on the girl has often suggested to me that the reports from various groups are descriptions of ideal behavior, not manifest. If so, all efforts to prove such a reaction to be correct have failed.

The emphasis found among the Han for child betrothal appears somewhat accidental. At least, if the percentages of such cases were really high, that would be a distinguishing facet of Han culture. This is not to imply that the custom was uncommon, however, as it is also regularly reported from neighboring tribes (Osgood 1936a: 142–3, 148, 151; McKennan 1965: 56). A similar statement on cross-cousin marriage should also be indicated (McKennan 1959: 121–3).

Finally, I cannot conclude this commentary without a word on the disposal of the dead. One major source of confusion with respect to that complex is undoubtedly the great emphasis on burial in the ground caused by the influence of Christian missionaries. Obviously, abandonment was the easiest method of disposal, and one which at some times under special conditions was certainly practiced by every Northern Athapaskan group. Of the normal forms of disposal, two are outstanding: cremation with the ashes often raised on a pole, and the disposal of a body in a wood container, usually a hollowed split log, but sometimes a box of sewn boards or a canoe. It would be simple to hypothesize on the basis of considerable evidence that cremation, easy to undertake, was the common aboriginal Athapaskan method of disposal, and that deposition in a wood container or in a log coffin, a great deal more work, was reserved for chiefs and the rich. Certainly, evidence of aboriginal cremation was widespread among the Pacific Drainage Athapaskans. Thus the late cremation of chiefs such as reported by Schmitter could be explained on the basis of conservative values, and the rise in scaffold coffins due to the introduction of steel tools. One becomes uneasy with such simplifications, however, when one realizes that the evidence for cremation appears to be practically negligible among the eastern, or Arctic Drainage, Athapaskans.

Ceremonial Life

The arrival of the first salmon was celebrated among the Han, as among most tribes for which the salmon was an essential food. Walter, at Eagle, said the first salmon caught each year, normally a king salmon, was boiled and at least the broth was shared by everyone except females who were observing menstrual taboos and women nursing babies. The latter had to wait two weeks after the first salmon arrived before they were allowed to eat the fresh fish. At Moosehide it was claimed that everyone was given a little piece of the first king salmon by the man who caught it. The simple explanation for this behavior was that everyone was so happy to see the salmon return after having eaten dried fish for so long.

Also typical of the Pacific Drainage Athapaskans was the ceremony following a death, which was commonly termed the potlatch after the Nootka word connoting "giving." Schmitter (1910: 14–15) describes one for us in the first decade of the nineteenth century.

> Last winter the Eagle chief died. He had hoarded up much wealth of skins, blankets, traps, rifles, and other property and, since it is not customary among the Eagle Indians for relatives to inherit the property of the deceased, his kinfolk received nothing of his belongings. By common consent Old Peter took charge of the effects. It was then announced that there would be a "pot-latch" in the spring, when the goods of the deceased man would be given away. Invitations were sent east to the Moosehide Indians up the river, west to Charlie Creek Indians down the river, and south over the hills to the Ketchumstock Indians. The Porcupine Indians [Takkuth Kutchin] to the north were not invited, because they were not related to the tribe. All the goods were kept intact in the caches until the arrival of the guests. Then Isaac, the Moosehide chief, took full charge of the ceremonies, which lasted several days, during which there was much feasting and dancing. At the dinners, the men first gorged themselves, allowing the women to come in after they had finished and take what was left. Between the ceremonies they assembled in groups about the village and gossiped or sung to tunes resembling those of Japanese operas. Time was kept by one of the Indians beating upon a caribou-skin drum, while everybody swayed to the time, alternately bending the right and left knee. For the final ceremony a fence about seven feet high was built about an enclosure thirty by sixty feet. The "potlatch" proper was held in this enclosure during one afternoon, the people sat about near the fence facing the goods of the deceased, which were displayed at one end by Chief Isaac, who stood in their midst and presided. The first hour of the ceremony was very much like a church meeting, all talking in their native language. The chief then opened with a speech, and when he sat down others rose and spoke as the spirit seemed to move them, apparently eulogizing the great chief. At times the speaker became much wrought up, his gestures showing that he was illustrating a fight with an animal. After the speechmaking the goods were distributed one article at a time. The chief would pick up a blanket, walk down the center of the assembly, and with a few remarks toss it to some one, the recipient smilingly responding with brief remarks. Articles were only given to the visitors; the Eagle Indians received nothing.

After watching the ceremony several hours, I was about to leave when the chief called me and handed me a pair of moose-skin moccasins, saying, "This is because you were good to my people."

Next day the food became scarce, so the visitors began to depart for their homes, their toboggans laden with goods from the deceased chief's cache.

No attempt was made in 1932 to obtain a detailed description of the potlatch, which is a time-consuming process and not satisfying except with a good inform- ant. After ascertaining the existence of the custom, a few direct questions were asked. In response, Walter was confident that the potlatch was associated only with death. Furthermore, only a chief, or rich man, gave a potlatch, and he was as- sisted by all the members of his own clan. The exact time at which a potlatch was given in relation to the death of the person being commemorated was uncertain. That was because the preparations, including the collecting of food and gifts, re- quired months of effort that could be affected by many factors such as the wealth of the family, the number of supporting clansmen, and general economic condi- tions at the period. About a year was suggested as the average intervening period. Things mentioned as being given away were skins of various animals, articles of clothing, and various types of lines. There was no actual limit on the kind of material that might be contributed, and used objects were included as well as new.

Two Han informants at Moosehide in 1932 said that the fence surrounding the ceremonial ground was made by the moiety giving the potlatch. It was constructed of upright poles placed only four or five inches apart, with a horizontal pole tied on at the top and another near the bottom. Such a fence was made only for a pot- latch, and afterward people, irrespective of moiety affiliation, helped themselves to the wood.

In considering other details, the use of the plank drum, a characteristic of the Peel River Kutchin, was denied at Eagle, the more usual tambourine drum with a caribou-skin head being the normal instrument for the accompaniment of singing and dancing (cf. Osgood 1936a: 122). Faces were specially painted for the pot- latch.

When I tried in 1932 to find out if any of the commonplace contests, such as pulling on caribou skins, occurred, Walter responded by saying that he knew of pole-pulling across a fire engaged in by Indians near Whitehorse (Tagish?), but that he did not know of the Han doing so. He did mention a game played with pemmican, but notes apparently made to stimulate details in an ethnographer's memory no longer do so. Finally, the role of grease, so often important at potlatches, was raised (cf. Osgood 1936a: 126, 138–9). Walter immediately recognized its use, stating that grease was drunk to make people vomit which they did into a fire, but only if the deceased person being honored was particularly well loved. Among the Peel River Kutchin, the noise of this act was interpreted by someone present as the drinker asking for a specific object among the potlatch gifts (cf. Osgood 1936a: 122). Walter did not confirm this.

Slobodin's data of the 1960s do not deal primarily with the culture at the period of contact. He does, however, refer to stakes set up in a row to hold potlatch gifts, and to visitors being given presents, even when of the same clan—or equivalent sib. Furthermore, it is noted that a potlatch might be given for a woman if she was important enough. More significant with respect to detail, Slobodin (1963a: 17–8) provides the following statement based on information from Mary McLeod. "However, there was no dancing at the memorial potlatch. Instead, the women put on a march. They went around and around to the beat of a hoop drum. Every now and then they made hand motions: hands extended, palms down, thumbs touching, moved slowly downward in front of the chest—a soothing or quieting gesture. The marching women wore two streaks of red paint horizontally across their faces. The purpose of the dance was to honor the deceased and to end the family's mourning."

Commentary. The restriction on sharing in the first salmon by women observing menstrual taboos brings to mind the possibility, instilled by some forgotten article, that menstrual blood contains the chemical menotoxin toward which fish are highly antagonistic—indeed, one that was used in a compound to inhibit the attack of sharks upon survivors of World War II disasters who found themselves precipitated into dangerous waters. The theory that Indians once learned empirically that menstruating women who worked in water around fish weirs would affect their catch is just too neat but, with the thought in mind, some scientist may be in an easy position to evaluate the facts.

We should note in Schmitter's description of the potlatch that the articles specifically mentioned as being given away are European trade objects, but in the later resumé and discussion of the period of culture change among the Han, I shall present evidence that these were available before 1850. Also Schmitter's statement that relatives inherit nothing is not quite accurate—for if they did not, how could they give it away? Undoubtedly, in the case of a chief or rich man, property was accumulated for distribution in anticipation of the potlatch following his decease, and those responsible for giving it away regarded it as the expected and proper obligation to do so. On the other hand, some things were inherited and not given away, while potlatch material may have been regarded more as property of the clan. Ownership is often an unclear concept among the Athapaskans. Perhaps what Schmitter meant to make clear was simply that potlatch gifts were not made to members of the deceased person's clan or moiety.

It is also significant that Schmitter notes the restriction of those invited to the potlatch to the Han themselves. Although true in this case, the extent or limitation on the guests invited was probably a correlate of the amount of food and gifts available. This, I believe, could range from primarily the residents of a single settlement to all those within the greatest distance practical for travel. The Indians, of course, would not be likely to give a potlatch during either the busiest or the coldest seasons of the year.

When Schmitter tells of the chief illustrating by gestures a fight with an animal, the chief was probably recounting some brave deed of the deceased, such as killing a bear. Without doubt, the Indians were prone to giving long speeches; some too long for the first trader (Murray 1910: 48, 87).

Finally, I offer a warning for the reader not to be fooled by Mary McLeod's assertion that there was no dancing at the potlatch, surely a confusion of terminology as is shown in both the third and last sentence of her account. Perhaps she was thinking of the European dancing that became so popular at Dawson after the great Klondike gold rush. In any event, it should be remembered that the potlatch was a social affair, certainly never duplicated exactly on any two occasions, and one greatly affected by the economic and social impacts on the particular situation.

Arts and Amusements

Schmitter (1910: 16) tells us: "The Indians do not write, but make signs of one sort or another, a few of which follow. The sign (a) drawn in the snow means a moose in the direction of the end of the line to which the head is attached (Fig. 5). The sign (b) in the snow means caribou on the mountain in the direction of the straight line.

"Along a trail, where it divides, if one sees a leaning pole with grass tied to the end, it means no 'grub' in that direction, or a pole with willow tied to the end means plenty of 'grub.' "

The art of healing was largely, but not entirely, in the domain of the shaman, as has been indicated in the section on religion. Schmitter (1910: 19) has a good deal to say on the subject, his interest no doubt being stimulated by being a doctor himself. "Disease is not always the result of the medicine-man's evil spirit, but sometimes comes of itself, so the Indians have certain actual medical remedies. If they have a cough they chew grass roots or spruce bark to stop the illness, and sometimes the old women boil bark, roots, and brush to make tea, which is drunk for all forms of illness. Originally many kinds of bark were infused in the same mixture, making a sort of general remedy, for it seems probable that the specific use of these herbs was not acquired until later from the whites; at least the medicine-man never used them or any other drug, his practice being limited to psychotherapy."

Slobodin's (1963a: 19) informant Charlie Isaac contradicts this last statement, however, when he states: "The medicine man knew all kinds of plants for curing

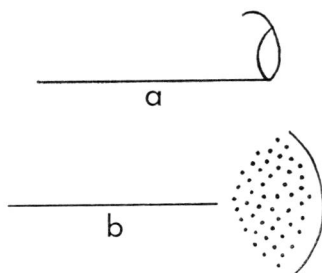

Fig. 5. Signs in snow indicating (*a*) moose in direction of end of line with head attached; (*b*) caribou on mountain in direction of end of line with dots (after Schmitter 1910: 16).

and also could do doctoring. If somebody broke an arm or leg, he could set it, then wrap it in fresh birchbark. The birchbark would dry hard and be like a cast; stronger than a cast. They used spruce gum for a salve and also for chewing, and made tea from different plants for curing."

As for the shaman's psychotherapy, Schmitter (1910: 19) goes on: "Their treatment of wounds is most interesting. If a wound bleeds profusely, the medicine-man gets a piece of king salmon skin the size of the palm and cleans it of scales. He takes this between his palms and has another Indian hold his hands together for security; then, as the medicine-man blows, the salmon skin disappears, going into the wound, where it forms a membrane and stops the bleeding. This is extracted again when the wound is healed. This method is also employed when there is a pain but no bleeding."

Again, after a discussion of the weasel as a shaman's fetish (cf. p. 00), Schmitter (1910: 18) goes on:

> The good medicine-man works in the opposite way from a bad one; he cures a sick man by drawing the weasel skin out of the ailing part. I was shown how it was extracted from the ribs, neck, or head. With the skin concealed up his sleeve, or hidden in his clenched hand, the medicine-man reached to the affected part, whence he jerked it [the weasel skin] forth in the twinkling of an eye. Sometimes in sickness, when all the friends are assembled to assist the medicine man in singing, he will brush the affected part with his hand as he sings until, with a puff of breath, he blows the disease away. At other times he will firmly grasp at something invisible and appear to pull it out and throw it into the air, driving it away with a puff of breath. The medicine-man, after extracting the evil spirit, returns to the animal its own spirit and sends the evil spirit back to its original sender, whom it kills, because he sent it first.

To this important descriptive statement, Schmitter (1910: 19) adds a more unusual one: "An odd test used in case of sickness is to put a frog on top of the man's head; if the frog soon jumps away the man dies soon, but if the frog remains on his head for any length of time the man will live a long time."

Finally we find the notion common among the Athapaskans that sickness did not exist aboriginally. Charlie Isaac expressed it when Slobodin (1963a: 20) asked him "whether, whenever someone became ill, it was thought he had been attacked by a medicine man." Charlie answered: "But people never died of sickness in those days, only of old age, or accident, or sometimes starvation—but not that so much because they usually got by. The people were very strong. They run all the time, getting game, and they had no liquor, no smoking."

The importance of red paint to the Indians is well known. Schmitter (1910: 10) asserts that "their wood work is nearly always painted with red ochre, which is secured from the banks of a creek [Seventymile] near the village of Nation, about thirty miles down the river from Eagle. They say that this creek is red from the ochre, which can be gathered in handfuls from the mud in the swampy places along the banks." He adds, "They used it also for painting their faces in the dances." Walter, discussing the importance of red paint, said that it was made by putting the "mud" that had been gathered into the fire in order to refine it. The red ocher thus obtained was mixed with water when it was to be used on wood, but mixed with grease when intended for painting the face.

As for dyes of various colors, Schmitter (1910: 4–5) tells us: "Porcupine quills, which are used for decorating their clothing, were dyed red by boiling in cranberry juice, or blue by boiling in huckleberry juice. When any quills were found which were pure white, they were left so. Various colored flowers were also boiled and their coloring matter used in dyeing the quills." These colored quills comprised one of the most important, if not the most important, method of decorating clothing and accessories. Schmitter (1910: 5) provides some detailed information on the quill work.

> Small geometrical figures were made by sewing the flattened out quills to a backing of skin, and long stripes were made by rolling the quills into spirals about a sixteenth of an inch in diameter and sewing them side by side. The backs of mittens and insteps of moccasins were decorated with these quills. Flat strings of caribou-skin one-fourth of an inch wide were sometimes wound with porcupine quills. These strings were either sewed to, or tied about the coat wrists and about the breeches below the knees. The coat of a chief was decorated down the front and back, and had a special color, significant of his office, which consisted of a strip of moose-skin about two inches wide and nearly a yard long with one margin fringed by cutting it into strips. On this was sewed strands, and strings of quills were suspended from the ends. The collar hung around the neck and down the front like a scarf (this specimen could not be found). A special hunting belt was made of caribouskin decorated with porcupine quills, and from it hung an ornamented moose-skin sheath containing a hunting knife (this specimen also could not be found).

Jones (1872: 321), in describing Han woven baskets, not only writes that porcupine quills were woven into them but that hair was woven into them as well.

I have already noted one or more references to the use of the tambourine drum among the Han. Walter stated that the head might be made of either caribou skin or moose skin. He also knew of the willow-bark whistle, essentially a plaything of children.

As for songs, Walter recognized the following categories: those sung by individuals in love, war songs of several kinds, songs made up for the occasion of a potlatch, and finally, songs associated with shamanistic practices.

Possibly the Han Indians engaged in fewer sports and amusements than some of the surrounding tribes, or so one might judge from the number of negative responses. Fortunately, we have what is probably an eyewitness account of Han wrestling from Schmitter (1910: 17): "They wrestle 'catch-as-catch-can,' but they usually try for a hold in the following manner: Putting the right arm around the oponent's waist and grasping the breeches at the thigh with the left hand. It is only necessary to throw a man, for as soon as he falls he is beaten. As a mark of friendship on separating, after this sport, the Indians exchange coats or other articles of clothing regardless of value." Walter, also at Eagle, said that there were two types of wrestling. The first was distinguished by each opponent starting with his right hand over (or outside) his opponent's left. Then they closed together. Perhaps Walter was trying to communicate the actions that Schmitter described. In the second type, the wrestlers grabbed at each other's clothes at the shoulders with the arms outstretched. Regrettably, a match of neither kind could be arranged during my visit.

Among games, the Han ran races, proud of their fleet-footedness. They also engaged in a tug-of-war by having contestants in turn pull on a stick about eight inches long held by one hand. The loser gave the winner a little tobacco. Also, people in groups pulled on the ends of a stout line with a marker in the middle which had to be drawn past a pole or post, near one or the other side, in order to win.

Adney (1900a: 503, 506) describes and illustrates a favorite game called "kli-so-kot" or "throwing-the-stick." He says: "A row of five or six small stakes is set up in the hard-packed snow of the village street, and another row thirty or forty feet distant. Each contestant provides himself with two clubs [which appear to be about a foot long], and taking turns, they throw these at first one, then the other, of the group of upright stakes, the one who knocks down the greatest number of stakes being the winner" (Pl. 1, *top*).

Walter knew of boys playing shinny on smooth ice by hitting a puck-like piece of wood with a stick. Apparently, as recognized, the game was informal for no good posts were erected. Men were sometimes bounced in a moose skin, but Walter denied that the Han engaged in the specialized bouncing game on a small square of skin held by lines from the corners as reported for the Peel River Kutchin (Osgood 1936a: 98).

Schmitter (1910: 16) recorded the hoop-and-pole game as follows: "The boys had a game that not only furnished sport, but gave them practice in throwing the spear as well. One person would roll a hoop made of willow before a number of Indian boys standing in a row, each with a long spear-like stick, which he threw at the hoop as it rolled past him, and when one went through the hoop it counted as a caribou killed."

Walter knew of the ring-and-pin game as played among the Peel River Kutchin, but said that the Han did not have it.

As for the hand game, Schmitter (1910: 17) states: "The nearest approach to gambling among the natives is an old game, the rules of which are as follows: Two rows of men sit opposite one another, each man holding in his hand a bone marked with a notch. The bones are secretly passed from [a player's] right to left [hand] and vice verse. Some one on one side would call out which of the opponents' hands contained the bone, and the calling side would get as many sticks, from a pile of about sixty, as the number of opponents' hands guessed correctly. Each side called the other alternately. Sometimes they would hold another unmarked bone in the opposite hand so as to confuse the guesser. The side which lost or got the fewer sticks had to give the other something as a forfeit." Curiously, about a quarter of a century later, when Walter was asked about such hand games, he thought they were not played at Eagle, although he knew of them among the Chilkat on the coast (cf. Helm and Lurie 1966). He also denied that the game was ever played among the Han in which a boy drags a moose skin along the ground while his playmates try to pin it to the ground with sharpened sticks (cf. Osgood 1936a: 96).

Walter knew of swings being made by suspending a long rope between trees. Also boys played the snow-snake game in winter, driving a spruce pole about three feet long out of a snowbank with a club like a baseball bat with a flat end.

Schmitter (1910: 16) tells of what has been termed the ball-in-air game. "The Indians had an outdoor game similar to volley ball in which several [Indians] took part. A ball the size of a baseball, made of caribou-skin stuffed with hair, with a marten tail attached, was used in this game. A party of about ten Indians would take up their position on each side of a line, batting the ball with bare hands from one side over the line to the other, and every time the ball touched the ground it counted against the side on which it fell." When Walter described this game, he said the ball was about the size of a fist and made with a cover of moose skin stuffed with hair until it was hard.

Another somewhat unusual game was recorded by Schmitter (1910: 16). "For an indoor game they had one which is not uncommon nowadays. In this game the men sit on the ground with their legs arched in front of them and the women sit tailor fashion, each person having a cloth similar to a handkerchief. Any small article is started down the row; the men pass it under the knees and the women pass it behind their backs, the object being to conceal the article in the cloth or stealthily pass it on without being caught. It was the duty of one [individual of the same sex on each side] to catch a person with the article in his possession. Men and women sit separate in rows opposite each other and watch the other sex play the game."

Adney (1900a: 506) writes of the activities of small children: "Most of their play is out-of-doors, where they make play-houses in imitation of the large ones, and roll about in the snow like little polar bears. Sometimes they take papa's snow shoes and slide down some little bank, but they did not use the toboggans for that purpose."

Walter said that children played blindman's buff. Making string figures and story-telling were also important, but there was no ownership of the latter. Gambling appears to have been relatively rare, an assumption that the above evidence supports.

Interestingly enough as an unusual practice among interior Athapaskans, Walter claimed that some of the Han men went swimming, first building a big fire on the beach to warm themselves when they came out of the water. This does not strike me as aboriginal, and I must note that Jones (1872: 323), while speaking of the Han canoe, says none of the Kutchin, presumably including the Han, could swim.

Commentary. Schmitter's statement that shamans did not use herbal remedies must be discounted to some extent in light of Slobodin's data. Nonetheless, there seems to be surprisingly little evidence in the Athapaskan ethnographies to indicate that shamans made use of medicinal plants. We should note that Schmitter does make a distinction between a good and bad shaman in so many words. Also the account of a frog being placed on a man's head as a prognostication of health is odd but not unique, as a similar behavior has been reported from the Ingalik (cf. Osgood 1959: 29). Finally, with reference to health, the statements on the lack of sickness in aboriginal times probably reflect favorable conditions at least relative to the contact period when Europeans brought in such devastating diseases as diphtheria.

It is perhaps interesting that when my information on red ocher being derived from *mud* was recorded in 1932, it was not understood, whereas the later comparison with Schmitter's statement made clear what Walter was referring to.

We should record that Jones's (1872: 321) comment that hair was woven into Han baskets suggests some kind of moose-hair work, a technique which was highly developed among the Slave of the Mackenzie River and used in lesser ways as, for instance, decorative edgings, among various tribes.

Fortunately, Schmitter was able to send a few specimens of material culture to the U.S. National Museum which are invaluable as samples of Han art. On the other hand, it is curious that so little description of dances has survived, especially as relatively so much is available on the neighboring Kutcha Kutchin. To say that these two peoples were probably much alike in this respect is simply to guess, for there are often surprising contrasts between them and their neighbors. One case is that of the drum, the Han using the widely distributed tambourine type, while a close neighbor like the Peel River Kutchin had a predilection for the plank drum, and the Crow River Kutchin used no drum at all (Osgood 1936a: 94, 100). If this seems merely to illustrate the weakness of negative statements, one might take note of the absence of the drum among the Ahtena in a situation where it might be expected (Allen 1887: 133).

It is possible that the Han Indians were less given to games and amusements than some of their neighbors. When among them in 1932, I had been working primarily with a better group of informants who were Peel River Kutchin, and it was consequently possible to make direct comparisons of the data recorded just previously in these matters. The proportion of negative statements given for the Han by Walter seems high, and it must be remembered that, without further study, such negatives are far from conclusive.

War

There seem to be two points that are clear from my limited data on war— one is that when any intertribal fighting took place it was usually with people to the southwest; the other is that shamans were often involved one way or another in causing the conflicts. To begin by delineating the enemies of the Han, we might first note a statement by Murray (1910: 61) in speaking of the Gens du fou who were visiting Fort Yukon in 1847: "They said, the Russians were once the same, they would not give them what they wanted, but they (the Indians) killed a number of their people and pillaged one of their Forts on the coast, and ever since then they had been refused nothing. I had before heard of their murdering some Russians at a small outpost but took the repeating of their story here as a rather bold threat." Murray (pp. 27, 51) records his own anxiety with respect to the Gens du fou whose threats to burn the traders' houses had been reported to him, and later he was again warned to be on his guard against them at Fort Yukon.

Walter in 1932 said that the Eagle Indians fought with the ma hu nai [Nahanni?] south of (or above) Whitehorse, and that these people cut off the heads of their victims and threw them into the snow, a practice he happily reported that the Han never followed. Coincidentally, he admitted that he had never heard of any kind of armor, the slat and the skin types having been explained to him. Angus stated that Indians whom he called ma ho ni (Nahanni?), who lived in the upper Stewart River country, fought with the Yukon Indians, by which expression he seemed to be including the Tutchone. Unfortunately, the ramifications of questioning that would have been involved in clarifying the matter were too much for me then, as they would probably be now, so I subjected him to no irritating probe. Interestingly enough, John Semple, a superior Peel River Kutchin informant at Moosehide, volunteered the information in 1932 that the Moosehide and Eagle people—and thus specifically the Han—fought with Indians whom he called Slaves. Being more articulate, it became clear that he was referring to Arctic Drainage Athapaskans who must have been either the Mountain or the Kaska group (cf. Osgood 1936a).

Charlie Isaac gave Slobodin (1963a: 20–1) some additional information.

> Our people were not fighting all the time. Mostly they were pretty friendly with the other tribes.
>
> I know of only one fight the Klondike people had. One of our young men was off hunting by himself in the mountains and met a bunch of strangers. No—first he saw their tracks and noticed it was a different kind of snowshoe [from ours]. He wanted to find out about them. He followed up the tracks and came to where they camped. He sat down in their circle and tried to talk to them. He wanted them to come with him to see his people, so they could all be friends and maybe do some trading.
>
> But while he was sitting there, one of them got behind him and shot him in the back with a muzzle-loader. Then they cut off his arms and legs and threw them here and there. Then they beat it.
>
> After the boy was missed, our people went to look for him and found his remains. What they minded most was the way he was cut up. Why did those people do it? Just savages. So our people chased them. We had muzzle-loaders then,

but so did they. Finally our people caught up with them near Ross River, and we killed eight of their men. Then it was finished.

We call those people nah?ɛ. I do not know what they are. We also call them Ross River Indians, but that's because they were heading for the Ross River.

The attribution of murders carried out at a distance by a shaman in one tribe on a member of another is common among Athapaskans and the Han were no exception. Murray (1910: 51) writes of such a case in late June of 1847 when he says of the Gens du fou who had arrived at Fort Yukon that they "were greatly displeased to find a Peels River Indian with us, most unfortunately a great number of their [Han] women had died lately, and many were sick when they left their camp, one of their women had been stolen from the Loucheux [Kutchin] of Peels River, and they believed that 'Vandeh' our hunter, to revenge the loss of said woman who was a relative of his, had made *medicine* to kill them, and now wished to kill him that no more of their wives might die." Murray adds, "I did not attempt to persuade them of the absurdity of their belief, for all the tribes in this part of the country believe as gospel, that certain individuals have necromantic powers to cause the death of others, though a great distance apart." And again (p. 52): "The other Indians were all present but took no part in this, as they did not wish to displease the Gens-du-fou, who they say are very strong, the two bands nearest this numbering upwards of a hundred men." Another incident illustrating the same belief is given later (p. 59): "It was early in August that a large party of 'Gens-du-fou' arrived. We had previously been informed of the sudden death of their chief, whom I met at Lapiers House, a young man who had great influence with the nation, and reports were circulated by the Indians that his death was imputed to our being here and also to the 'Kootcha-Kootchin.' "

Schmitter (1910: 19–20) not only confirms the shaman's role in war but also introduces what is perhaps a novel technique into the procedure. "In war times the medicine-man performs his magic against the enemy. In experiments of this nature a medicine-man uses for a fetich two pebbles, a few inches in diameter, with natural holes in them, tied to the ends of a string about a foot long, made of caribou-skin wound with porcupine quills. In demonstrating the use of the pebbles, the magician pointed to an imaginary enemy in the distance and, assuming an attitude of forward charge, his countenance showing fierceness and his eyes the glassy, vacant stare of the mystic, he suspended the pebbles by the middle of the string, swing them forward three times, blew on them a puff of breath, and with full strength threw them at the enemy. Immediately relaxing, with a smile of satisfaction, he said, 'They run'."

These stones were acquired about 1906 from a shaman named Luke living at Eagle. Each stone is about 2 inches in diameter and weighs 3 ounces (Plate 2, *E*). The connecting cord is 17 inches long and about ⅛ inch wide. The stones are of dark color and each has a hole through it. There is bead work on the cord, mostly white, but in three places along the two parallel rows, red and blue beads occur in groups of three.

Whatever one may think of the power of the shaman's stones in warfare, certainly the common weapon used primarily was the club made from a heavy caribou antler by cutting off the tines four or five inches from the beam. The antler is then boiled to straighten it, as has been reported for the Peel River Kutchin (Osgood 1936a: 86). Walter also said the club could be used against bears, but I presume only in a situation of some desperation.

I have only one point to add which is that Angus told me that when a raiding party had been decided upon, a young war leader called nabati was appointed by the council to lead it.

Commentary. Although from custom we use the term war to refer to intertribal conflicts, it must be understood that what actually took place were the activities of raiding parties, disconnected from one another except in the sense that one attack might be related to another from a motive of revenge or general animosity toward a certain group. Furthermore, out of a sense of chauvinistic enthusiasm informants tend to exaggerate when they tell of specific conflicts.

In Murray's report of the attack on the Russians, we must presume that the Gens du fou were speaking of Indians in general as it seems unlikely that any Han were ever on the coast. The great massacre at Sitka in June 1800 (Tompkins 1945: 113–6), seems to be one likely source of the story, although several other destructive raids on Russian posts occurred closer to Murray's time. An example would be the earlier of two attacks on Nulato which took place about 1841 (not to be confused with the more widely mentioned one of February 16, 1851, when Lieutenant Bernard of the British navy was among those killed) (Osgood 1940: 39–41). The latter occurrence, four years after Murray was writing, gives justification for his anxiety.

The cutting off of heads, or other body parts, of course, is distinctive of the North Pacific Coast tribes. On the other hand, we seem to have something approaching confirmation of the reports of the Han fighting with the Kaska, for at least there is evidence that the Kaska fought with the people of the Pelly River. They are reported not to have practiced decapitation, however (Honigmann 1954: 92, 95; also 1949: 158).

Charlie Isaac's account, insofar as the enemy are concerned, also suggests the Kaska (Nahanni). A problem, appears, however, when we realize that in the several specific cases of conflict referred to, the opponents who have been distinguished are not members of tribes adjacent to the Han. This leaves us with the question of how such conflicts came about when they involved more than one border. One factor was the distance of the European trading posts from many of the tribes, which apparently stimulated unusual travel as we shall see in considering that subject.

Tools and Implements

Adney (1900a: 502) provides a description of a tanning of moose skins by the Han in the Klondike River country. "The hides were brought in-doors, and women at once set to work dressing them. The hair was shaved off; then the skin was turned over and all the sinew and meat adhering was removed by means of a sort of chisel made of a moose's shin-bone; and finally scraped, a work requiring a whole day of incessant and tiresome labor. The skin was now washed in a pan of hot water, and then wrung dry with the help of a stick as a tourniquet. After which the edges were incised for subsequent lacing into a frame, and then hung out-doors over a pole. The tanning, with a 'soup' of liver and brains, is done the next summer. After which the skin is made into moccasins, gold-sacks, etc."

In a later paper, Adney (1902: 631) contributes several additional points. For example, he mentions specifically that the skin to be tanned was laid across a slanting pole inside the shelter, an undertaking that was rather unclearly depicted in his earlier paper—which is unusual for one with his skill in drawing (Adney 1900a: 501). He also speaks of the edges of the skin being "slit" rather than "incised," and he makes the important addition that the skin was washed in hot water in which rotten wood had previously been boiled. Finally, he states that after the application of liver [and/or brains?], the skin was smoked. Schmitter (1910: 5) adds to this information that hair is scraped off moose skins after they have been soaked in water in order to soften them.

Among other techniques, the weaving of basketry was known to the Han, although the details of the process are not available. Simple mats were made of willow rods tied together in parallel rows, according to Walter, who added, however, that such mats were not as common among the Han as they were among the Peel River Kutchin. None of the 1932 informants knew of any pottery being made by the Han. Rabbit-skin line was apparently netted to form material for certain articles of clothing.

Lines of all the usual kinds—babiche (semitanned skin), rawhide, sinew, willow bark, spruce root, and whole willow—were available to the Han. Adney (1900a: 502) specifically mentions braided rawhide (babiche?) being used as packlines, and twisted lines were also undoubtedly known. Schmitter (1910: 10), we may recall, defines babiche in his limiting way as "a tough string made of walrus hide, secured in trade from the lower river Indians and used for making snow-shoes and fish-nets."

Walter had heard of gill nets being made of willow-bark line but did not know of their actual use by the Han. This was not taken as negative evidence, however, for willow-bark gill nets were supplanted very early among most Athapaskan groups. One of Slobodin's informants (1963a: 6) said gill nets of spruce root were used. On the other hand, it is clear that the Han depended primarily on dipnets and fish traps.

Jones (1872: 323), one of our earliest sources, noted this fact. After describing fish traps among the Kutchin he goes on to say:

> The Hong-Kutchin [Han] have another way [to fish], but this is only used for killing the big salmon [i.e., king salmon], while the bar [weir] is for the smaller fish, such as pike, white fish, etc. The largest salmon weighs from forty-five to fifty pounds, the smaller from eighteen to twenty-five pounds. In salmon fishing

a stage is erected on the bank of the river, and a man stationed upon it gives notice when a salmon is passing; this he knows by the ripple it makes when ascending the strong current. The other men, each in the middle of his small canoe, push out, all provided with a [netted] bag at the end of a pole; the bag is about five feet deep, and has an oblong frame around its mouth three feet long by one broad; the pole is eight or nine feet long. The Indian paddles his canoe in front of the fish, and pushes his net right to the bottom in front of it; as soon as the salmon enters the [dipnet] bag the man pulls it to the surface and stabs the fish with a knife fastened to a pole about five feet long; he then either lifts the salmon into his canoe, or drags it ashore in the net. . . .

The fish makes the water foam when it is first hauled up; if it strikes the canoe it will knock a hole in it; if it goes under the canoe it will upset it; and as none of the Kutchin [Han] can swim, the consequences might be unpleasant.

Schwatka (1885a: 258) also describes and illustrates the dipnet used by the Han at Eagle (Fig. 6). "The mouth is held open by a light wooden frame of reniform [kidney] shape . . . [which] is of great advantage in securing the handle firmly by side braces to the rim of the net's mouth." He adds: "Further down the river (that is in the 'low ramparts' [below Fort Yukon]), the reniform rim [of the dipnet] becomes circular; thus of course increasing the chances of catching the fish; all other dimensions, too, are greatly increased." Schwatka had noted two pages earlier that the pole handle of the dipnet was nine or ten feet long (also cf. Schwatka 1900: 342).

It is somewhat disconcerting to find that in an article published the same year, Schwatka (1885b: 825), instead of these dipnets, reports seeing at Eagle what he calls "scoop nets." Their construction is not clear and must be judged in part from his description of their use. "The fish are caught with scoop nets three or four feet long, fastened on two poles from ten to twelve feet in length. A watcher,

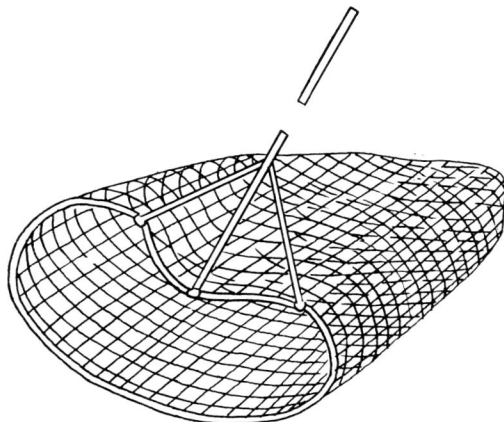

FIG. 6. King salmon dipnet (after Schwatka 1885a: 258).

generally a squaw, standing in front of the cabins, hears the approach of a fish, perhaps a half-mile down the river. Never more than one fisherman starts. Paddling out to the middle of the river, he guides his canoe with his left hand, as the voices from the shore direct, and with his right dips his net to the bottom. Upon his careful adjustment of this [net] depends his success. Failures are rare. As the fish swim near the bottom, I do not understand how they are detected in the muddy water of the river." Jones has already explained, and Schwatka's theory on the subject I shall present later.

Schmitter (1910: 10) casually refers to the "frames for fish-nets" (dipnets) being made of birch wood, while Walter said the netting was made of line cut from bull caribou skin.

Henry Harper at Moosehide in 1932 reported that basket traps made of willows tied with spruce-root line were used in the side streams of the Yukon. The diagram drawn at the time shows a weir set all across a stream, with three baskets, openings upstream, set in the angles, but there might be more (Fig. 7). The fish proceeding upstream would be swung sidewise at the weir and turned back into the trap. Each man had a basket, or sometimes two men would share in one as a basket sometimes caught so many fish that it would break unless regularly tended. The installation of the weir was undertaken by all those concerned in the fishing.

Slobodin (1963a: 6) also supplies a sketch of a weir with a fish trap after a drawing by Simon McLeod whose father had helped to build such equipment (Fig. 8). It should be noticed however, that in this case the opening of the basket is set against the current next to or near an opening of the weir which crosses a side stream. The traps are said to have been made of spruce wood [splints] and spruce-root line. Again we have a confirmation from Slobodin (1963a: 6): "During fish runs, the traps had to be attended constantly; otherwise the weight of captured fish would break the trap."

At this point we might note that the native name of the Klondike River, crudely spelled "thron-duik" with many variants, has sometimes been translated as

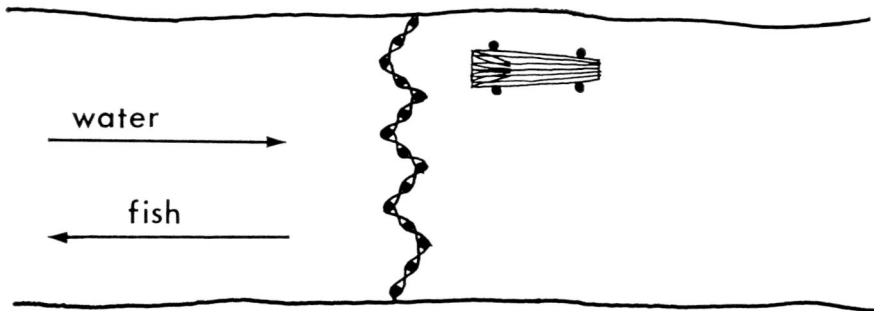

FIG. 7. Diagram of salmon trap.

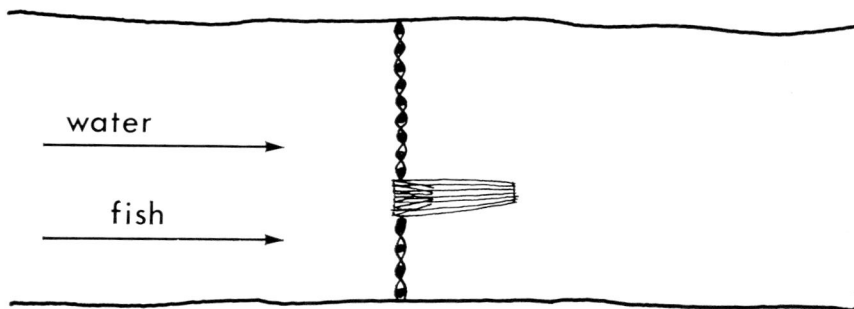

FIG. 8. Diagram of fish trap (after Slobodin 1963a: 6).

"hammer-water" with reference to the many fish-weir stakes hammered into the stream (cf. Mathews 1968: 148–9).

Henry Harper of Moosehide reported the use of a fish spear, or lance, with a detachable bone point which fitted into a socket and was tied to the end of a dried wood shaft about twelve feet long. This implement, called *ι dι zaι* was made for the purpose of spearing king salmon. Walter at Eagle confirmed its use, but it was Charlie Crow, a Vunta Kutchin born in the 1850s, who later in the same summer of 1932 gave the most interesting confirmation of its use among the Han. He contrasted its effectiveness to the toggle-headed point adopted by the Kutchin, explaining that the simple Han point had to penetrate all the way through the fish to be effective.

When taking sizable fish such as salmon, a club is needed to stun them before removal from a net or trap, and Schwatka (1885a: 259) provides us with an illustration of one seen at Eagle. It appears to be made of two pieces of wood, but no description is furnished (Fig. 9). Slobodin (1963a: 7) tells us that also the "tibia of a moose's hind leg was used as a fish-killer."

Snares and deadfalls of various kinds were set by the Han, but specific details of their use have not been recorded unless we count as such Schmitter's (1910: 8) reference to snares set in connection with caribou surrounds and their application in capturing moose and eagles, which will be described in the section on food.

Schmitter (1910: 10) writes of the Han: "One of their most useful weapons, the spear, was made by binding a hunting knife of caribou-horn to the end of a pole about 6 feet long." This is an almost identical description of the lance

FIG. 9. Club for killing king salmon (after Schwatka 1885a: 259).

described by Jones (1872: 323). Jonathan Wood at Moosehide spoke of a very similar weapon which he called a t'at, and said that it consisted of a birch pole five to six feet long, and of a convenient diameter to hold. At one end was a point made of caribou horn which he guessed to be about eight inches long, but he was not sure. This implement served to attack a bear that had been aroused from its den. Walter also knew of such a lance.

The bow is an ancient weapon and fortunately the Han type is excellently described by Jones (1872: 322), who writes: "the bow is about five feet long, and that of the Hong-Kutchin is furnished with a small piece of wood, three inches long by one and a half broad and nearly one thick, which projects close to the part grasped by the hand. This piece catches the string and prevents it from striking the hand, for the bow is not bent much. There are no individuals whose trade it is to make spears, bows, or arrows." Jonathan at Moosehide and Walter at Eagle both confirmed the Han use of the bow with the guard which Jonathan called či kaı, and the string, klul.

A bow 57 inches long and 3 inches wide with a 2¼-inch guard colored red lashed onto it and a string of two-strand babiche may be seen in the collections of the National Museum of Canada (VI-G-76). It was made by Tanana Silas of Moosehide and obtained in 1912 with the information that such bows were used by the Indians along the Yukon River below Dawson to kill ducks and other small game.

Charlie Isaac described the making of a bow for Slobodin (1963a: 9–10) but the guard, not mentioned, was perhaps simply overlooked. Nonetheless, the account is clearly worth quoting.

> Bows were about five feet long, made of birch, the best wood around here for them. A young man would carve himself a bow and shape it as best he could . . .
>
> In the evening an old man would take the young man's bow, the one he was making, and sight along it toward the fire. In the firelight he could see any lumps or rough places. He would take out his knife and make maybe one stroke (making motion of shaving toward the body) and knock off a little lump, or smooth the bow down. Then he would pass it to another man. Later the boy would take it to another wigwam, and after a while every one of the old men had a shot at it. They might even go around the camp again with it. When they were through, the bow was perfectly smooth and even and balanced. Then it was strung with sinew about so long (indicating eighteen inches to two feet). How the women made a perfectly smooth, very strong string about six feet long, I do not know. Nobody knows any more. People have asked me, and I used to ask about it, but nobody knows.

Bows must have arrows, and Schmitter (1910: 10) mentions one kind when he states: "Arrow-heads are about five inches long and made of caribou-horn or bone, and bound into split shafts with fine sinews." Elsewhere on the same page he says the shafts were made of birch. Informants at Moosehide in 1932 together provided descriptions of three types of arrows, but there were probably others. The first, called simply ƙɛ a', originally had a barbed stone head, although similar points were cut from bone, and very early in the nineteenth century multibarbed copies in iron were substituted. The second, called nu ƙɛ a', had a spikelike head of bone several inches long sharpened to a point at the striking end. The third type, called taγ, simply had the end of the wood shaft left as a blunt knob. These last arrows were used to knock down birds or small animals. Schmitter (p. 8) more specifically says: "Grouse, ptarmigan, ducks, rabbits, owls, hawks, and other small game are killed with a dull, round-pointed arrow, sharp-pointed arrows being used only for big game."

The length of the shafts, usually of spruce, was given as the distance between the middle of the chest to the end of the closed fist (or perhaps 28 to 32 inches). Actually, $2\frac{1}{2}$ feet was suggested as average. The shafts sometimes had two feather vanes and sometimes three bound onto the end near the nock with sinew line. Eagle and hawk feathers were commonly used.

In shooting the bow, Jonathan Wood said that it might be held in either a vertical position or one approaching the horizontal, with the palm upward. The nock of the arrow was held between the first and second fingers (not counting the thumb) which, together with the third, are also used to pull the string (Mediterranean release). Walter at Eagle claimed that both two- and three-finger releases were used (the latter being simply a variant of the Mediterranean release).

Walter said that the sling, such as was known among the Peel River Kutchin (Osgood 1936a: 68), was not made by Han children as their mothers did not want them to cut animal skins for the purpose; instead they used light, whole-willow line.

Bone knives are mentioned by Schmitter (1910: 10), who writes: "Hunting knives are made of bone ground flat and sharp on both edges." In the same paragraph, he mentions a hunting knife of caribou horn and also says, "they occasionally have copper knives of the same pattern, which were secured in trade from the White River Indians [Tutchone?]." He also collected a copper hunting knife at Moosehide near Dawson, that was owned by Chief Isaac, who said that such knives were used long ago and that he procured his from a White River Indian, the latter saying that copper was abundant at the head of White River. The handle of the knife is enclosed in two pieces of wood and wrapped with rawhide (babiche). The knife is $14\frac{1}{2}$ inches long, the blade $1-1\frac{1}{2}$ inches wide (Pl. 2, *B*). A moose-skin hunting belt with knife sheath attached which would hold the copper knife was acquired from Eva, the daughter of Alex, at Eagle. The belt is 34 inches long and $\frac{3}{4}$ inch wide, the sheath 10 inches long. The belt is decorated with porcupine quills colored with dyes extracted from colored textile fabrics which came into Eva's possession (this specimen could not be found). Another copper knife from the Dawson area is described and illustrated by Rogers (1965: 3, pl. G) in his article on such specimens.

Murray (1910: 85), speaking of the Indians at Fort Yukon, said their arms included the Russian knife "made of iron, but the fancy handles and fluted blades are of more value to them than the temper of the knife; they complain of ours being too hard and the difficulty of sharpening them." Since Russian trade knives of iron seem to have been common at Fort Yukon before 1850, it is hardly possible that the Han Indians did not have them if the Kutcha Kutchin did.

On the basis of the same kind of statement by Murray (1910: 85), it is equally certain that some of the Han owned guns before Europeans reached their territory.

Skin scrapers were a necessity for the Han. Adney (1900a: 502) indicates an end scraper used in tanning moose skins when he says "the sinew and meat adhering was removed by means of a sort of chisel made of a moose's shin-bone." Apparently Schmitter (1910: 5) had the same tool in mind when he stated that the hair of a moose skin was "scraped off with the end of a sharp bone spatula."

The sewing awl was of equal importance, and Schmitter (1910: 5) tells us: "as in primitive times, all sewing is still done with bone awls, bones from the fore leg of the caribou or moose being used for coarse work, and for fine work a bone from the fore leg of the lynx or of a bird is used." Walter said of the sewing awl that it was made from a small bone (fibula?) in the lower leg of the lynx. He added that he had never heard of the penis bone of the marten being used for this purpose, as reported by a Peel River Kutchin informant (Osgood 1936a: 70). He immediately suggested, however, that a canine tooth of a marten was set in a wood handle and used as an awl in the construction of snowshoes.

Schmitter (1910: 10) reported that his interpreter said: "stone axes [adzes?] for chopping down trees were used some time ago, although he never saw one." Walter told us that stone for adzes was obtained at Fifteen Mile Creek and that trees were cut down by pounding a ring around the base of a tree.

About hammers, Schmitter (1910: 10) is more explicit. "They still have hammers made from a rounded stone fastened to the end of a stick with a string of caribou-skin. These are used to break up bones for cooking and to make arrowheads. My interpreter has seen stone hammers in use."

Walter claimed that the pump drill was made and used by the Han, and in the same form as that described for me by the Peel River Kutchin in 1932 a week or two earlier (cf. Osgood 1936a: 70).

As for making fire, Schmitter (1910: 9–10) gives us a clear statement: "One method of starting a fire was by the flint and iron-pyrites method, in which a piece of flint fastened to a stick about three inches long was struck against a piece of pyrite to produce a spark. Punk to catch the spark was usually secured from a fungus growing on birch trees. The Indian word in the Porcupine language for flint was 'vetrih,' and pyrites 'tshi tlya.' Another method of fire-making was with the whirling stick. The stick was braced between the body and a piece of punk. A string was wound round the stick, so that pulling would revolve the stick rapidly in either direction, starting a friction fire on the punk."

Henry Harper and Johnathan Wood gave me essentially the same facts in 1932, but one of them said that the use of the fire drill was older—or at least it had been displaced earlier—than the strike-a-light. Walter, interestingly enough, a short time later at Eagle reported the iron and pyrites method of making fire, including the use of fungus from a birch tree. Furthermore, he said that the fire drill had a separate piece that was held between the teeth and that the vertical rod was twirled by a skin line held in the hands, not by a bow. When asked if this instrument was not borrowed from the Eskimo, he replied that he knew the Eskimo used it but denied that it was borrowed within the period of European contact.

In considering the containers used by the Han, I might first say that none of my 1932 informants knew of any folded and sewn wood boxes being made.

Wood spoons were made by the Han. Adney (1902: 631; also 1900a: 503) mentions a large communally used one: "The hot fat which rises to the top [of boiling moose meat] is skimmed off in an immense wooden spoon and passed around the circle [of Han hunters in one house], each taking a sip." Walter said that wood spoons were cut from a crooked piece of birch, and that some were made from mountain-sheep horn as well.

Spoons of mountain-sheep horn are perhaps the commonest single item in collections of ethnological specimens from the upper Yukon River area but unfortunately their provenience is generally only so given, if noted that specifically at all. Four spoons have been found from, in, or around Dawson, however, and they may be presumed to be Han. These specimens vary from $21\frac{1}{4}$ inches in length down to $9\frac{7}{8}$ inches with bowl widths from $4\frac{3}{4}$ to $3\frac{3}{8}$ inches. Decoration, consisting of incised patterns filled with red pigment is commonplace. Two of the more ornate of these spoons have been illustrated (Pl. 2, *C* and *D*).

Birch-bark baskets provided commonplace containers and were constructed in various sizes and shapes.

More important were the woven baskets first described by Campbell (1958: 97). He says: "their 'kettle' was made of the small fibers of the roots of trees, mostly split & then knitted up tight & close like a blanket; after using it for a time it becomes water proof & is then fit for cooking purposes; the method being to heat stones in the fire & throw them into the 'kettle' with a pair of tongs formed by bending a stick, & keep on doing so until the water is boiling & the food cooked. By the time this is accomplished to the satisfaction of the 'chef,' the water is converted into a pretty thick soup—not with vegetables like Scotch broth—but with sand & ashes conveyed into the cooking utensil by the hot stones." Jones (1872: 321–2) was also impressed by these baskets and adds further details: "The kettles were, and still are, made, by the Hong-Kutchin [Han] at least, of tamarack roots woven together. These kettles are very neat; hair and dyed porcupine quills are woven into them. The water is boiled by means of stones heated red hot and thrown into the kettle." About fifty years later Schmitter (1910: 9) mentions both the basket and the stone: "Baskets for cooking are made of spruce roots, and, though they leak when new, they soon shrink and the crevices become filled with grease. Each Indian woman keeps near at hand during the winter a stone which is used in cooking, as follows: First it is heated in the fire, and when it is red hot the ashes are brushed off and the stone dropped into a basket of water, making it boil in about a minute. These stones are hard to procure in the winter and are guarded most carefully. Sometimes birch-bark baskets are used, but, since they break easily, are of little service except for cooking and drinking utensils on a hunting trip. The spruce basket is preferred, since it is collapsible and can be rolled into a small package." Walter also mentioned baskets woven from spruce-root line but could not describe their manufacture.

Fortunately, two bags that can be attributed to the Han were collected at Dawson in the first decade of the twentieth century. The more curious of these has as its principal material the leg skins and claws of the jaeger (*Stercorarius* sp.), a rapacious gull-like bird whose abilities to kill were no doubt conceived of as transferable to the owner of the bag. The specimen is not completely aboriginal as is shown by a tassel of pink wool and a cotton lining. Nevertheless, its most visible features are of native origin and deserve illustration (Pl. 3, *B*).

A second bag collected at the same place and period has the appearance of the common sinew bag made with a loose netlike mesh. In this case, however, tiny beads have been strung on the sinew thread so as to produce bands of various colors at the top and bottom between which appear beads of assorted colors (Pl. 3, *C*).

Plain netted bags of fine babiche line in various sizes were used by the Han for carrying and storing materials. One specimen obtained for Yale in 1932 is about 11 inches across and the same deep when lying empty in a flat position. The construction is simple, each row of the fine babiche line simply passing through the loop above and then twisting against itself before moving on to the next loop, each loop thereby taking on a diamond shape about a half inch on each of its four sides. Around the top edge is a 2½-inch-wide band of smoked moose skin ornamented at the two edges with notched narrow bands of white caribou skin. A pair of softly tanned strings of white caribou skin alternately lace in and out of vertical slits placed parallel to each other and more or less 2 inches apart in the moose-skin band. With some difficulty, these strings can be pulled to close the opening of the bag (Fig. 10).

Decoration on this bag appears in the form of small, paired, white trade beads and paired black trade beads on opposing sides of nine netted triangles more or less evenly spaced in one row around the bag about 2½ inches below the band, plus a second row of nine about 6 inches below the band. Finally, in three roughly equidistant places just below the band there are pairs of tassels 3 inches long, each pair comprising the two ends of a tanned skin line and each line bearing two unidentified seed (?) beads between a black trade bead at the top and two at the bottom.

Adney (1900a: 499) tells of Han women using long-handled wood shovels to remove the snow in preparation for camping. Thirty-odd years later, Walter also told of wood snow shovels being made by the Han at Eagle.

Commentary. Adney's account of tanning, taken in its entirety with the accompanying illustrations, can be regarded as one of the best eyewitness descriptions of that activity among the Athapaskans, but nevertheless it will be the more appreciated if read in conjunction with other accounts of tanning from neighboring tribes (cf. Osgood 1936a: 67; McKennan 1959: 83–4; 1965: 38). Also, in referring to braided rawhide, what Adney almost certainly meant is braided

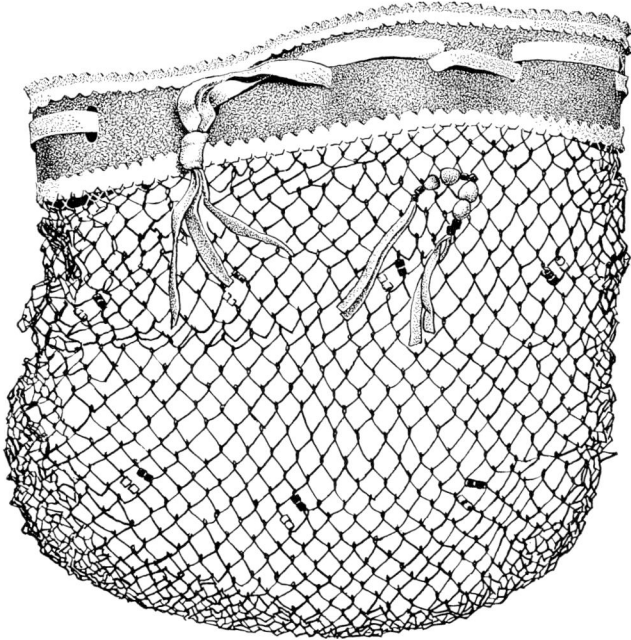

Fig. 10. Netted babiche bag.

babiche (semitanned skin line) (e.g., cf. Osgood 1940: 104 n). Also I find it difficult to understand how a gill net could be made out of spruce-root line and the question is thus raised whether willow-bast line was not actually the material.

Schwatka's description of catching salmon in two kinds of dipnets which he presents in two different publications, each without reference to the other kind of dipnet, leads me to the opinion that they are actually the same and that the one in the article (Schwatka 1885b: 825) was not accurately described. At least, the latter seems confused, and it is difficult to understand how an Indian could handle the two poles of the scoop net in one hand, quite apart from, locating the fish.

Fish traps are difficult to make and they were probably much less used after the Indian received the gun. Consequently it has been difficult to obtain much detailed information about them. Indeed, it is notable that both Schwatka and Schmitter fail to mention them with respect to the Han, but in the former's case, this is probably because they were not located at Eagle where he stopped. From the fact that the basket mouth is set downstream in the Slobodin drawing (Fig. 8), it seems more than likely that the informant was not reporting on a trap set for salmon but rather for other fish, as suggested by Jones a few paragraphs above.

Schwatka's illustration of a club to kill fish seems extraordinarily elaborate for that purpose, as one would presume a short section of graspable wood should suffice.

About the bow with the guard, it is noteworthy that Jonathan Wood said it not only occurred among the Han but also among the Tutchone (at Fort Selkirk), the Tanana, and most interestingly, among the Kutcha Kutchin where Jones (1872: 324) implies that it is absent. Negative statements are often unreliable, and I note that at the same place Jones says the Kutchin bow is the same shape throughout all the tribes and that the bow is made of willow, whereas there is reliable evidence that at least the Crow River Kutchin had the bow with the guard and made it of birch (Osgood 1936a: 72–3). I might add that Walter said he never heard of a bow with a tube attached, such as had been reported among the Peel River Kutchin a short while before (Osgood 1936a: 68). The latter was possibly an experiment in imitation of the first guns seen.

The use of copper knives by the Athapaskans of Alaska is apparently very old, although it has been questioned whether the distinctive Y-shaped handle with spiral ends is not Russian (cf. McKennan 1959: 58). For the acquisition of copper in various locations and the use of caribou-horn picks by Indians, one should see Brooks (1900: 377–82). The mention of iron knives also leads one to the thought that some iron also may have been used very early in the area (e.g., cf. Drucker 1965: 23, 110).

In speaking of axes, Schmitter may have been confused, as the ax does not appear to have been an aboriginal implement of the Athapaskans in that region. On the other hand, it is not impossible that a European ax was sometimes copied in stone (cf. Osgood 1940: 96–8).

I find it somewhat strange that Schmitter gives the native terms for flint and pyrites in the "Porcupine language" which I take to be that of the adjacent Tukkuth Kutchin of the upper Porcupine River (Osgood 1934: 174). The possibility of his using a Tukkuth informant is disturbing, although there might well be a number at Eagle. It reminds me that he caused a basic confusion by speaking of the Han by their Tukkuth name, or Vuntakutchin. It is a problem no one is likely to resolve, but we are safe in concluding that most of his data referred to the Han, as there is independent confirmation of almost all the basic facts, if not always the same detail of description.

It is quite possible that Jones made a mistake in singling out tamarack roots as the material for baskets. Certainly, spruce root was in commoner use among various Athapaskan groups. Also, Schmitter's statement that these woven baskets were collapsible deserves emphasis, as it gives a key to the technique of their manufacture. Offhand, however, it does seem a little strange that a collapsible basket would serve to boil water.

Finally, we come to the question of the relative use of birch and spruce. In this matter it is timely to quote Schwatka (1900: 343) where we find the statement about the Tadush of Charley Village: "In regard to the timber of this region, it is the same as that spoken of previously, the birch being the only wood used in the manufacture of any useful articles." This is such palpable nonsense that I might even have disregarded it altogether had it not led to the general problem of the credibility of Schwatka's work. I do not intend to be unappreciative of this somewhat extraordinary traveler, and I still believe that what is reported by him with internal evidence of being seen is, on the whole, valid. Generalizations, however, such as that given above are another matter.

After some investigation of the several reports under his name, I find in what was apparently the original one this rather easily overlooked statement by Schwatka (1900: 323): "The part of this report devoted to Indians, the most important in a military sense, is due almost wholly to Dr. [George F.] Wilson, the surgeon." Hence all the references to Schwatka 1900 may be considered the report of Wilson. Apparently, Dr. Wilson was assigned the task of describing the culture of the Indians through whose territory they passed and, as among the Han, when no interpreters were available, he apparently collected his information from anyone who would supply it, but particularly, a Russian Creole named Waniuk, who was McQuesten's interpreter at Fort Reliance. The Schwatka party probably encountered him at Fort Yukon where they met McQuesten himself during their stay of a day and a half in July 1883 (Schwatka 1900: 316, 341; McQuesten 1952: 7, 12). Over four quarto pages are devoted to the Han in which we find such comments as: "these Indians [the Takon opposite Fort Reliance] like many others, are generally opposed to violent exercise of any kind in which there is any element of work" (Schwatka 1900: 340); and "these Indians [at Johnny Village] are not at all brave or manly, but on the contrary are great cowards" (p. 34). He also mentions that the only difficulties with them would occur "on account of the avariciousness of the Indians, who, besides many other faults, are very improvident indeed" (p. 342). For the ethnographer, sufficient are the quotations; others may correctly conclude that Dr. Wilson was not very sympathetic toward the Indians on whom he was reporting.

I must admit that we cannot consider Dr. Wilson a very reliable source on the Han except when he supplies potentially perceptible data that relate to relatively static time periods. I also suggest that Schwatka's self-contradictions— as in the case of dipnet fishing—resulted from his confusing Dr. Wilson's accounts with his own observations in the haste, as some have thought, to publicize his journey (cf. Sherwood 1965: 99–105).

Travel and Trade

It becomes quite clear from over ten observations made by Murray with respect to the Han (Gens du fou) at the time Fort Yukon was established in the middle of the nineteenth century that these people had distinguished themselves as traders. Perhaps it was their aggressiveness as well as their central position between the Hudson's Bay Company posts in the Mackenzie drainage, or near it, and the Russian redoubts on the North Pacific Coast and Western Alaska. We should again note the reported anger of the Han when Fort Yukon was established sufficiently close to affect their own trade (Murray 1910: 41, 53). Before that time they were seen on the Porcupine and up the Bell River at least as far as La Pierre House (Murray pp. 28, 52). It is even reported that the caribou lands of the Chandalar Kutchin were "within reach of a band of the 'Gens du fou,'" although this is a little hard to understand unless they did not hesitate to go north of the Porcupine River or down the Yukon through Kutcha Kutchin territory (p. 36). Perhaps one of Murray's most significant comments (p. 53) is that "One band of the 'Gens-du-fou' have, *of late years,* had much intercourse with the Loucheux [Kutchin]." The italics are mine and I take the phrase to indicate the then recent impact of a two-way trade in English and Russian imports.

It also seems clear that the Han were on the Pelly and probably at Frances Lake soon after Robert Campbell had moved into that region in 1840, which we might note was the same year that John Bell established Fort Macpherson near the mouth of the Peel River (Murray 1910: 2, 8, 75–6).

With respect to travel in still another direction, we note the Schwatka (1885a: 247) mentions the trail from Nuklako, just below the Klondike River mouth, which ran southwesterly over the mountains to a tributary of the Tanana, as well as Tanana Indians who had come to the Yukon over it. This was probably the old route to and from Tetling, and the people seen were from the upper Tanana River. No doubt, the Han on the Yukon River used the same trial when occasion demanded.

Certainly, the Han lost no time in visiting Fort Yukon the summer of 1847 when it was established, and an account of their arrival by Murray (1910: 59–60) is obviously worth quoting.

> All the canoes (twenty-five in number) soon appeared in sight gliding down along the bank on account of the swell in the river, but there was no noise nor singing as with the other [the Kutchin apparently], they landed a little above our encampment assembled in silence on the bank: I went forward and presented each with the usual token of friendship, a small piece of tobacco, and expressed my happiness at seeing them here. As soon as I had stepped to the one side, they started off at full race all in a body to the lower end of the encampment and back again to their landing place, shouting and whooping in a peculiar manner; they immediately formed into a half circle and danced with great vigour for a few minutes, keeping time with their outlandish songs. They had a very extraordinary and wild appearance with their greasy dresses covered with beads and brass trinkets, and long cloated [coated?] hair fluttering in the breeze. These fellows had pipes of their own, pipes made of tin or sheet iron traded from the Russians, more than half of them had brought nothing to trade, and the others had comparatively little—six bear skins, a few badly dressed but otherwise good martens, some moose and carribeux skins, some pieces of fresh meat, and upwards of 100 geese killed with their arrows while ascending [descending?] the river.

As Murray pointed out later (p. 83), the Han were the largest group reckoned on the trade at Fort Yukon.

In payment for the furs which the Europeans wanted, beads were among the principal items appreciated by the Indians. In support of this statement we again turn to Murray (1910: 94), surely an authority on this subject. "There is not an Indian here, and very few even at Peels River but wear fancy beads, that is blue and red of various sizes, they cost the Indians nearly double what they pay for the common white beads, all these fancy beads are traded from the Russians, or by the Peels River Indians from the 'Gens-du-fou' and natives of this quarter."

There was an even older article of trade than those that have been mentioned. Schmitter (1910: 10) makes a clear statement on the subject. "In former times this pigment [red ocher] represented an important article of commerce, and was carried to a great distance [by the Han] and traded with other tribes." On the same page, he adds "they occasionally have copper knives . . . which were secured in trade from the White River Indians [Tutchone?]," and a little farther on: " 'Babiche' is a tough string made of walrus hide, secured in trade from the lower river Indians and used for making snow-shoes and fish-nets." There is also little or no question that the Han had acquired metal knives, axes, files, needles, and pails, as well as guns, ammunition, snuff, and pipes and tobacco before white men had reached their territory.

In considering the methods of travel, let us now turn to one of the most important traits of Athapaskan culture, the birch-bark canoe. Apparently because of its peculiarities, it was singled out for description by one of the early traders in the middle of the nineteenth century. While reporting on the specialized dipnet fishing of the Han, Jones (1872: 323) writes: "the canoe is flat-bottomed—is about nine feet long and one broad, and the sides nearly straight up and down like a wall." He also supplies an outline not only showing the craft in cross section but what appears to be a gradually heightening deck line as it approaches the prow (Fig. 11).

Schwatka (1885a: 242–3) must have been referring to somewhat longer canoes when he writes that on July 18, 1883, he saw sixteen birch-bark canoes a few miles above the Klondike River, each associated with one Takon (Han) Indian from Nuklako. He writes: "Already we observed an increase in the size and a greater cumbrousness in the build of the birch-bark canoes, when compared with

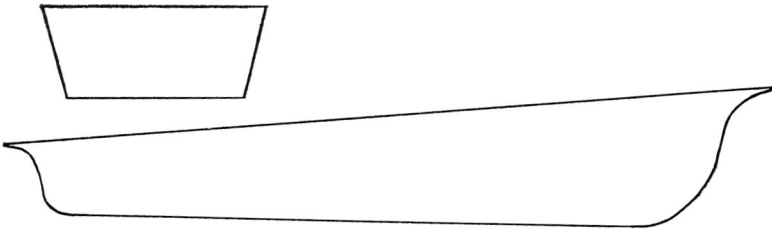

FIG. 11. Profile of birch-bark canoe and cross section (after Jones 1872: 323).

the fairy-like craft of the Ayans [Tutchone]" At Johnny Village (Ktat-ol-klin), here called Eagle, a few days later (p. 259), he elaborated on the relative size. "Up to this time the birch-bark canoes on the river had been so fragile and 'cranky' that my Chilkat Indians, who were used to the heavy wooden canoes of their country, felt unsafe in employing them for all purposes, but these [Han canoes] were so much larger and stronger in build, and our old Tahk-hees [Tagish] 'dug-out' so thoroughly worthless, that we felt safe in buying one at this village, but for a number of days 'Billy' and 'Indianne' paddled very gingerly when making excursions in it." Perhaps he had encountered a birch-bark traveling canoe for the first time. Such a craft might have been thirty feet long.

Wilson in Schwatka (1900: 343) tells us something of the manufacture of Han canoes: "A framework is made of a light wood, generally birch, which is securely fastened together with moose-skin string or roots of the spruce, split. A covering is then made of birch bark, fastened, wherever joints occur, with stitches made by splitting small spruce roots, which are very flexible, and the cracks are then closed with pitch, put on with a firebrand, in the same way that solder is used." As to their use, he states (p. 340): "The Indians, in their light canoes, keep well toward the shore; in fact as near land as possible, and push themselves along by means of two small sticks held in the hands and used like poles. In this way quite a fair speed is maintained, but not a great distance accomplished during the day."

Adney (1900b: 454) gives his own view of the Han craft. He writes: "Their canoes are made of birch-bark, but in construction are less like the birch canoe of the East than [they are like] the Eskimo *kyak*, or skin-boat. They are slender and graceful in appearance, with high, upturned ends, the forward part being decked over with bark for about five feet. Like the *kyak*, a man's canoe usually carries but one grown person; the women's or family canoe is not decked over and is somewhat larger. The occupant sits in the middle of the canoe and propels it skilfully by means of a single-bladed paddle deftly dipped from side to side. When going up-stream in shallow water the canoe-man uses two slender poles, one in each hand, with which he digs his way along." We have reproduced a photograph of what is probably a Han canoe, from the same volume (Pl. 1, *middle*).

Since it conforms in important points to verbal descriptions given above and was recorded as coming from Fort Reliance at an early date, I have illustrated a model of a birch-bark canoe in the National Museum of Natural History, Washington, D.C. (Pl. 2, *A*). It was catalogued on December 30, 1879, having been obtained by E. W. Nelson, who had been commissioned to obtain specimens for the museum in 1877 and later gained distinction for his work on the Eskimo around Bering Straits.

Schmitter's (1910: 10) description is important because it provides more data on the manufacture of birch-bark canoes at the beginning of the century. "The natives still build a style of canoe characteristic of the upper Yukon. It is of birch bark, fastened to a frame by lacing with the slender roots of trees. The bark is fitted over the frame, and then about a dozen squaws hold a sort of sewing-bee, as they sit along the sides of the canoe and lace the bark through the holes punctured along the edges by a sharp bone awl. The cracks are filled with pitch by the supervisor to make the canoe water-tight. This is a product entirely free from the influence of civilization." On the same page he notes that birch wood was used in making canoes, presumably for the frame.

Some additional data were given by Walter in 1932. He said that the frame of canoes was made from straight-grained spruce wood, although from various sources it would seem that either birch wood or spruce could be used. Bark for the cover was peeled off birch trees by means of wood chisels and warmed near a fire immediately afterward so that a sheet could be rolled up and carried home. Three pieces were needed, one for the bottom and one on each side. Walter added that pitch taken from spruce trees was melted in a birch-bark basket and applied with the bare hand over the seams which had been sewn with spruce-root line. The pitch when properly heated is reported not to stick to the hand, the latter being first dipped in water.

Walter said that moose-skin boats were also constructed, for example, at the head of Fortymile River where they were launched in order to bring down caribou meat taken in a surround that had been built in that area. He added, however, that only paddles were used, oars having come in with the white men. Also, he said that the Han never used sails. Slobodin (1963a: 5) mentions boats of moose skin being used to descend the Klondike River in the spring.

In Schwatka (1910: 340), we find the statement that rafts were used in going downstream. Walter said that pointed rafts were constructed of logs tied together with whole willow lines, but that square rafts were not made in aboriginal times.

Schwatka (1885a: 259) mentions the snowshoes of the Han as a compromise between the hunting and packing (trail) shoes of the Chilkoot. Walter reported that snowshoes were made of birch in various sizes, as might be expected of people in the middle Yukon area. Adney (1900b: 224) did not help much when he wrote: "the snow-shoes are long and narrow, with upturned toes, the frame being of white birch, filled with caribou-skin webbing," but he did when he provided a sketch of a hunting snowshoe side by side with a trail shoe (Fig. 12).

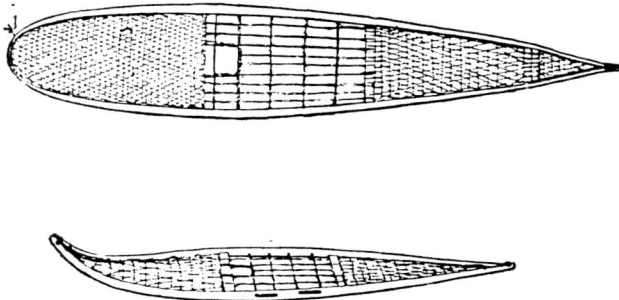

FIG. 12. Hunting snowshoe (*above*) and trail snowshoe (*below*) (after Adney 1900b: 224).

Schmitter (1910: 3, 10) notes that snowshoes were made in the fall, under-standably enough, and likewise reports that the basic material was birch. Walter added that when birch was not available, willow was substituted. More important, he claimed that aboriginally only snowshoes with a round front (Loucheux type) were constructed, and that the frames were painted red (cf. Osgood 1936a: 77–82, 99). Walter also stated that women ordinarily did the lacing of the snowshoes. From Schmitter (1910: 10) we also learn that walrus-hide babiche, originally secured in trade from the Eskimo, was used as lacing.

Walter seemed certain that the Han had no toboggans in aboriginal times, the sled, ordinarily pulled by a combination of dogs and women, being the common method of winter transport. A description given previously by Henry Harper at Moosehide was discussed with Walter, who added a point or two besides confirming that account in general. According to Henry, the xal, or sled, was about 10 feet long with both ends flaring upward. It was about 1½ feet high in the middle and about 2 feet wide. The wood used was birch and, if the informant was understood cor-rectly, each runner was made from two pieces of root, all the parts of the sled being tied together with babiche (semitanned-skin line). The runners had no extra fastening on the bottom, the surface being iced, according to Walter, by a woman melting snow in her mouth, then spitting the water into her hand and immediately rubbing it over the bottom of the runners. This could be done only in extremely cold weather when a sled was hard to pull.

Henry said there was a single line from the front of the sled. The woman took her position directly in front of the sled and one or two dogs were fastened to the line in front of her by looping the line around their necks, old clothing first being wound around that part of their anatomy to serve as a collar. A drawing (Fig. 13) made of the Han sled was scarcely distinguishable from one sketched by Murray before 1850 (Murray 1910: 85, or Osgood 1936a: 50). When necessary, other women, or men, pushed the sled from behind.

As might be expected during the seasons without snow on the ground, dogs were used for packing when the Indians traveled away from the rivers (Schmitter 1910: 3). They were also mentioned in Schwatka (1900: 343) as pulling canoes: "The dog is to them what the horse and other beasts of burden are to the civilized races; and is not only used to pack on his back and draw sleds in winter, but is employed like the proverbial canal mule in drawing their canoes up stream, not, however,

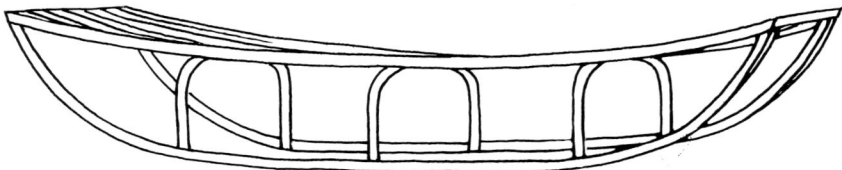

Fig. 13. Sketch of Han sled.

when a single member wishes to go on a journey, but when any number of the family moves, with the various household goods, etc."

Commentary. It is perhaps worth noting the potential sources of European trade objects that might have had a meaningful impact on the Han in the sense of affecting their economy and material culture. In my opinion, the primary source was Russian, and the direction of first penetration was from Cook Inlet where these Europeans had settlements among the Athapaskans as early as 1786 (Osgood 1937: 19; Tompkins 1945: 97). Cook Inlet is not too great a distance from the Kechumstuk area to permit one to conceive of some trade articles reaching the Han. Then we must note the settlement made by the Canadians about 1800 at Fort Norman on the Mackenzie. The Mountain Indians traded into Norman and they were neighbors of the Han, albeit with some high country to cross in order to meet. Early in the nineteenth century goods must have also started to come in from the Russians at Sitka with the Chilkoot and Chilkat as middlemen, as well as from the coast via the Ahtena. Then, in the decade beginning in 1840, a great flow must have begun and from several directions—up the Yukon and down, as well as from the Mackenzie via the Liard and Bell rivers. By that time the Han probably had enjoyed a generation or two of trading advantage which was quickly to disappear and true acculturation to begin.

With respect to canoes, Schwatka (1885a: 253) presents a drawing of an Indian fishing with a dipnet from a birch-bark canoe. The general outline seems correct, although the ends may be pointed upward a little too much, but the cover extending to the central area from both ends is most likely an error by Schwatka or Wilson, due to some confusion with a kayak. We recall Adney's (1900b: 454) specific statement that the hunting canoe had only its forward part decked over, while the traveling canoe was not decked at all. Bow and stern covers have been reported for the Nabesna (Upper Tanana) by McKennan (1959: 93), a trait which he says seems to distinguish them from their neighbors, but a craft as completely covered as a kayak is not likely to have passed without comment by other informants on the Han.

I must also mention the fact that Adney made a special study of birch-bark canoes, perhaps beginning it while he was on the Yukon. Unfortunately, the publication with its meticulous drawings, issued fourteen years after his death, fails to identify the sources of information adequately for my purposes. Nevertheless, I wish to draw attention to the section in that volume entitled the "Kayak-Form Canoe" (Adney and Chapelle 1964: 158–68).

I also might comment that the propulsion of a canoe upstream by means of a pole in each hand seems to have a limited distribution among the Athapaskans, and one that depends on the nature of the waterway, shallow water being the obvious and necessary requirement. For a more detailed description of the procedure, I recommend the account given by Allen (1887: 97–8) when he was among the Koyukon.

As for Schmitter's report on walrus-hide babiche being used for snowshoes, we must presume that this material served only for lacing central panels of those useful appendages. The trade in such items as walrus-hide babiche must have involved other Athapaskan groups. It has been described between the Ingalik and the Unaligmiut Eskimo (Osgood 1958: 62–3), and similar activity occurred between the Koyukon and the Malemiut Eskimo (Dall 1877: 27). Schwatka's (1885a: 259) mention of the Han snowshoe being a compromise, presumably in size, between the hunting and the trail shoe of the Chilkoot, I presume to be an error of delimitation due to his lack of opportunity to observe various sizes of snowshoes during his brief summer stop at Eagle.

I have found considerable information on dog-driving and toboggans in the literature, all of which, however, seems clearly to pertain to the historic period. It will consequently be presented in the section on the period of culture change.

Shelter

Even as late as 1932, informants on the upper Yukon seemed more familiar with the aboriginal forms of shelter than with many other aspects of their culture, while I myself had been impressed by the dome-shaped movable winter house of the Kutchin that had been sketched in 1847 or 1848 by Murray (1910: 85) and reproduced as a colored lithograph by Richardson (1851: frontispiece). Consequently, considerable time at Moosehide was devoted during my 1932 visit to obtain an overall comprehension of this aspect of Peel River Kutchin life. Although the effort was not as successful as it might have been had pertinent comparative material been available, the general outline, as well as many significant details, seemed clear. This I report here because during the following days at Eagle, after Walter had given support to his affirmation that there were few significant differences in the construction of shelters used by the Han and those used by the Peel River Kutchin, the latter data were simply read over and checked. This was not the most satisfactory procedure, but as has already been stated, the primary work of the summer was directed toward a study of the ethnography of the Kutchin, not that of the Han.

Walter stated that there were three main types of shelter occupied by the Han according to the season of the year and the activities of the people. The most substantial of these was the nà kún, or moss house, which served as a permanent dwelling during the colder part of the year except when people were ranging over the country on hunting trips which occurred seasonally, as will be seen, but also somewhat irregularly as a result of various circumstances such as the special movements of game, or weather conditions, or the scarcity of food. Presumably, most moss-house settlements were found on the banks of the Yukon, but not all of them. A description of their construction will be taken essentially from that given for the Peel River Kutchin.

Two families generally unite to build and occupy the moss house. When houses are built in the same vicinity they are segregated sufficiently so that the respective owner's dogs will not be brought into too close a fighting proximity and so that the children will have room to play. The occupation of the moss house is correlated with periods when there is little or no travel, when the cold of a new winter brings a climatic change, and when snow falls soft and heavy to block up the trails. Generally a new house is built every fall.

The Han begin the construction of the moss house by excavating a 25-foot square to a depth of $1\frac{1}{2}$ feet (or actually to frozen ground). Then posts, about a foot in diameter, are raised at each corner to a height between 4 and 6 feet. Next, two more posts are erected to stand about 10 feet high, halfway between the two corner posts at the ends of the house. A ridgepole is then laid up between these center posts. It is so cut at the ends as to fit into parallel V-shaped grooves made at the tops of the center posts. Horizontal beams, parallel to the ridgepole, likewise connect the corner posts and, like the ridgepole, are lashed in place. Following this, principal rafters are extended and lashed between the ridgepole and the horizontal beams connecting the corner supporting posts. When this framework is completed, split poles, 6 to 8 inches in diameter, are placed vertically, side by side, all around the house and lashed to the horizontal beams and at the ends of the principal rafters. A door is left at one end, apparently by omitting a few of the upright poles. This door faces to leeward if there are strong prevailing winds, but the direction is not important. The lashing on of a few purlins and numerous common rafters made from trimmed poles finishes the framework of the roof, a space being left on each side of the middle of the ridgepole for the emission of smoke. Finally, squares of moss, cut as large as possible, are piled high against the sides and ends, dirt being added as a support. There is always ventilation at the ends. Moss is likewise laid, roots upward, on the roof and covered with dirt. When a bull caribou or bear skin has been hung over the doorway and a dirt mound built up in the center of the house for a fireplace, the dwelling may be said to be almost complete. The final touch comes with the laying of a few willow mats. These are put down in all the more or less permanent shelters except under the beds, which are prepared with small spruce boughs. The brush in the home of a well-to-do man is changed at about weekly intervals but the poor are less particular.

Since references to the moss house are rare, I might mention that Schwatka (1885a: 245) during his brief stop at Fort Reliance mentions the abandoned post as "consisting of one main house, probably the store, above ground, and three or four cellar-like houses, the ruined roofs of which were the only vestiges remaining above ground." Although a dozen Europeans had wintered at Fort Reliance before Schwatka's visit in 1883, the "cellar-like houses" seem to have been moss houses of the Han (McQuesten 1952: 11; Mathews 1968: 96). Walden (1931: 59) specifically mentions the moss house by name, and describes a deserted village which may have been Tutchone, however, rather than Han. He writes of "three or four houses, built of tiny poles laid one on top of the other, as the timber was very small in this section. The poles were notched together like those of a log house and made into double walls about eighteen inches apart. The intervening space was crammed hard with moss and a small amount of earth, [and the house had a roof] with a smoke-hole in the middle. These made warm and comfortable dwellings."

The second main type of shelter was the somewhat elongated, hemispherical, skin-covered, winter traveling house Walter named nɩ bɛl sʒo, but here I shall retain the Peel River Kutchin term, nivaze, which is simpler to write and to pronounce. Adney (1900a: 499–501) provides an excellent description of the nivaze itself as used by the Klondike band of the Han, as well as the manner of living in it which he experienced in January 1898 and, finally, illustrations (Fig. 14; Pl. 1, *bottom*).

Two miles from the Yukon, above the mouth of the Bonanza Creek, the head of the caravan stopped, and Isaac marked the place for the camp at the edge of the river, alongside a dense grove of spruce-trees. As we turned off the smooth miners' trail every person old enough to walk slipped into snow-shoes, as the snow was about two feet deep. The women took long-handled wooden shovels and removed the snow off the ground an elliptical space eighteen feet long by twelve feet wide, banking it all around two feet high. While some covered the exposed river gravel with green spruce boughs and kindled a fire in the centre, others cut sticks three to five feet long and set them upright a foot apart in the bank of snow, the long way of the intended house, leaving an opening at one side two feet wide for the door. The house-poles, an inch thick and ten or twelve feet long, whittled out of spruce and previously bent and seasoned into the form of a curve, were then set up in the snow at the ends of the camp to the number of sixteen or twenty, their upper ends pointing toward the middle in the form of a dome ten feet high. These were strengthend by two arched cross-poles underneath, the ends of which were lashed to the side-stakes with withes of willow twigs thawed out and made pliant over the fire. Over this comparatively stiff frame-work next was drawn a covering of caribou-skin, tanned with the hair on, made in two sections, and shaped and sewed together to fit the dome. The two sections, comprising forty skins, completely covered the house, except in the middle, where a large hole was left for the smoke to escape, and at the doorway, over which was hung a piece of blanket. The toboggans with the balance of the loads were hoisted upon pole scaffolds each side of the house, out of reach of the dogs, who looked and acted as if ready to devour anything from a moccasin to a rawhide toboggan-lashing. Not until the house was done and enough wood stacked before the door to last until morning did any one stop for a moment. In a climate where the temperature remains not higher than thirty

FIG. 14. Sketch of pole framework of nivaze (after Adney 1900a: 496).

degrees below zero, and occasionally drops to fifty or sixty below, it is dangerous to dally, as white men are prone to do under the same conditions.

In our little village there were seven lodges. In the chief's house were nine persons and seven dogs, divided into two households, each having a side of the fire to itself. On ours were Isaac, his wife, Eliza, with a nursing boy less than a year old, myself, and three native dogs—Chicken (child), Gagul (broken-leg), and John; also a tawny "white man's dog," Beaber, taken to board, a small black native pup, and an extremely miserable short-haired white man's pup, wrapped in a blanket to keep from freezing, and weighing just fourteen pounds by Isaac's spring scales. On the other side were a middle-aged, stockily built man known as "Billy," or "the missionary's man," and his wife, with two girls respectively about eight and ten years of age, and a boy of the same uncertain age, four large native dogs, and two pups. The human occupants kneeled or reclined before the fire, which was ingeniously built to throw the heat in two directions and to draw well, notwithstanding which latter, I soon discovered that it was often necessary to lie close to the ground, and when the smoke became too thick, to lift the lower edge of the skin covering.

The following morning before daybreak word was given "All go." Toboggans were rattled off of caches, and houses taken down and loaded as swiftly as they had been set up.

Unfortunately, Adney did not tell us exactly how swiftly that was. In comparison with my data, we discover that the nivaze I described was smaller, the area being about ten by seven feet as compared to his eighteen by twelve feet. The length of the house poles was exactly the same, but only ten to twelve poles were used, rather than sixteen to twenty as might be expected in a larger dwelling. More significant, in the smaller nivaze the poles were shoved into the snowbank rather than lashed to sticks three to five feet long which were cut at the camp and set up in the snow to be lashed to the long, prepared poles. We also note that in the larger nivaze, willow-bark lines were used for this lashing. Possibly, some type of skin line served for the main fastenings, as was reported for the smaller dwelling.

Both accounts clearly mention the two-family occupancy and the skin cover in two sections, one for each end of the elliptical dwelling. Adney's description indicates twenty caribou skins for each cover, while twelve or thirteen was the number given for the smaller construction. We might also note that the seams of the covers might be painted red and have feathers attached at intervals if the owners were families of high prestige. In the description of the smaller nivaze, the point is made that the size of the smoke hole could be controlled by separate skins on each side overlapping the area left between the pair of covers. Also we note the caribou covers had the hair turned in, while Walter said that moose skins might be used if they were more plentiful than caribou skins.

Finally, there is the matter of the fireplace. Adney reports that the snow was simply cleaned off the gravel bed of a stream. It would seem that when a given location was to be occupied for a longer period, a fireplace was provided by camping on terrain with a small knoll in the center, or by finding some dirt or stones to bring in.

Schmitter (1910: 3) mentions the nivaze but was apparently not really familiar with this segment of Indian customs. He says for example, that the Han took the covers with them, but left the "wicker framework." This notion he apparently derived from the fact that the poles "are sometimes seen still standing where Indians have not been for years." He also states that the Han "had no permanent dwellings," by which he apparently meant that the Indians did not stay in one place all year.

The third type of shelter, which Walter called a di tᵧ szo, was really a variation of the nivaze, the cover being different in having the hair removed. Walter claimed that no smoke hole was left and that the covers overlapped, the interior being dark as a defense against mosquitoes. This type of shelter was used when the Indians traveled in mild weather and what fires were needed were built outside. Walter added that sometimes, when skins were not at hand, this same type of basic construction was used with a cover of spruce bark.

Among secondary, or more temporary structures, a tipi without hoop supports was erected when families failed to bring bent and pre-dried poles with them. Also a man caught alone in the snow might make a snow house just large enough to crawl into for the night simply by heaping up a pile of snow, then digging it out, freezing the interior surface by inserting a small fire for a few minutes, then, after removing the fire, adding brush, crawling in, and closing up the entrance sufficiently with a block of snow or other material so that body temperature would remain tolerable.

A small nivaze four or five feet high was constructed as a sweat bath, according to Walter, especially when a person was not feeling too well, heat and steam being believed to have a salutary effect. Hot rocks were placed inside at the edge of the structure and the occupant dripped water on them to create steam.

The open brush camp used especially by men traveling without their families is so characteristic of the Northern Athapaskan that only its use need be recorded here.

One of the more important types of buildings was the smokehouse in which fish and, more occasionally, meat was dried. During the summer months it also seems to have been used for sleeping in order to avoid some of the biting insects which could make life unpleasant at fishing camps. The buildings in Schwatka's (1885a: 251–5) description of the Indian village at Eagle in the summer of 1883 seem to be smokehouses of that period. Since it is a unique bit of evidence it is quoted in full.

This was the first Indian village we had encountered on the river deserving the name of permanent, and even here the logs of which the cabins, six in number, were built, seemed to be mere poles, and by no means as substantially built as it might have been with the material at hand. It was perched up on a high flat bank on the western side of the river, the gable ends of the house fronting the stream, and all of them very close together, there being only on or two places wide enough for a path to allow the inmates to pass. The fronts of the houses are nearly on the same line, and this row is so close to the scarp of the bank that the "street" in front is a very narrow path, where two persons can hardly pass unless one of them steps indoors or down the hill; and when I visited the village the road was so monopolized by scratching dogs that I could hardly force my way through them. This street may have been much wider in times of yore—for it seemed to be quite an old village—and the encroachments of the eroding river during freshets may have reduced it to its present narrowness. If so, it will not be long before the present village must be abandoned or set back some distance. Further up the river we saw a single pole house projecting over the bank about a fourth or a third of its length, and deserted by its occupants. The body of the houses is of a very inferior construction, in which ventilation seems to be the predominating idea (although even this is not developed to a sufficient degree, as judged by one's nose upon entering), and the large door in front is roughly closed by a well-riddled moose or caribou skin, or occasionally by a piece of canvas so dirty that at the distance of a few feet it might be taken for an animal's skin. The roofs are of skins battened down by spruce poles, which, projecting beyond the comb in irregular lengths, often six and eight feet, gave the whole village a most bristling appearance. A fire is built on the dirt-floor, in the center of the habitation, and the smoke left to get out the best way it can. As the occupants are generally sitting flat on the floor, or stretched out at full length on their backs or stomachs in the dirt, they are in a stratum of air comparatively clear; or, at least, endurable to Indian lungs. The ascending smoke finds ample air-holes among the upper cracks of the walls, while that dense mass of it which it retained under the skins of the roof, making it almost impossible to stand upright, is utilized for smoking the salmon which are hung up in this space.

The Han made platform caches to protect their equipment and food supplies from marauders varying in size from mice to bears. Walter also mentioned a ground cache constructed by digging a hole with sharpened sticks. When of a suitable size, dry willows were put on the bottom as a lining. After the fish had been put in, heavy poles were laid parallel across the top and then lighter ones crosswise. Finally, a layer of birch bark or spruce bark was added, after which the entire top was covered with the dirt extracted in making the hole. This left a slight hump, the only sign of the location of the cache. According to my notes, this cache was used for dried fish.

Commentary. It seems highly probable that the use of the moss house was affected to a considerable degree by the acquisition of the gun and the shift to a trapping economy after the beginning of the fur trade. These factors will be discussed in the final section on the period of culture change. In any event, the character of the construction was such as to seemingly make a poor impression, if any at all, on early travelers. In fact, the moss houses might have been viewed as

FIG. 15. Han houses at Klatolklin, or Johnny Village (after Schwatka 1900: 312).

poor adaptations of the Euro-American log cabin. Descriptively even worse, we have two statements from Dr. Wilson in Schwatka (1900: 340, 343), which are included in this section to indicate awareness of them. The first is: "The houses are not substantially built, being of logs and brush piled up, and are placed almost at the waters edge." The second is a description of Johnny Village (Fig. 15, sketched after an engraved photo): "it consists of only 5 or 6 houses, which are built after the general plan of all the native houses on this portion of the river, of sticks and brush; and with just enough room to accommodate the various members of the family, including the dogs, which are by no means few in number. Had they any other domestic animals to provide for, doubtless an entirely different style of structure would be adopted." Apart from the speculation, Dr. Wilson might have done better even using Schwatka as an informant.

From the Indian point of view, the moss house must have been regarded as the most permanent type of house. At least it was not normally moved and appeared in locations in which these semi-sedentary people spent most of their time in winter when not traveling and, under aboriginal conditions without the gun and the impetus to trap, we may argue that they traveled less. It seems probable that each band had a specific location for moss houses which had something of the special meaning of home and from which they spread out in smaller groups in summer to be closer to fishing weirs, and in perhaps larger groups at other seasons in order to hunt. At least the Han give the feeling of being somewhat more sedentary than the Peel River Kutchin, but if with such ideas we go skating around, we must be careful while presenting the facts of aboriginal culture to stay off thin ice.

In any event, with the benefit of hindsight and the suspicion of original responsibility, I would now not present the two, skin-covered, more or less dome-shaped, shelters as two different types but merely as variants of one. The type of shelter used aboriginally during the fishing season remains a problem, for there is reason to suspect that it was closer in form to the moss house than to the nivaze. Of the facts, we may never be certain.

Dress

As did all Northern Athapaskans, the Han dressed in tailored clothing of skins, that of the caribou being the most important. Walter was confident that the Han never made garments either of fish skins or bird skins with their feathers, or any kind of animal intestines. Furthermore, they did not weave hats from spruce-root fibers.

Aboriginal dress was in most respects soon replaced by European-type clothing, and consequently it is not surprising that descriptions of items attributed directly to the Han are rare. As perhaps might be expected, however, the longest comment on the Han Indians that was made by Robert Campbell (1958: 111–2) during the first trip through Han territory which took place between June 5 and 10, 1851, was on dress. In his journal for the same period, Campbell writes briefly about the Indians and one can hardly doubt that they were Han. He says: "Their dress which when new is pretty & picturesque, is made of the skin of the moose or the reindeer, principally the latter. The skirt [shirt] or coat is finished in a point, both before & behind, & reaches down to the knees, being frequently ornamented with coloured beads, porcupine quills or long hair. The coat has a hole large enough to admit the head, but does not open in front, & is provided with a hood which can be used, when wanted, as a head-dress. The trowsers or leg covering, & shoes are made of the same material, & the garment made with the hair inside for warmth" (Campbell 1958: 97).

Fortunately, we also have the sketches of Murray (1910: 82, 87, 89, 90, 94; and see the corresponding colored lithographs in Richardson 1851, *1:* 384, 397, 391, 381, 377) and his statement (1910: 84) that "the dress worn by all [the Indians] I have seen is nearly the same, the only difference being in the fashion of wearing the hair and some of their ornaments." If I were not sure he was including the Han, one of the main trading groups at Fort Yukon, I would become sure as it is the Han that he specifically mentions as wearing their hair differently. Therefore, I feel justified in quoting his descriptions and, in general respects, attributing them to the Han as well as to the Kutcha Kutchin.

Let us begin with the main upper garment of the summer costume. Murray (1910: 84) writes: "They wear a capot or shirt of dressed deer skin, pointed in front and behind something like the tails of a dress coat." He is obviously speaking of a man's dress as is shown in his drawing of hunters (Murray, 1910: 94; present Fig. 16).

As for the comparable female garment, Murray (p. 85) states: "The women dress nearly the same as the men, only the capot is a *leetle* longer, and with no point in front." This costume is clearly shown in another drawing (p. 82; present Fig. 17). It perhaps should be emphasized that Murray uses the word *capot* in the sense of a shirt that does not open all the way down the front and must be pulled over the head, and certainly does not mean a long overcoat, to say nothing of meaning a cape in the original French sense. Also, he writes deer skin for caribou skin, a common substitution among fur traders in his day.

Campbell (1958: 97–8), used the word reindeer for caribou, and he says: "The woman's dress is very similar to the men's only the leather garment comes down square to about the ankle like a gown."

Describing the lower summer garment, Murray (1910: 84) informs us that the

FIG. 16. Men's costume (after Murray 1910: 94).

people wore "simply a pair of deer skin pantaloons, secured by a narrow band around the lower part of the body; a strip of beads about two inches broad is worn on each side of the *trousers* from the hip to the ankle, bands of beads are fastened around the legs and ankles. The shoes and pantaloons are of the same piece, the stripes of beads on the legs are in alternate squares of red and white, but frequently only single fringes are worn, and those who are poor use only porcupine quills." These pantaloons, or trousers, and he seems to use the words synonymously, are shown in the same drawings that illustrate the shirts, and more colorfully in Richardson (1851, 1: 377).

About the comparable items of winter clothing, Murray (1910: 85) merely states: "The winter dress is a rabbit skin capot [closed shirt] and deer skin trousers with the hair on, the hair is always worn next the skin."

One wishes that he could have been a little more generous with his description of these main items of winter dress, and I shall consider the data from later sources before going on to other aspects of the subject. Let us mention before doing so, however, that Murray, unlike Campbell, does not tell of any hood being attached to the shirt which, if it were, could then be described as a parka. Visually, however, he shows us (p. 82) a child wearing what is apparently a parka in one of his sketches. Richardson's (1851, *1:* 384) colored lithograph makes the style even clearer.

FIG. 17. Women's costume (after Murray 1910: 82).

Fifty years after Murray's time, Adney (1902: 625) comes to our aid with some elaboration on the winter costume. He writes: "The men are variously dressed. The older men wear shirts of caribou skin (tanned and made up with the hair inside), which reach to the middle, with a curious rounded point at front and back extending lower; or a shirt of plaited rabbit skins, split, plaited, and sewn together, making at once the lightest and warmest garment known, which they wear next the skin in the coldest weather, with nothing else!" No hood is mentioned and his illustrations rarely show them, although in his book Adney (1900b: 355) provides a photograph of an Indian (?) woman at Dawson (?) wearing an elaborate parka apparently of Eskimo style, no doubt the *haute mode* of 1898.

Schmitter (1910: 4), on the other hand, is quite definite when he states: "The original native upper garment was the caribou pelt 'parka,' a combination of hood and coat reaching to the knees and without buttons or laces. It was pulled on over the head like a shirt, the hood generally hanging down the back and covering the head only in severe weather. Sometimes sealskin 'parkas' were secured in trade from this lower river natives."

This would seem to make things clear except that Walter at Eagle was equally definite in saying that the aboriginal dress of the Han did not include the parka and that there was no hood on the shirt. His insistence is perhaps meaningful as he was aware of the problem and there is no evidence that Schmitter had been apprised of it. None the less, to support the position that the parka was not aboriginal among the Han we are faced with negative evidence, always dangerous, and from a man born as late as 1882. Still, the subject is one that might easily have come up when Walter was a boy which is probably the time the parka of true Eskimo pattern was introduced.

Returning to descriptions of the summer costume for men, Walter said that it consisted of two pieces, one a shirt (without a hood) which was open a few inches down the front and had flaps extending before and behind in the area of the upper legs, the other a garment combining trousers and moccasin-like footwear. The material of both pieces consisted primarily of caribou skin without the hair and bleached white by hanging in the sun at the end of the tanning process. The soles of the lower garment, however, were made of moose skin because of its superior wearing quality.

The summer dress of the women varied in no obvious particulars except that, according to Walter, the bottom of the shirt reached below the knees and was cut off square. It is only here that we find Walter's description not conforming to the impression given by Murray's drawings.

As for the corresponding items of winter dress, Walter said they were the same as those for summer except that they were made from skins with the hair left on which was turned inward toward the body.

It is significant to add here that Han informants at Moosehide a few days earlier had reported that the aboriginal costume consisted of *coats* made pointed before and behind, reaching a point just below the crotch. Looking at the notes at this late date, it would seem certain that shirts, not coats, should have been recorded by the ethnographer, for the mistake seems incongruous. Perhaps he was working too fast.

Moccasins were apparently known to the Han in aboriginal times, even if not regularly used as they were when Schmitter (1910: 4) wrote: "Moccasins were of moose-skin, with caribou-skin strings to lace and tie them on, and they were of generous size, so that grass or other soft material could be placed in the soles to protect the feet. The moccasins usually reached several inches above the ankle, although low slipper-like moccasins were also worn in camp."

To protect the feet, Campbell (1858: 97) says: "Their socks [duffel] in winter consist of grass & hair over which is drawn the shoe." Walter specifically mentioned rabbit skins serving as duffel (inner linings) to protect the hands and feet, but there is no reason to believe that grass or sedge was not also used, especially in footwear when it was likely to become wet, a not uncommon occurrence in the spring and summer.

Schmitter (1910: 4) states: "Large moose-skin mittens were made with gauntlet-like wrists, and these are now used and prized by whites as an article of comfort." This was certainly true in the decades around the turn of the century and since, but Walter said that the aboriginal mitten reached to a point only a little above the wrist.

Schmitter (1910: 4) said of the Han: "They wear no head covering in summer, but marten or rabbit skin caps are worn in winter." Walter also mentioned hats of rabbit skin, and described them as hemispherical in shape. Headbands also were worn and by individuals of both sexes.

Robes were reported in 1932 and said to have been made of caribou skins, mountain-sheep skins, or rabbit skins. Slobodin (1963a: 10) says that "rabbitskin blankets, manufactured by the loop twining technique reported for a number of Athapaskan tribes, are still [in 1961?] occasionally made for infants."

With respect to the appearance and decoration of clothing, Campbell (1858: 98) states that the Indians "decorate their dress freely with ermine or squirrel skins or tails, duck wings, long hair, & c." Also we may recall Murray's (1910: 60) early comment when he spoke specifically of the Gens du fou making "a very extraordinary and wild appearance with their greasy dresses covered with beads and trinkets." Later on, Murray (p. 84) adds more specific details of the decoration of the summer shirt saying: "a broad band of beads is generally worn across the breast and shoulders, and behind a fringe of fancy beads, and small leathern tassels wound round with porcupine quills and strung with the stones of a white berry common in the country."

Schmitter collected one specimen specifically used to decorate clothing. This was moose-skin string ¼ inch wide and 42 inches long with white, red, and blue porcupine quills. It was intended to be tied, or sewed, either below the knees of the lower garment or around the ends of the sleeves. The piece was made by Sarah, wife of Luke, a shaman at Eagle. Schmitter was told that she used cranberry and huckleberry juices as dyes. Walter said that the decoration of clothing with porcupine quills, or beads, was a characteristic of the rich.

As for personal adornment, tattooing was practiced principally by women, according to Walter, who said that they made a few vertical lines on the chin and a few horizontal lines on the front part of the leg below the knee. Men who were exceptional marksmen with the bow and arrow sometimes made a tattoo mark on the back of the wrist. Information is not available to indicate by which method this was done.

Face painting was common among the Han, according to Walter, who said some paint was put on the face every morning. Campbell (1958: 98) noted: "They also often daub their faces with red earth or ochre." Grease was appreciated as a coating for the skin, and it apparently spread over the clothing as well.

I have found no evidence of labrets being worn, but earrings were popular. Campbell (1958: 98) wrote: "These Indians are very fond of ornaments of any kind such as earrings." Walter said that rich men in particular wore long earrings made of beads. Murray (1910: 90, 94) shows men in his sketches with earrings of dentalia shell and other beads suspended not only from the lobe but also from additional holes in the helix above it.

An ornament was also inserted in the septum of the nose. Walter claimed that both sexes wore straight bone ornaments horizontally in the nose. Curiously, he knew of only the Selkirk (Tutchone) and Whitehorse (Tagish?) Indians wearing rings in their noses, a fact that shows the weakness of negative evidence, for not only did Dall (1870a: 202) note that among the Han "a metal ring is sometimes used in the nose instead of the dentalium ornament of the western Tinneh [Athapaskans]," but Schmitter (1910: 4) tells us: "Another custom was to pierce the nasal septum and through it insert rings of small bones from birds."

Necklaces were worn by the Han, and Schmitter collected a specimen of one type of neck ornament. It was made from a strip of moose skin, 1¼ inches wide and 38 inches long, with five rows of wound-up porcupine quills of red, blue, and white running its entire length. Tassels of skin 2 inches long hang in groups of five at 1-inch intervals along one edge of the piece. This ornament was reported to have been made by Maggie of the Indian village at Eagle (Pl. 3, *A*). Many of Murray's sketches show Kutchin wearing some kind of necklaces or collars. An informant at Moosehide in 1932 claimed that a line of beads was put down the middle of the front and rear shirt tails, but of these there is no indication by Murray. Walter also mentioned bead necklaces.

On the basis of considerable evidence, one can conclude that the hairdress of the Han Indians was one of their most obvious cultural distinctions. Campbell (1958: 97) said: "Most of the men wore their hair long in a queue." Murray (1910: 85) makes a special point of saying: "The 'Gens du fou' and lower Indians mix their hair with red earth, greese and the down of geese and ducks, by continuing this from their infancy the *tail* attains an immense length, often as large as the head, and becomes so heavy loaded as it is with beads and shells and accumulated dirt, that the neck is bent forward, and gives the Indians the appearance of stooping."

Schmitter's (1910: 4) description adds details: "The old method of hair dressing was to allow the hair to grow long and tie it in a bunch behind [the head] with a small bunch over each temple. Swan feathers were chopped fine and applied with grease to the rear bunch daily until it became a large mass."

Walter added some further details, pointing out that individuals with little hair tied it behind the head, while those who had more hair tied some of it at the sides. In the latter case, the hair was parted in the center of the head and the part smeared with a line of red ocher. The use of grease and fine feathers was mentioned by Walter, and he added that rich men bound beads around their hair. Furthermore, one or two white eagle feathers, tipped with black, were placed in the hair as a designation of clan affiliation, as has been mentioned. Also it was made clear that women dressed their hair essentially as did men, but they did not insert the eagle feathers or use as much of the cut-up feather material smeared over the coating of grease. Finally, shamans did up their hair as did ordinary people except when performing, as heretofore noted.

Commentary. One basic question concerning the principal garments of the Han is whether the winter shirt normally had a hood attached to it. The problem is a complex one. Certainly, Campbell's evidence is weighty, but at least one wonders how he obtained this information without an interpreter in a brief passage through Han territory in July. Still, the Peel River Kutchin wore the parka in winter, but the Crow River Kutchin apparently did not (Osgood 1936a: **39, 43**). Nevertheless, considering Walter's insistence, plus the fact that Schmitter might reasonably consider the parka as the aboriginal garment unless the possibility that it was not had been brought to his attention, and most of all, Murray's failure to indicate such distinctive dress, I feel confident that the hooded shirt, or parka, was not the exclusive winter dress of adult Han Indians. The use of a hooded shirt or combination garment for children has a wide distribution among the Athapaskans, however, and there can be no question but that the Han knew of the parka and apparently sometimes used it in aboriginal times.

Since it seems certainly to have been adopted by the Indians after the coming of the Europeans, why did not all do so before? Several suggestions can be made. Perhaps it was partly a matter of style, and a style, especially when reinforced by long usage in a culture, can exert a singular force. The Han may not have wanted to look like an Eskimo, for the parka is certainly an Eskimo garment. From a more practical point of view, the advantage of the hood, which is warmth, may be offset by its restrictive effects with respect to seeing and hearing. For the Eskimo on the barren coast this may be a small matter compared to the comfort afforded a person who has to accept the cold whenever he is out of his house. For the Athapaskan, however, sight and sound in the forest are of the greatest significance. Furthermore, his attitude toward the cold, which is generally more intense in the interior Athapaskan country, is different from that of the Eskimo. It is too cold simply to dress warmly and accept the winter environment in the manner that the Eskimo does. The Indian wears lighter clothing and makes up for the difference by running to keep warm with the necessity and assurance of finding wood for a fire to prevent him from freezing when he stops. With heavy hair coated with grease and fine feathers thickly covering the back of his head and neck, his thoracic heat loss would be considerably lowered and the need for head covering would be small. Finally, in the extreme cold—and the middle Yukon is one of the coldest areas in the world that have been aboriginally populated—Athapaskans tend to stay close to their shelters, and this may well have been even more true before historic contact. So much for theory.

A second question that the data raise is whether the Han had an aboriginal coat that opened down the front. Here again one recognizes the potentiality of impact from European sources. It again seems reasonably certain that such a garment was not a part of their regular dress in the first half of the nineteenth century. On the other hand, it seems more than likely that one or more Russian or English coats had been secured in trade from other tribes before any of these Europeans had been actually seen by the Han. This is opinion; beyond this one would merely be guessing.

I would also like to draw attention to Campbell's (**1958**: **97–8**) statement that the woman's costume came to about the ankle. This does not seem to be a practical dress for ordinary Athapaskan wear, and the reader is referred to the blanket parka of the Ingalik (Osgood 1940: 256–7).

Although it is not certain, because of the unclear meaning of the word *plait* as used by various authors, I judge that one technique of working rabbit-skin line served for both clothing and robes. (For an attempt to clarify it with an illustrated description, see Osgood 1936a: 71–2.)

The value of grease in personal adornment must be related to the extremely cold temperatures, and the Han seemed to have used as much of it as any Athapaskan group. That fact, with their elaborate hairdress, must have given them an outstanding appearance among the Indians of the Yukon.

Food

It will be helpful before beginning a compilation of the data on food and related subjects to present some picture of Han life as it progressed through the seasons. To begin with the period of salmon fishing, for nothing else seems more certain as to time, in the middle Yukon there are three varieties of salmon that are mentioned as important to the Indians and they arrive in the following order. First come the king salmon, *Oncorhynchus tschawytscha* (Walbaum), also known as chinook or tyee salmon; second according to Adney (1900b: 449), are the silver salmon, *O. kisutch* (Walbaum), also known as coho salmon; while the third to appear are the dog salmon, *O. keta* (Walbaum) which are in some areas referred to as chums. Adney (1900b: 449), who had the interest to record such things, gave the date (later proven erroneous) for the first king salmon to arrive at Dawson as between June 10 and 15, so I might have taken the last date for the beginning of the salmon fishing season. Schmitter (1910: 6) simply says of the Indians of Eagle: "During July they catch king salmon and later the dog salmon," a statement I take to mean that July is the principal period when the Indians were devoted to king salmon fishing. In 1932 Walter's opinion was the same, but John Semple at Moosehide, when asked for dates, suggested that the king salmon season was between July 10 and August 15. If Adney was correct, it would seem likely that either Walter meant to say June or I myself erred. Adney continues: "By August the biggest [of the king salmon] have passed," and I take this line to mean "by the beginning of August."

With the timing of the first king salmon still in mind, I turned to the oceanography library at Yale where a record was found of the date of capture of the first king salmon at numerous localities on the Yukon River in 1920. An indicative ten are listed in the table on p. 99, with the distances as given from the sea (Gilbert and O'Malley 1921: 133).

Since it is unlikely that the time of arrival of the first king salmon at Dawson varied a full month, I should perhaps have had more respect for my informant, if not for myself. Some time later I found another professional authority who states: "Both king and dog salmon reach the Yukon Territory. The kings enter the mouth

	Date	Miles
South mouth of Yukon	June 13	
Marshall	June 20	144
Paimiut	June 22	259
Kaltag	June 28*	491
Ruby	June 27	659
Tanana	June 28	804
Fish Creek, above Rampart Rapids	July 3	841
Charlie Creek	July 12	1,317
Eagle	July 13	1,402
Dawson	July 14	1,504

* Authors say the record is probably defective—it should be June 24.

of the river in Norton Sound early in June, and take about three weeks to make the first 1,250 miles to Dawson, where the run is expected to begin about June 28. The date varies from year to year: in 1945 the first was taken on July 9. The main run lasts only a week or ten days, after which the condition of the stragglers rapidly deteriorates" (Wynne-Edwards et al. 1947: 13). If the authors had read Gilbert and O'Malley, they might well have concluded, even on the basis of their own statement, that the journey of the king salmon up the Yukon requires closer to four weeks than three, the latter apparently having become the popular number. Moreover, Wynne-Edwards makes no mention of silver (coho) salmon in the Yukon River.

Finally, I am happy to note that no less a source than Campbell (1958: 131) mentions in his diary that the Han (apparently near Charley Village) had obtained their first five salmon on July 9, 1852. By coincidence, I have discovered not only that Warburton Pike (1896: 213) was told on July 9, 1893, at an Indian camp not far from the mouth of the White River below Fort Selkirk that the first of the salmon had arrived, and apparently at about the same time as he did, but also that Sheldon (1919: 13) states king salmon had just begun to run up Coal Creek, a short distance below Fortymile, on July 11, 1904. Little doubt should remain as to when the first salmon arrive in Han territory, but if there is, see Spurr (1900: 106).

John Semple told me that the dog salmon run through August and September but, when asked about silvers, he said only that they ran in the fall. This uncertainty on the part of an informant who could give exact dates for the visit of king salmon may have made me uneasy, as it should have then and has done since. Therefore it is of considerable importance to interpolate the following statements in the article found by chance as mentioned above. "Near the mouth of the Yukon, where the influence of the cannery has been felt, the coho is generally and properly designated as the silver salmon, which is one of the two names by which the species is known in other fishing centers of Alaska. Unfortunately, as will later appear, elsewhere throughout the Yukon the term 'silver salmon' is generally but mistakenly applied to an entirely different species" (Gilbert and O'Malley 1921:

100

YUPA 74—OSGOOD

131). Later we have the explanation (pp. 136–7) which should be more generally available to Athapaskanists:

It is unfortunate that confusion should have arisen in the Yukon from a failure to recognize that the dog salmon and the so-called "silvers" represent different phases in the development of one and the same species.

The "dog salmon" are the individuals furthest advanced toward spawning. They exhibit the elongated hooked jaws and enlarged teeth in the male, the bright nuptial coloration, and the impoverished condition of the flesh, which is light in color, largely devoid of oil, and possessing very little substance when dried.

In the "silvers" the eggs and milt are less developed, the jaws of the male are little or not at all hooked, the external coloration is silvery, or with a light flush of red, and the meat is red in color when dried, rich in oil, and valuable both for human food and for dogs.

In general, the "dog salmon" along any stretch of the river consist of those individuals which will turn into some adjacent tributary to spawn, while the "silvers" [which] are on their way to the upper reaches of the river, show relatively little of the sexual changes they will exhibit on their spawning beds, and are still richly provided with the oil which serves as fuel and principal source of nourishment during the long journey still before them.

Many fishermen recognize the difficulty of distinguishing sharply between "dogs" and "silvers" and relieve their embarrassment by recognizing a third class, the "half-breeds." But the term "silver salmon" has acquired a fairly definite and useful significance in the trade. "Dog salmon" are so poor in nourishment that they have indifferent value even for dog feed, and will not be purchased except during times of extraordinary scarcity. The natives will feed them to their dogs, but will not eat them themselves unless king salmon and "silver salmon" are unobtainable. . . .

It became evident, as we were ascending the river in August, that the "dogs" and the "silvers" were in general keeping apart from each other and were following distinct migration routes. Throughout the entire lower course of the Yukon, from Tanana at least as far as Anvik, the "dogs" predominated on the right (north limit) of the river and the "silvers" on the left limit. This is generally recognized by all the fishermen of that region, who also agree that the "dog salmon" turn into all the creeks and smaller tributaries, while the silvers "dislike the taste of fresh water," as a native fisherman stated the case. It is also recognized that a heavier run of kings and of cohos is found in company with the "silvers" along the left limit of the river. It appears, therefore, that there is a prevailing use of the left shore [as one faces down river] by those fish which are bound for the upper reaches of the river. This may have connection with the fact that the majority of the tributaries of the lower river enter on the right bank.

Having done my duty, I return to the question of timing. The same authorities (pp. 137–8) tell us that the dog salmon—I shall not succumb to the un-Indian term chums—started up the Yukon in numbers on June 22, 1920, or eight days behind the kings while "in the district between Circle and Dawson, the first chum [dog salmon] was recorded 11 to 17 days later than the first king." This would seem to confirm John Semple's date of the beginning of August for dog salmon fishing at Moosehide. Then there is the relatively recent statement by Lotz ([1964?]: 151): "The fish run at Dawson occurs in early July for three weeks (for king salmon) and then the chum or dog salmon run commences and lasts until near freeze-up [or apparently until about October 1]."

For the reasons given above, it is easy to understand Walter's possible confusion when being asked about silver salmon, for whereas the "silver" dog salmon might be seen early, the true silvers, or cohos, would be late, and one might add that there does seem to be a late run of the latter fish, but whether it reaches Han territory is not clear. This same problem of nomenclature will also make Adney's positioning of the "silvers" before the dog salmon understandable. I can now summarize by saying that the salmon-fishing season consists of the months of July, August, and September. Obviously, the people undertaking the fishing were located on the banks of the Yukon or tributary streams during this period.

Although the annual round of activities is not as clear for the other nine months of the year, Schmitter was conscious of a seasonal perspective and makes some reasonably concise statements about it. The first problem arises from the fact that, in the intermittent sense, it is possible to say as Schmitter (1910: 6) does of the Han: "At all seasons they hunt caribou, moose, bear, and mountain sheep." Such a remark certainly does not mean that in all seasons the Indians were *primarily* engaged in hunting, as his specific descriptions of fishing make clear. At times during the fall and winter, if not spring, there were periods of concentration on hunting but, almost certainly, whenever caribou or moose were seen in the vicinity, some Indians would go after them. The second problem to be faced is that of changing conditions in time brought about by the introduction of the gun and trapping, by the Pax Britannica which ended Indian raids on each other and allowed a wider movement of the hunters, and lastly by the effect of repeating rifles and a large white population on the game supply. These factors will be discussed in the section on the period of culture change, but they are mentioned here to indicate how difficult it really is to be certain of the aboriginal pattern of Han life.

With this said, let us return to Schmitter's (1910: 2–3) view of the animal round as seen from Eagle: "In the early fall," and he clearly means September as we shall soon see, "the entire family goes hunting and when a good supply of game is accumulated they cache it on the spot." It appears almost certain that in the early days, this hunting trip was related to the caribou surrounds which were built on that animal's migration routes, for Schmitter (p. 8) describes this activity in a later passage as taking place in the fall.

After hunting in September, Schmitter (p. 3) says: "In October they return to the river for about two months, when they make snow-shoes, toboggans, and other things for winter use." He is presumably speaking about the second half of the nineteenth century, from his mention of the toboggan, although perhaps he is taking it for granted that the toboggan was an aboriginal construction, unaware of the role of the sled. One should add that probably the most important items made during the fall were the basic articles of dress cut from caribou skins obtained on the hunt.

Schmitter goes on to state: "About the middle of January they have a big time—'all same Christmas'—when they get out all their cached meat and bring it to the river." Read over several times, this sentence seems to mean that sometime in late December the Indians returned to the caribou hunting grounds and brought back to the Yukon all the caribou meat they had left in caches. The "big time" was about the middle of January, hence the transportation and preparations must have been carried out beforehand. Also one can deduce from the earlier statement that if the Indians returned to the river in October for two months they would still be there in December. Although there is the suggestion that the behavior may have been affected by the Christian festival, I do not believe it was necessarily or significantly so.

Then Schmitter continues (p. 3): "They stay there [on the river] till the meat is nearly gone, and again go in search of game until the middle of March, when the weather moderates, at which time they return to the river banks." How long it would take for the meat to be "nearly gone" obviously involves several factors. We might reasonably presume several weeks, however, as were the procedure much shorter, we would have to find a reason for Indians packing the meat all the way back to the river rather than consuming it where it had been stored. At least by some time in February, it would seem from the account that the Han were out hunting again and did not return until the middle of March, after which a period of extreme temperature changes in a twenty-four hour period can make travel extremely unpleasant, if not dangerous.

This brings us to the next segment in the cycle which Schmitter (p. 2) covers with the statement: "In the spring they go to the river bank, where they make canoes and nets in preparation for salmon fishing."

Finally, he continues: "and during the summer [the Han] dry and cache large quantities of fish."

This conscious and continuing explanation of the annual cycle of subsistence activities can be summarized by saying that, in the general sense, at least the Indians at Eagle in the central part of Han territory were in residence at their homes on the Yukon, or possibly tributary streams, from the end of March to the beginning of September, then from perhaps late in October until late in December, and again from perhaps the middle of January to some time in February, making a total of up to seven months for the more or less sedentary period. I say more or less sedentary because it becomes quite clear that at least some of the people were off hunting at almost every time of the year. Indeed, before setting forth his picture of the annual round, Schmitter (p. 2) writes: "During the winter season they move about wherever game is plentiful." Of course it is not clear whether "they" refers to a couple of families whose men preferred to hunt, or to the Han in general. He merely continues to say: "The men go to a place, cache their packs, and then proceed to hunt. The next day the women come, pitch the camp, and prepare to cook." What he does not tell us is the duration of the moving about. On the other hand, his description of the annual round immediately follows this passage. With the admission that I have been dealing with one account referring to one period which perhaps was influenced by European contacts, as other periods certainly were, let us now go on to describe the subsistence activities themselves.

Before doing so, however, I must insert two statements, presumably by Dr. Wilson, in Schwatka (1900: 340, 342) which may, in some degree, seem to contravene what has been written above. The first pertains to the Indians of Nuklako Village across from Fort Reliance. "Caribou and moose abound in quantities throughout this region and furnish the tribe almost their only means of subsistence, except the root of a small vine, containing considerable sugar, which is largely eaten. Quantities of rabbits are also found during the winter and in sufficient numbers to sustain a few men, or at least furnish sufficient fresh meat to guard against any chance of disease, if due care be observed in other respects. Salmon is about the only fish caught to any extent in the river, and as the season only lasts during July and August of each year, they are not [sic] depended on for food only during those months, and are not [sic] dried and stored away for consumption during the winter." Then he says of the Han of Eagle: "In Winter these Indians leave the river and scatter out in different directions in quest of game, principally moose and caribou, which, in reality, provide them with their only food. Besides these, however, great numbers of bears are found, particularly the black variety; also deer, mountain sheep, and rabbits.

"While the salmon are running in the river, they settle down at their village, which is situated close to the water's edge, and do nothing but fish."

It is clear from the data presented in the discussion of dipnets that king salmon were most commonly taken by the use of them, and the reader is referred to some of the descriptions of so-doing that accompany the accounts of the dipnets themselves in the section on tools and implements (pp. 66–8). King salmon are large fish averaging perhaps thirty-nine inches in length and fifteen to twenty pounds in weight; examples taken on the coast have reached from eighty-five to over a hundred pounds, and Adney reports one of eighty-pound weight being caught at Fort Reliance below Dawson (Adney 1900b: 449; Evermann and Goldsborough 1907: 246; Mathews 1968: 289). I recall, however, that Jones (1872: 323) noted the largest salmon as weighing only between forty-five and fifty pounds, but he seems to be setting them off against the smaller king salmon weighing eighteen to twenty-five pounds and not referring to maximum weight.

Schwatka's (1885a: 256–8) description of dipnet fishing by the Han at Eagle on July 21, 1883, is one of his most important ethnographic contributions and it is quoted here. He himself says: "It was at this village [of Klat-ol-klin] that what

to me was the most wonderful and striking performance given by any natives we
encountered on the whole trip was displayed." We then have his lengthy account.

The salmon I saw them take were caught about two hundred or two hundred
and fifty yards directly out from the shore in front of the houses. Standing in
front of this row of cabins, some person, generally an old man, squaw or child,
possibly on duty for that purpose, would announce, in a loud voice, that a
salmon was coming up the river, perhaps from a quarter to a third of a mile
away. This news would stir up some young man from the cabins, who from his
elevated position in front of them would identify the salmon's position, and then
run down to the beach, pick up his canoe, paddle and net, launch the former and
start rapidly out into the river; the net lying on the canoe's birch deck in
front of him, his movements being guided by his own sight and that of a half
dozen others on the high bank, all shouting advice to him at the same time. Evidently, in the canoe he could not judge well of the fish's position, especially at a
distance; for he seemed to rely on the advice from the shore to direct his movements until the fish was near him, when with two or three dexterous and power-
ful strokes with both hands, he shot the little canoe to a point near the position
he wished to take up, regulating its finer movements by the paddle used as a
sculling oar in his left hand, while with his right he grasped the net at the end
of its handle and plunged it into the water the whole length of its pole to the
bottom of the river (some nine or ten feet); often leaning far over and thrusting
the arm deep into the water, so as to adjust the mouth of the net, covering about
two square feet, directly over the course of the salmon so as to entrap him. Of
seven attempts, at intervals covering three hours, two were successful (and in
two others salmon were caught but escaped while the nets were being raised),
salmon being taken that weighed from fifteen to twenty pounds. How these Indians can see at this distance the coming of a single salmon along the bottom
of a river eight or ten feet deep, and determine their course or position near
enough to catch them in the narrow mouth of a small net, when immediately
under the eye a vessel holding that number of inches of water from the muddy
river completely obscures an object at its bottom, is a problem that I will not
attempt to solve. Their success depends of course in some way on the motion of
the fish. In vain they attempted to show members of my party the coming fish.
I feel perfectly satisfied that none of the white men could see the slightest trace
of the movements to which their attention was called. Under the skin roofs of
their log-cabins and on the scaffoldings upon the gravel beach were many hundred salmon that had been caught in this curious way. The only plausible theory
which I could evolve within the limits of the non-marvelous, was, that the
salmon came along near the top of the water, so as to show or indicate the dorsal
fin, and that as it approached the canoe, the sight of it, or more likely some
slight noise, made with that intention, drove the fish to the bottom without any
considerable lateral deviation, whereupon they were inclosed by the net. But my
interpreters told me (and I think their interpretation was correct in this case,

roundabout as it was), that this superficial swimming did not take place, but that the motion of the fish was communicated from the deep water to the surface, often when the fish was quite at the bottom.

We judge from the date of the description and the many hundred fish already caught that the run was at least a week old at that time in the latter part of July.

Schmitter (1910: 7) says of dipnet fishing: "To catch [king] salmon they generally use hand-nets which are let down to the bottom of the river [from canoes?] in rather deep places. When the fisherman feels a pull he draws in the net, although the salmon sometimes pulls the Indian into the water." From this we learn that the competition with king salmon was not always one-sided.

If king salmon were most often taken with dipnets, the more abundant dog salmon were undoubtedly caught in traps placed in the rivers in conjunction with weirs. Jones (1872: 323) had noted that fact for the Han, we will recall, when he said that the dipnet was used only for the big salmon whereas the weir was used for the smaller fish, and dog salmon are implied along with the other species actually mentioned. Dog salmon, I might add, are about twenty-nine inches in average length and eight to nine pounds in weight (Evermann and Goldsborough 1907: 242). The fish traps have already been described in the section on tools and implements (p. 68). As to some of the locations, there is Slobodin's (1963a: 6) statement: "Traps were set in shallow eddies near the banks of the Yukon, or at the mouths of its tributaries," and in placing some more exactly (p. 5): "In the summer, the largest concentration of people was at the mouth of the Klondike, where a number of fish traps were set, and where there was a very large fish camp, located—after spring floods had subsided—on the low shore of the Yukon just upstream from the Klondike's mouth. Later, during the gold rush, this place was the site of Klondike City, locally known as Lousetown. There were smaller fish camps along the Yukon elsewhere." And, I hasten to add, possibly larger ones as well.

Salmon were also caught in the gill nets which have been previously mentioned, but these probably were never as effective for this purpose as were fish traps. Simon McLeod told Slobodin (1963a: 7) "People got forty to fifty fish at a time out of a trap when the salmon were running—more than they get from nets. In the Spring [fall?] the traps were taken up; the weirs were broken by high water and running ice."

Although salmon were by all accounts the most important food fish, other kinds were caught, some in the salmon traps and nets; others were taken in special sets or by hook and line. Early information on these minor types of fish is rare and, by 1932, Indians could supply few details about secondary fishing in aboriginal times. Whitefish, perhaps the most important fish after salmon, Adney (1900b: 449) tells us were caught in both lakes and the Yukon River, and that they weighed up to forty pounds. Actually, there are several species of *Coregonus* in the Yukon and adjoining lakes, but here I speak of them only in general. Schmitter (1910: 7–8) says: "White fish is occasionally caught in the nets, and is even preferred to salmon, which is the staple fish food." Preferred as a change, or delicacy, no doubt.

Curiously, Walter had no knowledge of whitefish at Eagle, whereas John Semple said they were caught at Moosehide, and specifically referred to one with a crooked back, as likely as not *Coregonus kennicotti* (Milner).

John also knew of the inconnu, or *Stenodus mackenzii* (Richardson), which he said was small. An example ten inches long was reported for the record in 1898, having been taken at Eagle through an air hole in the ice, and possibly another on Fortymile Creek weighing three or four pounds (Evermann and Goldsborough 1907: 236).

No evidence of any kind of trout in the Han area has been found. Walter claimed the nearest trout could be found in Mayo Lake at the headwaters of the Stewart River.

Grayling, or *Thymallus signifer* (Richardson), a fish about eight and a half inches long, is probably the commonest fish other than salmon in the upper Yukon River drainage. Adney (1900b: 449) says they are taken in the spring on a hook and line, while Schmitter (1910: 8; also cf. Sheldon 1919: 13–4) notes that they are caught in mountain streams and prized as a delicacy. John Semple even distinguished two varieties, one, with a small mouth, which has a yellow color and is rare, and the other with a big mouth and a blue color, but perhaps he was confusing two different fish.

Pike, or *Esox lucius* (Linnaeus), occur in the rivers and lakes. Adney (1900b: 449) says they were taken in great numbers at Medicine Lake, on the trail to Birch Creek, and that they weighed up to fifteen or eighteen pounds. This may have been under special conditions, for according to informants in 1932, pike were of negligible importance for food.

The burbot, or *Lota maculosa* (Le Sueur), also known as ling or loche among other names, is generally appreciated by the Athapaskans for its tasty vitamin-rich liver and its eggs. Adney (1900b: 449) reports this fish being taken on set lines in the spring. John Semple said the Han caught them, but again, Walter did not classify them as food fish.

The sucker, or *Catostomus catostomus* (Forster), on the other hand, a fish easy to recognize, was immediately placed on the list of Han foods by both Walter and John. The latter, I should add, said that he knew of no shellfish in the Han country.

Probably few fish except salmon were preserved by drying, but the drying of salmon was of the greatest importance as the process made that food available over long periods (Pl. 1, *middle*). Schmitter (1910: 7) describes the method: "The salmon are brought to the shore where the women, squatting at the water's edge, dress and wash them in the flowing current, split them lengthwise, make transverse cuts about an inch apart through the meat, and put them on pole-racks to dry in the sun until ready for caching." We have also already learned that the dressed salmon were also smoked in a shelter. Henry Harper at Moosehide added the specific point that the heads were not cut off [dog?] salmon when preparing them for drying. He also said that salmon eggs were preserved for the winter in special sacks made from the skin of king salmon. Mary McLeod was apparently referring to the same preparation when she told Slobodin (1963a: 7): "Sometimes fresh fish eggs were placed in a sack made of fish skin, and some hot water was added. In time the eggs turned into a paste with high taste, 'like some cheese.'" She also told him that: "Fish eggs, especially salmon eggs, were sometimes dried for storage, on the same stages that fish were put up on."

Caribou, although most important in supplying skins from which to make clothing, likewise were an important source of meat during the winter. Caribou are migrating animals that formerly moved in large herds. Adney (1902: 631–3), who showed a special interest in hunting, makes some general remarks which will serve as a background for the discussion.

> The so-called caribou seems to be the Barren Ground species, which is none other than the native "reindeer" of Alaska. The woodland caribou is found in the mountains to the south of Klondike, but I am informed that it does not occur south of Big Salmon River, where the Indians know it by name and distinguish it from the Barren Ground caribou of the North. The caribou of the Klondike region occurs in small bands over the country on the higher hill tops where it feeds on the gray moss; but it is generally local in its range, migrating at times in bands so vast as to stagger belief. One such range is on the head of Forty Mile River, and from there they migrate, it is said, across the Yukon in winter to the eastern or Klondike side, and are found on the bald foot-hills of the Rocky range. Once in their migration they passed by the mouth of Forty Mile and 400 were shot by the miners. In the fall of 1897, two or three small parties of white men ascended the Klondike to a point above where the Indians went. They reported the "deer," as the caribou is called, exhausted their ammunition in killing forty-seven, and brought back the almost incredible story that the deer were there in numbers that would easily reach ten or twenty thousand. Another party, a member of which I came to know intimately, and to know him as a perfectly reliable man, said that he, too, found the deer, which seemed to be moving in bands of twenty to thirty in a general direction, and that some of the main roads which they traveled were beaten by their hoofs "as smooth as the trail on Bonanza Creek." Thus they occur on Porcupine River and Birch Creek; yet so variable and uncertain are these eccentric animals that the Indians sometimes fail to strike them, and in two cases while I was in the Yukon, a village, one at Porcupine and one at Tanana, was obliged to flee for very life [because they were starving].

Thus, besides learning of the huge numbers of animals in the caribou herds, we find that Indians could become completely without food while in search for them.

Discussing their habits with John Semple at Moosehide in 1932, he told me that the customary route of the caribou was a westward movement about the middle of May and a return eastward in July. Toward the end of August they began to move northward, starting to scatter for the winter at the end of October. Then, in April or May, they gathered together again. Walter, at Eagle, was less explicit, simply saying that the caribou appeared in a large herd for about a week and a

half to two weeks in the spring and again in the fall. It was this latter time which
was important for hunting because of the skins. Surely, the basic method involved
the surround and we have a description of such a hunt provided by Schmitter
(1910: 8).

> During the fall, when a run of caribou is expected, two long rail fences are
> built converging into a corral. Snares are placed in the fence about fifty yards
> apart and also thickly interspersed in the corral space where the herd is driven.
> The Indians line up at the entrance and shoot with their arrows those that try
> to escape. Some are caught in the fence snares, but most are captured in the
> corral. The snare consists of a loop of strong braided moose-skin rope, the end
> tied to a loose log, the loop being held in place by small strings of caribou-skin
> that break easily. It is set in a natural opening through which is is presumed the
> animal will try to pass. As the caribou jumps through the loop the string breaks,
> the loop tightens, and, thus caught, he tries to run, dragging the loose log after
> him. If tied to something firm, the rope breaks too readily; hence a loose log is
> preferred.

Adney (1902: 633) tells of a related method which might be referred to as the
human surround. "In the days of bows and arrows, when Indians were also more
numerous, sometimes as many as one hundred hunters would surround a band of
caribou. Leaving the village in the valley, the Indians would mount the hills, and,
as they neared the band, one went cautiously ahead until he located the herd slowly
feeding, perhaps brought down one [caribou], then stole back unobserved, and
then the hunters spread out each side, keeping an equal space between them until
the unsuspecting herd was entirely surrounded. Then they closed in, and, as they
came near, the startled deer would rush off only to meet them. The hunters rushed
in with shouts, and the poor creatures, knowing not which way to go, fell easy
victims to the arrows. In this way (the old men say), as many as four or five
hundred deer have been killed at a single time."

Charlie Isaac gave Slobodin (1963a: 7–8) a nearly duplicate account but, being
more personally oriented, it also is worth quoting.

> Most caribou hunting was done in the mountains in winter-time. The people
> would be moving along, looking for caribou sign. Then they might find some
> caribou tracks that might be one, two, three days old—maybe weeks old. They
> would look around for the nearest open space of clear ice, maybe an overflow or
> a glacier. Most of the people would camp there. Five or six young men would be
> sent after the caribou. They would take very little food—maybe the people had
> very little food anyway—and would follow the caribou two-, three days, maybe
> a week. Young men were trained to be good runners and to get along without
> much grub. All this time they slept in the snow, didn't make fire, kept running
> all day.
>
> Finally they caught up with the caribou, and then they got on the other side
> of them and turned them and began to herd them back toward the camp. The
> first day, the caribou went fast, the next day slower; the third day they were

just walking along. Especially if there was deep snow, it was hard for them. As they got closer to the camp, every night one of the boys ran back to camp to give word how far away they were, and then ran back to the caribou.

Finally they got close. All the people made a circle around the clear ice [sic]—old men, women, children, besides the regular hunters. Some had bow and arrows, some spears, some knives. The young men drove the caribou into the circle of people, and then the circle was closed and all the people hollered and yelled: "Wow-wow-wow!" and kept the caribou running around in a tight-packed circle, around and around. The kids yelled and waved sticks and hit the caribou's legs. The men used the weapons. Usually they killed the whole bunch, maybe 35–40–50–60 caribou. Some would use just a knife. My father killed two caribou that way when he was young. You grab the caribou by an antler and pull its head up. You have to watch its front legs. It tries to kick you with its legs, and it could bust your chest in or kick out your guts. But you stand to one side and hold the head away from you, driving your knife into the side of its chest.

Walter stated that when the surface of the snow melted a little and then froze over so that men could remain on its surface, hunters with dogs went after caribou, and also moose, that were almost immobilized by breaking through the ice-topped snow. He added that game became scarce just before the fishing season began.

Moose was the animal next in importance to the caribou. Its skin was valued as being tougher than caribou, and hence better for mittens, boot soles, and semi-tanned lines. Also the amount of meat on a moose was many times greater than that provided by a caribou. Moose, of course, were more difficult to kill, but the Han seem fortunate to have had a greater number of them in their country during the period under discussion than had most Athapaskans. One thing seems certain: moose were hunted whenever they were seen by the Indians, and apparently intermittent efforts were made to go in search of them except during the summer fishing season (cf. Adney 1902: 633). The reader must be cautioned to realize, however, that moose probably have cyclical increases and decreases in number and move from area to area over long periods (not semiannual migrations like the caribou) for ecological reasons that are not always obvious.

Adney (1900a) would appear to be the principal source on moose hunting among the Han, but in examining his article on that subject I find that it tells much more about other things than the details of tracking and killing that animal. As he himself admits, the Indians did not consider him much of a hunter and consigned him to the company of a boy. Indeed, he apparently never did kill a moose, an omission which I, having a deep-seated affection for the animal, shall not hold against him. I shall merely state that moose are usually tracked on snowshoes, preferably without arousing their awareness. For a fuller account of aboriginal moose-hunting by tracking, I suggest that given for the Peel River Kutchin in territory adjacent to the Han (Osgood 1936a: 26–7).

Schmitter (1910: 8), as we have come to expect, adds details of importance. He writes: "Moose are usually stalked and shot with bow and arrow, aim being taken behind the shoulder; but sometimes the dogs get a moose at bay and the Indians attack him with pikes. In the springtime the moose can be caught with snares set in a creek, the dogs chasing him down the creek into a snare. The Indians say that a moose once shot with an arrow never escapes, as they sometimes do after being shot with a gun, for, though they may run for some time, they will finally succumb and be caught."

Charlie Isaac gave Slobodin (1963a: 8–9) an account of moose-hunting which is of special interest because it involves a particular kind of geologic structure called a cirque—a deep, steep-walled, amphitheatral recess in a mountain, caused by glacial erosion. Charlie said of the fall season:

> This is about the hardest time of year to hunt moose. Somebody would see moose sign in a creek. The moose was deep in the brush and there wasn't much hope of getting close to one. The men would go up the ridges to the head of the creek and wait along the ridge in the curve of rocks [the cirque] above the head of the stream.
>
> The boys would start through the brush along the creek, making a lot of noise. They were supposed to notice the landmarks at the head of the creek: a clump of trees, a scar from a landslide, a big round rock, maybe a patch of snow, and so on. Finally they came to the base of the bowl [cirque]. The hunters were hiding behind the ridge, and couldn't see the moose climbing, but the boys would watch the moose and would watch the moose and would call out, "By the patch of trees!" "By the scar!" The men would run along, bent over, behind the ridge. The moose would come up, sometimes within six feet of the hunter, and he would be shot with arrows.

Black bears, their brown variation, and grizzlies are reported to have been killed and eaten in the Han area. Schmitter (1910: 8) provides a clear account of the classic Athapaskan technique of killing bears with a lance. "A pike or spear is nearly always used in hunting bears. The hunter attracts the bear by making a raven-like noise, causing the bear, as the Indians say, to think the raven has discovered a dead moose. They also further explain that the big bears only would come, as the little bears would not know what the croaking meant. As the bear approaches the Indian holds the spear in position, facing the bear as it draws near to him, and as the bear springs the Indian sticks the spear into its throat at the top of the breast-bone, at the same time shoving the handle of the pole into the ground, thus causing the bear to spear himself with his own weight. Sometimes three men hunt in this manner, two of them attacking the bear on either side as it rushed forward. The meat of the young bear killed in the fall, when they feed on huckleberries, is considered a great luxury."

"Beaver," says Adney (1900b: 446–7), "formerly more plentiful than now, are taken by the Indians with a harpoon through a hole in the ice, the spot being baited with willow twigs, or else by means of a peculiar dead-fall of poles on the bank near their homes." Informants in 1932 at both Moosehide and at Eagle mentioned beaver as one of the animals being caught and eaten, among numerous others to be quickly touched upon now with occasional comments.

Lynx were caught anytime and anywhere, supplying one of the tastiest meats. Schmitter (1910: 7) also mentions the eating of lynx. Rabbits were appreciated to a lesser degree, as were porcupines. Groundhogs (marmots) were occasionally found along a river, but many more back toward the mountains. Walter said they were seldom killed.

About mountain sheep, John Semple stated that there were plenty in the mountains on both sides of the Yukon, while Walter claimed that this was true only in days gone by (cf. Sheldon 1919: 43). On the other hand, Walter said that a few mountain goats formerly might be found in Han country, but John said there were none. These animals were appreciated both as food and for their skins.

Walter listed silver, black, cross, and red foxes as available, and John added gray. Walter said they were not eaten but John thought they were on occasion. Both men said a few otter could be found, but that because of their taste, they would be eaten by people only when starving. Walter said mink were plentiful but that no one would eat them; John thought poor people ate them sometimes. Ermine (weasels) were never eaten; "too stink," said John.

Wolverines were said to be numerous in certain areas according to both informants (cf. Sheldon 1919: 49). They were valued for their fur when taken at its prime, but in summer the fur became valueless. Walter said wolverines were not eaten, but John claimed that some people ate them when hungry. Schmitter (1910: 7) seems to agree with the latter.

Wolves, both 1932 informants agreed, were never eaten, although John attributed that fact to the bad taste of the meat. Dogs also were not eaten. Walter said that formerly there were relatively few of them, while John pointed out that the aboriginal dog was small. Here I should interpolate Schmitter's (1910: 7) typical and probably correct statement about most Athapaskans: "The Indians never eat dog meat or wolf meat; they would rather starve."

John said ground squirrels were caught in the summer and were good to eat. Walter noted that they could be found about thirty miles to the west of Eagle. The latter said there were no tree squirrels, but John said there were and that they could be eaten anytime. Of mice and shrews there were plenty, but only the fox eats them. The coyote was known to John, but he said that animal did not come into the Yukon River country until about 1920, while Walter thought perhaps 1910. Finally, as an interesting distinction, the closest place to find muskrats was said to be in the Kutcha Kutchin country around Fort Yukon; perhaps Walter meant in large quantities.

As might be expected, the Han enjoyed eating various game birds, some of which being seasonal were available only in the spring and fall. I shall deal with them in order.

Walter, to my surprise, said that there were plenty of sea gulls around, but that they were not eaten. Undoubtedly he was referring to one of the herring gulls, or *Larus argentatus smithsonianus* Coues. He also mentioned two kinds of owls, one black and one gray, which were occasionally appreciated as food. Schmitter (1910: 7) accounts for only one kind of owl being eaten. There are too many owls that might have been referred to by Walter for me to be certain which two he meant. I would suggest one of the great horned owls, or *Bubo viginianus lagophonus* (Oberholser), however, and perhaps the great gray owl, or *Strix nebulosa nebulosa* Forster, which are among the commoner owls on the upper Yukon. The excellent-tasting snowy owl, or *Nyctea scandiaca* (Linnaeus), is apparently rarely, if ever, seen.

The Canada goose, almost certainly *Branta canadensis parvipes* (Cassin), was shot in the springtime when it flew low, but not in the fall, as the flocks passed over the region at too high an altitude to reach. Naturally, they were highly appreciated as food.

Walter described two kinds of eagles, one being white and the other as being not very white. The white one was almost certainly the northern bald eagle, or *Haliaeetus leucocephalus alascanus* Townsend, and the not very white one was perhaps the American golden eagle, or *Aquila chrysaetos canadensis* (Linnaeus). It is of course possible that Walter was simply confusing the mature bald eagle with the young of the same species, but this seems unlikely. Sheldon (1919: 34, 54, 56) mentions golden eagles on several occasions. Neither was eaten but they were valued for their feathers. Schmitter (1910: 9) describes the capture of eagles as follows: "The eagle cannot be shot with an arrow, but is snared. For this purpose a small fence having a snare at one side is built on a mountain peak and baited with caribou lung. The Indians say that the eagle is very wary and will not go in at the top of the snare, but usually alights near it and inspects it carefully before entering, which he eventually does and is caught." Schmitter (1910: 7) also says that hawks were not eaten.

Ducks of all kinds were taken in spring or fall, whenever possible, according to Walter. Grouse and ptarmigan, on the other hand, were available all year and considered especially good to eat. Walter described the two species of grouse as pintail and chicken. In the first instance he was undoubtedly referring to the Alaskan sharp-tailed grouse, or *Pedioecetes phasianellus caurus* Friedmann, which has been reported numerous times in the Han area, and for which a common name is pintail. Two other grouse frequent the middle Yukon, however. They are the Hudsonian spruce grouse, or *Canachites canadensis canadensis* (Linnaeus), and the Yukon ruffed grouse, or *Bonasa umbellus yukonensis* Grinell. Walter's "chicken" might be the spruce grouse, which is famous for being easily killed, but then so is the ruffed grouse in Alaska, although perhaps less often come upon. Willow ptarmigan, or *Lagopus lagopus alascensis* Swarth, could be found anytime anywhere, but for rock ptarmigan, or *L. mutus nelsoni* Stejneger, one had to go to the mountains.

Swans and loons were formerly plentiful and could be caught in the spring and

THE RECORD OF HAN CULTURE

fall, according to Walter who spoke of two kinds of loons which I take to have been *Gavia immer* (Brünnich) and *G. adamsi* (Gray). On the other hand, *G. arctica viridigularis* Dwight, the green-throated arctic loon, is also known from the general area, as is the red-throated loon, or *G. stellata* (Pontoppidan).

Schmitter (1910: 7) noted that the raven was not eaten, and Walter gave the impression that killing these birds, which were plentiful in the Han territory, was taboo. The Canada jay, also a frequent visitor to Han camps, simply was not eaten.

Having exhausted the data on birds, let us now turn to vegetable food, Walter again being the principal informant. Blueberries, he said, were plentiful during the last week of July, while low-bush cranberries, or *Vaccinium vitis-ida* [?] could be picked in the middle of August. Of high-bush cranberries it is said there were none. Schmitter (1910: 7) states that "cranberries grow in abundance on the mountain sides and are gathered in large quantities."

Walter knew of wild strawberries growing close to the ground but said there were too few to be picked, and not many more red raspberries, although some could be found in the last week of July. On the other hand, gooseberries were very plentiful from the middle of July onward, while salmonberries were equally so by the last of that month. At the same time a berry, black in color, which was not identified, could be found in the mountains. It is probable that the huckleberry was being referred to since Schmitter (1910: 7) mentions it as growing in large quantities on the mountain slopes and being specially sought after.

Speaking of berries in general, Mary McLeod told Slobodin (1963a: 7): "In the late summer, berries were picked, cleaned thoroughly, and packed in split birch baskets sewn with spruce roots. These were stored in underground caches, 'like a cellar,' and covered with willow branches and moss." Walter said that he had never heard of storing baskets of berries in fish grease inside dryfish bundles in the manner reported for the Peel River Kutchin (cf. Osgood 1936a: 29–30).

Then there is the root plant, called čɩ naɩ ɩ in the Han language, and which I presume is *Hydysarum americana*, although no specimen was collected. Walter said that it is very plentiful and placed the height of its season as July 25. Schmitter (1910: 7) is undoubtedly referring to it when he writes: "Their nearest approach to vegetable food is the tuber attached to the root of a pennate-leafed weed that grows on the hillside in the shade of spruce trees in the midst of moss, through which the root extends a few inches, the tuber itself growing in the ground beneath the moss. It is six to nine inches long and from one-half to three-fourths of an inch thick, with fiber strands running through it. It has a slightly sweetish but indifferent taste. The natives originally ate it only when they could get no meat, though they say that it is quite palatable when boiled with grease."

Curiously, Walter denied that the Han ever ate the fibers under the spruce bark while he was equally certain that the Indians at Whitehorse (Tagish?) did so. Fibers under spruce bark, I had previously been informed, were eaten by the Peel River Kutchin (cf. Osgood 1936a: 29). The fibers under birch bark, on the other hand, were described enthusiastically as a Han delicacy. Taken about the first of July under the bark of a big tree when it was "good and fat," Walter said it tasted, "Oh fine, like sauerkraut sweet like sugar." It was edible only in July, and no birch syrup was known to have been made. Cottonwood fibers were good to chew also, Walter added, but again only in July.

Wild onions were said to be common, as was wild rhubarb. The [tops of the?] former were eaten raw, while the rhubarb was roasted a little or boiled.

Neither wild rose buds nor mushrooms were eaten, and wild rice was not available. Spruce gum, as might be expected, was chewed on occasions.

The smoking of tobacco and probably the chewing of tobacco and the use of snuff were known among the Han before the arrival of the traders on the middle Yukon (cf. Murray 1910: 60).

The methods of making fire and of cooking in spruce-root baskets with hot stones have already been described in the section on tools and implements (p. 73). Schmitter (1910: 9), however, has more information on the subject of preparing food: "Meat is roasted by suspending it on a string from a cross-bar on two supports near the fire, where it is continually twirled until roasted. Salmon is cooked a little differently. Usually it is hung at rest with the flat inner surface toward the fire. Rabbits, ptarmigan, moose-foot, and other small things are roasted in a pit oven, made by building a fire on the ground in the sand. After the fire has burned for some time it is brushed aside and a hole is dug beneath it in the sand. The meat is placed in the pit, covered with hot sand or dirt, and over this the fire is rebuilt and kept burning until the roasting is finished. Ducks, geese, and swans are boiled in a large basket of water by means of the hot stone."

Finally, we should consider the disposal of such large game as moose, caribou, bear, and mountain sheep. According to Jonathan Wood, except for taking some piece of the meat for the hunter's immediate needs, the rest is cached in a tree after the animal is skinned. The successful hunter then returns to his village and presents the animal to a man he respects in the opposite moiety (or another clan?). The latter goes, or sends, for the meat which is brought back and prepared for a feast in which everyone shares. Thus both the work and the food are distributed among the members of the group, irrespective of the skills of particular hunters. Naturally, successful hunters tended to make such gestures to their equivalents in other clans, and reciprocity ensued, so the advantage of their hunting ability was not entirely lost. We must presume that this procedure became inoperative when large numbers of caribou were killed in surrounds on a cooperative occasion. As Schmitter (1910: 6) says: "During the fall, when the caribou run in herds, the natives cache the meat for the cold weather. The other animals [and we might include caribou that have scattered] are scarcer, and when one is brought in it makes a treat for the village." Under any normal circumstances, if there was food available among the Athapaskans, sharing it in one way or another was inevitable. Schmitter continues: "It is customary, when one native is surfeited with meat, to give what is left to his neighbor." This, no doubt, applied under any circumstances.

Commentary. In thinking of the annual round of the Han Indians, I am cognizant of the fact that all groups of Athapaskans engage in both fishing and hunting, the latter necessitated by the need for skins from which to make clothing, since fish skins will not adequately serve. We know that salmon is the main food fish of most of the Pacific Drainage Athapaskans and that caribou skin is by all odds the most popular dress material. Finally, it seems generally true that the more salmon available, the less time was spent aboriginally in hunting. With these three factors in mind, we ask our total data to tell us where the Han Indian fits into the range of possibilities. They seem to indicate that the Han were somewhat more dependent on fish for food than they were on meat, the emphasis on hunting in some of the sources notwithstanding. Regarding these, the statements of Wilson in Schwatka (1900: 340, 342) need scrutiny. The assertion that caribou, moose, and roots furnish the Han with "almost their only means of subsistence" is not only unbelievable if accepted literally, but is also contradicted in his following sentences. Indeed, it does seem strange if caribou and moose abound in such quantities that it is the rabbits, by supplying fresh meat, that "guard against any chance of disease." As for salmon, the statement that "they are not depended upon only for food during 'July and August' and are not dried and stored away for consumption during the winter" leaves us with the question whether to delete the first "not" which would then leave the "only" in an illogical position, or whether more reasonably to substitute "but are" for "and are not." The reader is inevitably left in a quandary, and this ethnographer with the belief that Dr. Wilson was in a state of unhappy confusion about the subject on which he was writing, a judgment fortified by a later sentence with reference to the lower Yukon Athapaskan whose primary dependence on salmon has been verified so often that there is not space to list all the sources. Wilson, however, states: "Salmon are caught in considerable numbers, but the chief reliance is in a smaller variety, called whitefish, which is obtained in greater quantities and during a longer time" (Schwatka, 1900: 349). Apparently Dr. Wilson was given to simple statements with which he too often manages to confuse his readers. The above sentence becomes credible only if one substitutes the words "king salmon" for "salmon" and "dog salmon" for whitefish." Further comments on the relative roles of fish and game have been reserved for discussion in the section on the period of culture change.

Salmon, it might be noted, average 1,000 calories per average pound of the edible portion, which is half again as much as whitefish or halibut, double that of white perch or brook trout, three times that of pike or pickerel, and is approached only by lake trout or lampreys which average 800 calories (Rostlund 1952: 4). If we compute 15,000 calories for the average fish (Indians ate practically everything but the skin and bones), fifty of them would supply one person with 2,000 calories a day for a full year. Schwatka (1910: 7) makes the curious remark that the Han say they prefer dog salmon to kings because the latter are too oily. For me, that point of view has the color of acculturation, or perhaps it is a rationalization because dog salmon provided the more commonplace food.

Because there is so relatively little early information on caribou surrounds, I shall quote a description from an account of a journey taken by Hudson Stuck (1916: 276) in March 1910 from Lake Mansfield northeast to Eagle via the confluence of the Fortymile and Yukon rivers. He writes:

> The next day took us into and across the Ketchumstock Flats, a wide basin surrounded by hills and drained by the Mosquito Fork of the Fortymile. The telegraph line, supported on tripods against the summer yielding of the marshy soil, cuts straight across country. This basin and the hills around form one of the greatest caribou countries, perhaps, in the world. All day we had passed fragments of the long fences that were in use in times past by the Indians for driving the animals into convenient places for slaughter.
>
> The animal migration of the vast herd that roams the section of Alaska between the Yukon and the Tanana Rivers swarms over this Flat and through these hills, and we were told at the Ketchumstock telegraph station that upward of one hundred thousand animals crossed the Mosquito Fork the previous October.

That would have been in 1909 and, even allowing for exaggeration, the estimated number of caribou is impressive. I should add that these flats in the Fortymile drainage seem to be within Han Territory and probably the long surround fence lines were theirs.

Although the killing of bears with a lance (a term I prefer for a weapon like a spear which is not thrown) has been spoken of as classic, it must not be presumed that it was an activity engaged in very often. The method of placing the lance in the jugular vein of the bear and allowing the animal to press it in by its own weight has been described for various other Athapaskan groups and, if an ideal act of the brave, for some also a true one (cf. McKennan 1959: 49).

In the account of minor animals eaten by the Han, I may as well point out what the reader has no doubt observed, that John Semple at Moosehide viewed the Han as having more toleration for odd meats than did Walter Benjamin at Eagle. John was possibly more sophisticated in terms of Indian culture than was Walter, despite the fact that the latter was a few years older. On the other hand, John may have been leaning over backward a little when he said wolverine, fox, and mink were sometimes eaten. Of course, starving people will eat almost anything, and that may be the explanation of the difference in the evaluation of foods.

It should also be noted that marten are not among the animals commented upon. This seems to have been my oversight when going through the list of animals. Also informants responded negatively to my question whether there were any fisher, or *Martes pennanti*, in the country.

Mythology

To give balance to the presentation of Han culture, a sample of the mythology is needed, and this Schmitter (1910: 21–9) supplies. The following stories were collected by him from various individuals, and he presented them, as nearly as possible, in the style of the narrator.

Creation of the World

Long time ago the water flowed all over the world. There was one family and they made a big raft. They got all kinds of animals on the raft. There was no land, but all water, and they wanted to make a world. The man of the family tied a rope around a beaver and sent him down to find the bottom, but the beaver didn't reach bottom; he got only half way and drowned. The man then tied a string around a muskrat and sent him down; he reached the bottom and got a little mud on his hands, but he drowned. The man took the mud out of the muskrat's hands into his palm and let it dry, then crumbled it to dust. This he blew out all over the waters and it made the world. (All tribes about here are said to have the same story.)

Origin of the Wind

A long time ago, when all animals were men, there was no wind. There was a bear that used to go about with a bag on his back. Many people were curious to know what was in the bag and they often asked the bear, but he would not tell them. One day another man caught the bear asleep with the bag on his back. The man's curiosity to know what was in the bag was so great that he cut it open. The bag contained the wind, which then escaped and has never since been confined.

The Old Man and Old Woman

In the Yukon River between Eagle and Fortymile there are two large rocks which evidently were one before a geological cataclysm separated them. The natives call the one on the north side the "Old Man," and the one to the south the "Old Woman." These were the primogenitors of the Indians in this region. The story follows: These two old folks were once together in the middle of the river, but the old woman pushed the old man to the other side because he left her there. So he went north and she went south, but the children grew up around there. At that time this region was full of all kinds of animals, and they could talk like men. The old man killed off all the bad animals and saved one good one of each kind, which started the families. They have since been unable to talk.

The moose was the head game of the world, because the old man killed the bad moose first. The big swan was once the head of all birds and animals because it was stronger. All animals came together and had wrestling matches. The little teal duck was the strongest animal in the world. First the swan beat the moose, but the teal duck beat the swan after the swan had conquered all others.

Adventure of the Old Man

The "Old Man" (rock) in the Yukon went down the river where the bear, when bears were men, was fishing. He put his canoe on this side of the river where no one could see it from a point above where the bear was. Then he made a circuit on foot around the bear and reached the river lower down.

The old man then swam up the river, like a king salmon, to the bear's house, where the bear was spearing salmon. The bear tried to spear him for a salmon, but he grabbed the spear point, broke it off, and swam to his canoe and hid the spear point under the bow. Having disarmed the bear he now knew that he was safe. So he got in his canoe and went down to the bear's house to call. He concealed the fact that he had broken the bear's spear, but the bear believed that he did it, nevertheless. The bear wanted the old man to marry his daughter. The bear pointed to a mountain about a mile away, where there was no timber, and said that it was a good hunting place for bear, since a bear came up there every day. The old man went to the woods to get material to make some arrows. The bear had everything fixed dangerous about there, so that when a man touched a tree stump it would fall on him. The old man was cautious and would touch a stump and dodge when it fell. Then he secured the wood for arrows from the fallen stump. Now he wanted some feathers and the bear took him to a place said to be good for getting them. Here were big eagles that would kill men. The old man went to an eagle's nest in a big tree, where there were two young ones. He asked them which one could talk most. One said that he could talk most, and would tell the father and mother eagle about everything, so the old man killed him so that he couldn't tell. He asked the other young eagle how he knew when his mother was coming, and was told that she always followed a gust of snow. He asked when the father eagle came, and was told that he always followed a gust of hail. Then the old man hid under the nest with his spear. Then came the snow and the mother eagle appeared, carrying the upper half of a man. She asked the young one, "Where is your brother?" and he said, "It was too warm here and he went down where it was cool." She said, "I smell something here; what's the matter?" The young eagle said, "You smell that half a man"; but the mother eagle said, "I smell something different." Then the old man under the nest speared the mother eagle, piercing her front belly to crop. Then came the hail, and the father eagle followed and asked the same questions as the mother. He said to the young one, "Where is your mother?" and the young one answered, "She went down to look for brother." The father eagle brought with him the lower half of the man. Then he said, "I smell something," and the young one replied the same as to his mother. The old man was watching from under the nest, and he speared the father eagle too. This father eagle would kill any man he saw. The old man saved the young one. He got enough feathers to make his arrows. When he came back the bear said, "You're all right," which he always said. The old man wanted some pitch to stick the feathers to the arrows. The bear, as usual, led him to a dangerous place, where he told the old man there was plenty of pitch. Here the old man found a lake of pitch boiling like water. The old man wouldn't go near it, but took a long willow switch and dipped it into the lake. With this switch he threw the pitch all over the spruce trees about him. The spruce trees theretofore had never yielded pitch, but have done so all over the world ever since. Then the old man gathered enough pitch from a spruce tree and returned. Now he wanted sinews to bind the feathers and heads to the sticks of his arrows.

The bear led him to a moose lick where there was a bad moose. The moose didn't have much flesh, but was mostly bone and skin. His hide had such stiff hairs that it was hard for an arrow to penetrate. This moose would kill every man he saw. There was lots of high grass about there and the old man crept up to the moose on hands and knees through the grass, keeping out of sight of the moose. When the old man got near the moose he stopped and wished for a mouse to come along. He told the mouse to go to the moose and chew the stiff hair off behind the left shoulder. The mouse went to the moose and asked to chew the hair off behind the left shoulder, to use for his nest to keep the young warm. The moose refused, but told him he could chew the hair from his hind quarter. The mouse insisted that he wanted the hair from behind the left shoulder because it was soft and warm. So the moose allowed him to take it. As soon as the hair was off, the old man shot the moose through this spot into the heart, killing him. Then the old man got his sinew from the spinal ligaments of the moose. Then he returned to the bear camp and finished making the arrows. The old man made the arrows with birch-bark heads because the bear said the birch bark was the best. The old man knew that this was false, but he did it to please the bear. The bear said that upon the mountain where there is no timber a bear came every evening, and that the old man could get it. The bear was accustomed to kill men by this ruse. He sent his daughter up there dressed in a bear skin, and when a man came near she would hold him till her father bear killed him. The old man concealed bone arrow-heads in the back lock of his hair before starting. The old man and the bear started out to hunt bear. The bear said, "Walk slow" but the old man ran away. As soon as the old man approached the hill he saw the other bear and shot twice with his birch-bark pointed arrows, but they didn't penetrate. The bear when hit, instead of running away, as ordinarily, came toward the old man, who pulled the bone arrow-head out of his hair and shot the bear with it. He now saw it was the bear's daughter, for she hollered, "Father, that man hurt me." The bear said to her, "Catch hold of him," and as she tried to catch him she died. Then the old man ran away and the bear chased him all day. Then the old man ran into Ford's Lake. (Calico Bluff, six miles below Fort Egbert, on the Yukon, is called "Long Point." Clavath, pronounced "Klay-vay," and Ford's Lake, near by, is called Clavathmon, meaning Long Point Lake.)

The bear couldn't catch the old man, so he told the frog to drink all the water in the lake, and the frog drank it all. As soon as the water was gone the old man burrowed into the mud. The bear went all around digging in the mud to find the old man. As soon as he got near the old man, the old man wished for a snipe to come along and it came. He asked the snipe to go and hit the frog twice in the belly. The frog asked the snipe, "Did some one ask you to come?" The snipe said, "No, I am hunting for something for my children to eat." As soon as the snipe got near the frog he hit it twice in the belly and flew away. Then the water all ran back into the lake. The bear now was angry, and made a fish trap, which he put in the creek, from Ford's Lake to the Yukon River, to catch the old man.

The old man knew this and made a mud man, which he pushed ahead of him, swimming down the creek. The mud man went into the trap, the bear pulled it up, and the old man swam down to the Yukon and down to the bear's house below Calico Bluff, where he got his canoe and went down the Yukon, and the bear never saw him any more.

The Miraculous Little Man

Long time ago, before the "Old Man" and "Old Woman," lots of Indians were together and they fought until all were killed except an old woman and her daughter. This old woman cried every day because there was no man to help her do her work or get her wood. Every day when she had to get her wood from the brush she cried, and each day she had to go a little farther for the wood. One day she heard a sound like a baby crying in the woods. At first she did not go to see what it was, but told her daughter, for she knew there were no people there. Her daughter said, "Next time you hear it; go to it, and if you find a baby bring it." She went for wood again and heard it, and going to it she found a baby boy at the foot of a spruce tree. The boy was not born, but found by the old woman in the brush. When she brought it mother and daughter rejoiced, for bye and bye they would have a man. As soon as they got him home he became strong and could work. As a joke the old woman told him to take their dog and go out hunting, thinking that he didn't know how. She told him to tie a rope around the dog's neck. He tied it on the dog, then went out hunting, and on the way he pulled so hard that he choked the dog and dragged it back with him.

The old woman still had friends in another place. So she and her daughter and the little man went amongst these Indians again. The boy was small and didn't grow. When he went hunting he would put on an eagle-skin like a coat and fly. He was a pretty good hunter. People asked him, "How do you cut moose with a knife? You are too small." He said that when he kills a moose he is like a big man, but is small when he comes home again. He does all miracle work. He does not bring his eagle-skin home again, but leaves it two miles away on a tree. The daughter found the eagle-skin and took one tail feather to stick in her hair. The boy found it out and was angry, so he said to his sister, "I wish all your friends would be killed again." Then she said, "What are you going to do with your mother?" (the old woman), and he said, "I will put her in the corner of the birch-bark basket." In a little while war came and all were killed except the old woman and the daughter and the little man. Then the little man made lots of very small arrows and made a few from a bear's ribs. He worked all the winter making these arrows because he was going to fight the people all by himself. These people who killed his friends lived by a big lake. The old woman was with the little man, but the daughter had been captured by these people. He got lots of bags for arrows, and, being small, he walked under the snow and hid a bag of arrows about every 50 yards apart, so that when he shot away his arrows in fighting them he could run back to get some more. When he came near, the people thought that he was a raven because he was such a small black thing. His sister said, "You people didn't kill the little man with the old woman." There was one man who wasn't in the fight, so he was selected to kill the little man. The man took a small stick to kill the little man, thinking it would be easy, but the little man threw a small object at him, striking him in the chest and killing him. Then all the people, thousands in number, ran after him without their arrows, because he was too small to shoot. He ran back the same trail on which he came. He would come out of his hole and shoot some; they would rush after him, and back he would go and come up elsewhere and shoot again. Every time he shot he killed. He killed all those people in a day. He brought his sister back to the old woman at home.

After the fight he said he would make a big pot-latch (a celebration with feasting and giving of presents), because he had wounded and killed lots of people. Then he went hunting every day, and killed all kinds of game and saved the hide and meat. The mother and daughter tanned all the skins, dried the game and cached it. The little man said he was going to give the skins as presents to other people. The old woman said, "All the people are killed, so who can you give them to," and he said "Bye and bye lots of people will come." This was on a big island just this side of the Old Woman rock. When he collected his meat and fur he began to sing every day that he wished that lots of people would come from up and down the river to the pot-latch on the island, and they came without being told. They all moved about together and sung as usual at a pot-latch. When they did it the island cracked in two parts, because too many people were on it. The people feasted every day. After the feasting he gave away all kinds of skins and furs. He made the big time because he killed lots of people and was sorry for it. He killed the people because they killed his friends first.

THE BOY IN THE MOON

See the mark in the middle of the moon like a man? That was a little Indian boy when nobody had anything to eat. During the famine this boy dreamed that they were going to kill lots of caribou.

The boy said that when they killed all the caribou he wanted the leader caribou. The boy's uncle gave him the wrong caribou, because the uncle did not believe the boy dreamed it. Then the boy cried for two nights because he didn't get the right kind of caribou. The boy told his father, who brought home the hind quarter of caribou, to never cut the flesh off it to the bone, but to cut off what he needed, wrap it in a skin, and put it under his head to sleep on. The father did this and when he awoke he found a whole hind quarter, and thus forever he could eat caribou from this leg and always have it whole. Next night the boy, who always slept between his father and mother, was gone and nobody could find him. The boy wore marten-skin pants. In the morning the left leg of the pants was found on the tent-pole where the hole is in the roof for the fire. Hence they concluded that he went up through the hole and the left pants' leg was torn off going through. He went up to the moon and was seen there the next night, and it was proved, for he had a larger right leg than left, because the right leg has pants on. From his right hand hangs a little round bag with the wrong caribou meat in it. That night a big storm came and snowed all over where the caribou was cached. Then all the killed caribou came to life and went away, and the Indians couldn't find their meat. Then they all starved to death except the boy's father and mother. During the fall and winter with clear sky, one who has been properly instructed can readily make out the outline of this boy in the moon.

THE CAMP ROBBER

The camp robber is a slate-colored Alaskan jay, well known for its habit of stealing food from camps.

When all animals were men the camp robber was a medicine-man. One time the people had nothing to eat, and they asked the medicine-man to get them some food. For six nights a different man each night dreamed to find a way to get something to eat. The camp robber was the last and sixth man. He dreamed and called all the people together to bring their snares with them. He made a pack of the snares and put them on his back. The people made the snow in a big heap. Around this he went, chanting and saying, "Bye and bye meat will come." Then he reached into the snow heap and pulled a caribou's head out by the horns. He did not kill it, for it was not a real caribou; only a spirit. So he painted the horns and tail red, with red ochre, and let it back into the snow heap. Next day they got lots of caribou, and the one with red horns and tail was amongst them. That is why an Indian never kills a camp robber when he steals grub, but lets him go because he helped them in the days when he was a medicine-man.

THE RAVEN

The raven lies more than any other game. Long time ago all the animals were good except the raven. He was an habitual liar and robbed everybody. Whenever he found dead game he ate the eyes first. Once when the raven was like a man he came to a strange camp and told a man to kill his old dog and throw it into the river. The man did so. Then the raven followed the dog down the river and pulled it out and ate its eyes. Thus he went from camp to camp as a deceiver.

THE RAVEN RESTORES THE SUN TO THE SKY

The raven was the cleverest deceiver of all animals, but has one good deed to his credit. At this time, when all animals were men, a bear, who was a bad man, did not want the people of the world to have light, so he took the sun down from the sky and hung it with a string on his neck and kept it covered with his coat. The raven came to his house and pretended to be a friend, and soon married the bear's daughter. They very soon had a child who could walk as soon as born, and grew up in a very short while. The raven told the boy to get the sun from the bear, so the boy cried for it very much and finally the bear allowed the boy to play with it, but watched him carefully. There was no hole in the roof, but the raven made one, and when the bear's attention was away for a moment the boy threw the sun up through the hole into the sky and the bear couldn't get it any more. The raven then ran away and never came back, for the bear would like to kill him.

The Raven and the Coot (Mud Hen)

The raven wanted all the birds to look nice and he painted them with their various hues. He painted the coot last. The coot was then in turn to paint the raven, who wanted to be very richly variegated with colors. The coot was painting the raven gorgeously with his right hand, but had charcoal concealed in his left hand. Then, for a joke, while the raven's attention was away, he smeared the raven all over with charcoal. The raven was angry and chased but couldn't catch the coot, so he grabbed and threw a handful of white mud, spattering it over the coot. That is why the coot has white spots on his head and back. The coot flew away and the raven has remained black ever since.

The Woodpecker

The woodpecker was a very domestic sort of a man-bird. He used to get married lots of times. When he would get married he would go away from the people with his wife. After a while he would come back without his wife. He would say that she died. Then he would get another wife. One girl was very smart, so she married him to find out what he did with his wives. They went away together. When he found a good hunting ground he stayed there. Whatever game he got he only gave fat and grease to his wife and ate the meat himself. Whenever she wanted a drink of water he gave her grease to drink. Every time he went hunting he took about ten days, and brought back fat and grease and blueberries and cranberries and all kinds of berries, but no meat. The girl knew by this that he was going to make her so fat that she couldn't walk, for already when she would lie down she could hardly get up. Then, before he went hunting again, at her request, he prepared a dugout on the bank of a creek. She told him she was lonesome and wanted to be where she could see the creek running. The dugout was to be her home while he was away. The door was covered with brush. She told him to make a small, sharp spear for her, so she could keep the mice away with it. As soon as her husband went she took the spear and dug a tunnel from the dugout to the creek for her escape, for she knew he would kill her when she became very fat. She was too fat to walk, so she rolled down to the creek through the tunnel, and stayed in it a whole day, until the fat came off from her. Then she went into the woods and watched till her husband came back. As he approached she saw that he was picking a lot of berries. When he reached the dugout, where the hole was covered with brush for concealment, he ran his spear through the brush so as to kill her; but she wasn't there. Every time he jabbed the spear in and withdrew it he tasted of the point to see if it stuck her. Then he said aloud to himself, "Some spirit must have taken her away." The woman now was sure that he wanted to kill her, so she ran away back to her family. She told them all about it, saying that he killed his wives and ate them, and that he fed them berries to flavor their meat. The man came back then. His wife's mother previously put her in a sack and hid her. He cried much, pretending to be sorry for the death of his wife. He said to the mother, "My wife has died again." Everybody else cried, to deceive him into thinking they believed him. Next day everybody moved again. The old woman gave him a heavy sack to pack along and told him it belonged to his brother-in-law, who needed it. She told him to hang it high on a tree, so the dogs couldn't get it. She told the other men not to help him lift it up. He tried so hard to lift it up that he broke his back-bone.

When the man was injured nobody took care of him. The hunting party went away without him. When they returned and saw that he was sure to die, they let him see his wife, so that he would know that he was found out. His wife was in the sack. Her mother then arrived with other Indian woman, untied the sack, and let her out, and she was safe. He died then. They preferred to let him kill himself in this way.

The Robin

The robin had a husband, but she loved another man. She had a family of four—a husband, son, daughter, and self. When she sat on a tree she would laugh. Because she loved another man, she wanted her husband and son to die, so that she and her daughter could live with this man. Every time she sang she would say, "I wish my husband and son would die," then she would laugh. Then she would say, "I wish I and my daughter would live," then she would laugh. Her husband did whatever she said, and he died. The boy died too. Her husband and son died because she wished them to die. She wished this, so she could get the man she wanted.

The native still chants the words in his own language, meaning, "I wish my husband and son would die," to the tune of a robin whistling. The laugh referred to is the clattering noise which a robin makes when excited.

The Marten

The marten has a white or reddish bridge across his breast. Whenever he was in an Indian camp and they were sitting around the fire eating he always looked hungry and watched every one eat, looking greedily for something for himself. One Indian didn't like being ogled, and threw a chunk of king salmon grease which struck him on the breast and made this bridge-mark.

The Wolverene and the Traveler

The wolverene is supposed to be the marten's uncle and the wolf's brother-in-law.

One time a man was walking down along a creek. It was winter. He met a wolverene coming up. The wolverene had no sled nor toboggan nor anything except a caribou-skin blanket on him. As soon as the man saw him, the wolverene went into the woods and filled his blanket with brush from spruce trees and made believe he had a load of utensils. His family was following a few miles back. The wolverene sat on his load and made the spruce sticks break. Then he told the man that he had broken his utensils. The man sat on his snow-shoes. The wolverene was bad and reached a long copper hook under the snow to catch hold of the lower snow-shoe and trip him. The wolverene would eat men. The man watched the wolverene because he knew what the wolverene would do. The wolverene, after tripping the man, would kill him with his copper ax. The man put his rabit-skin cap under himself, so when the hook came under him it caught the cap and pulled it out instead of catching his leg. Immediately then the man jumped on the wolverene, grabbed the wolverene's ax, and killed him with his own ax. The man built a camp. He cut off the wolverene's right leg at the shoulder and hung it over the fire to cook. Then he laid the wolverene on his right side to conceal the cut-off shoulder. He put the hook in the wolverene's left hand, giving him the appearance of poking up the fire. This was to deceive the wolverene's family that, coming soon, would think he had something and was cooking it. Then the man hid in the snow about fifty yards away and watched. When the wolverene's family came the young ones tried to wake him up to tell him that the shoulder was cooked, but they could not wake him up. Then they ate up the shoulder, not knowing it was their father's. Then they tried to wake him up more, and found out that he was dead and his shoulder off. Then they knew that they had eaten their father's shoulder. They took their spears and hunted all around for the man. They knew he had come down the river to the camp by this snow-shoe tracks, but he concealed his last tracks. They went about stabbing their spears into the snow to find him. When they came near him he jumped up on his snow-shoes and they all ran after, trying to catch him. The man could not run fast enough, so he wished for a warm wind to come so that the young wolverenes would get overheated and have to throw their coats away. The mother wolverene followed them, and every time one would throw his coat away she would pick it up and eat it. The man now knew that the young wolverenes had no coats, so he wished that a cold storm would come. Then the storm came and they called to the man, "Partner, come and build a fire for us, because it is cold and we won't kill you." The man started to build a fire. He got wood together and started a fire under it. He didn't want it to burn right away, so he put a little snow on the fire. Then he told the young wolverenes to sit in a row and all blow the fire at once together. As they bent to blow it he struck all of them over the heads with a long pole, killing them all with the one blow.

THE WOLVERENE AND THE HUNTER

The wolverene used often to go out hunting with a man, but every time he would return without his partner. One man decided to go out with him and find out what he did with them. They traveled together all day. Every time they saw a moose track the man wanted to follow it, but the wolverene said, "That's no good; we must go long way to get good hunting." At dark they made a camp. There was plenty of wood about, but wolverene said that he would get a hollow rotten stump and a large squirrel's nest (the kind built on pine-tree branches). The man had stripes about his pants below the knees, made of porcupine quills. The wolverene didn't have any stripes on his pants. They both got wet. The man knew that the wolverene was going to do something bad with the rotten wood. They stretched a pole across the fire and hung their pants on it to dry.

The man turned his pants inside out, so the wolverene did the same way. The wolverene sat on the left of the fire and the man sat on the right, with their pants on their respective sides, so that they would know whose pants each were. They both went to bed without pants on, beside each other. This man was smarter than the wolverene. The man did not sleep, but pretended to. He would snore; then the wolverene would go to get up quietly; then the man would move a little and the wolverene would lie down. The man did not go to sleep, but kept awake till the morning hours, when he was sure the wolverene was asleep. Then the man got up and changed the place of the pants and went back to bed. The wolverene now woke up and took the pants which he thought was the man's. He put them inside the hollow stump and laid the squirrel's nest over it. Then he put it in the fire and burned it. At daylight the man got up. The fire was out, so he built another fire. After that he took his pants down. Then the wolverene got up and said, "Partner, that's my pants." The man said, "No, they are my pants." The wolverene tried to take them away, but the man said, "You haven't any stripes on your pants; there are the stripes, so they're mine." The wolverene was sorry he lost his pants, and said they must have fallen on the fire and burned. The man got lots of small wood, no large pieces, so that it would burn up quickly; then he told the wolverene he would go home to get a pair of pants and come back after him. When he started he got a few hundred yards away; then he called to the wolverene and said, "I have found out now what you do with your partners. I won't come back to you any more." Then the man went home and let the wolverene freeze to death.

The Period of Culture Change

As I TRUST has already been made clear, it is not my intention to deal fully with the problems of culture change among the Han. Such a study would be desirable and I hope that it can be carried out by some anthropologist while it is still possible to do so effectively. At present, most of the needed information has not been recorded. What can be done here is little more than to marshal the limited evidence that has become available as a result of sorting out the data on the aboriginal culture of the Han. First I shall present in the usual order such pertinent statements as have appeared in the sources, together with a personal commentary on the cultural changes affecting the Han.

If one pleases, the personal commentary may be disregarded, for it does not have the same type of validity as the factual data that have been previously presented with respect to the aboriginal culture. Indeed, the control on factors responsible for culture change is too limited and, furthermore, it also seems to be impossible to eliminate from the presentation ideas about Athapaskan relations with Canadians and Americans that have resulted from my own intermittent association with the contact scene over a long period beginning in 1927. The summary can thus perhaps best be considered merely as an introduction to what follows.

In the second part of this section, I shall add a few remarks on the Han attitude toward those changes. Finally, I shall treat of three special problems which have particularly challenged my attention. Having presented this guide to the procedure, I can now return to the summary of changes in Han culture.

Changes: The Periods

In the attempt to give some chronological perspective to the data pertinent to a consideration of culture change, I shall attempt to allocate the information among four periods: before 1847; 1847–1897; 1897–1947; after 1947.

The first period is obviously that of the founding of Fort Yukon, the first trading post within easy reach of the Han. Concern with a period before 1847 arises from the fact that Han material culture in particular was influenced by direct or indirect contacts with Europeans living well outside Han territory. A change in material culture inevitably affects the social culture of a people, and their ideas as well. Let us consider the evidence and see what can be deduced from it.

Changes: Before 1847

Murray (1910: 60) tells us in speaking of the first large group of Gens du fou who visited Fort Yukon that he presented them with tobacco, and there is no indication that they received it as anything but commonplace; indeed, they had pipes made of metal that they had traded from the Russians. Along with tobacco, apparently also came snuff.

Furthermore, it seems almost certain, although proof has not been found, that tea was one of the commodities traded from the Russians before direct contact. The popular belief has been expressed by Spurr (1900: 21–2): "The Russians, themselves the greatest tea-drinkers of all European nations, long ago introduced 'Tschai' to the Alaskan natives; and throughout the country they will beg for it from every white man they meet, or will travel hundreds of miles and barter their furs to obtain it."

With respect to clothing, Murray (1910: 72) wrote, "the Russians bring to this country blankets, capots, cloth (of the latter two almost none are traded)." Apart from the warmth they afforded, blankets undoubtedly were significant for the potlatch. On the other hand, the basic patterns and the material of the native clothing seem to have been little affected by these acquisitions during the first period.

Certainly one of the most important precontact trade articles was the large Russian blue bead. It readily fitted into the Indian conception of values with respect to material things because of the long-established native trade in dentalium shell beads which originated at the distant end of the North Pacific Coast area. One might wonder if the first barter of exotic items always involves what even at a later date might be called luxuries. In any event, Murray (1910: 94) was impressed by the Indian longing for the blue and red beads such as they had obtained from the Russians before 1847. We must also remember the brass trinkets and small brass coins already in the possession of the Gens du fou at that time (pp. 60, 72).

I do not conceive of the forms of shelter changing before 1847 in any significant way, but there may have been an increasing use of the movable types since trade and a trapping economy began to absorb more of the people's attention. This general sequence of influences will be mentioned in the later discussion of special problems.

Just how many metal tools and implements had reached the Han before 1847, we shall never know. Russian muskets, with their powder and ball were certainly in use, and Murray (p. 72) distinguished fine and common varieties of these weapons. Speaking of the Kutcha Kutchin (p. 85), he said that of the ninety men in the band, twelve had guns, but many more carried powder horns. It is inconceivable that the Han could have been without guns and Murray not mention that fact; indeed, there are reasons to infer that they were better equipped than the Kutchin. It is also certain that iron knives were in use, for Murray (p. 85) says that the Hudson Bay variety were not popular because they were too hard to sharpen; with knifes came files, iron hoops from which to make arrowheads, and flint and steel with which to make fire (p. 72). We were told at Moosehide in 1932 that multibarbed copies of arrowheads (ke ɑʔ) made of iron were in use in the early nineteenth century. Jones (1872: 322) also mentions such metal points among the Kutchin. Some changes were taking place even among introduced objects during the period before 1847, for Murray (1910: 72) tells us that the Russians at first "brought only sheet iron kettles but last summer ... copper kettles the same as ours." A metal container was almost priceless to a people who had to do their boiling in baskets, and almost as close a correlate of tea, it would seem, as ammunition was to a gun.

Of particular interest is the implication that the Han did not have axes before 1847, and a more understandable one when it is realized that the ax required the introduction of a new technique. Murray (1910: 72) states he was told that the Russians brought "no regular axes, only a flat piece of steel shaped something like a plane iron, which the Indians fasten to a crooked stick with battiche, and use it as we would an adze." Certainly Murray was being told about the old Athapaskan adz made from spruce root (near the trunk) with steel substituted for the original stone blade, and then being bound in place with babiche line (cf. Osgood 1940: 98–100).

I cannot resist interpolating the fact that Campbell (1958: 68) deposited a tin can in the Pelly River in June 1843 as an early record of cans being used, if not of pollution in the upper Yukon drainage.

The introduction of metal tools and implements usually begins the process of replacement of aboriginal counterparts among Athapaskans. For a complete displacement to occur requires time. When one considers the less static and less visible aspects of culture, the degree of change is more difficult to measure.

As has been mentioned earlier, the gun must have affected intertribal conflict in various ways, perhaps intensifying it in the earlier stages. Actually, one of the rare records of change among early behavior patterns was the firing of guns by the Indians as a greeting. Murray (1910: 46) mentions the procedure, while Schwatka (1885a: 247) explains it, not without reason, as a custom acquired from the Russians.

Although a few inferences might be made about the impact that a knowledge of foreigners beyond the horizon may have had on ceremonial life and religion, I shall stop before involving myself in undue speculation and now turn to the next period.

Changes: 1847–1897

From the establishment of Fort Yukon (1847) to the Klondike stampede (1897), changes in Han culture became more and more evident. The Hudson's Bay Company and the Alaska Commercial Company brought increasing varieties of foods. Flour, lard, sugar, and hard biscuits might be considered basic, but there were other items as well, although some of them were available only periodically (e.g., Adney 1900a: 505). Although the Indians became more attracted to such store foods as the economy shifted to trapping and hunting, they still depended primarily on fish and game.

The gun clearly played an increasing role in hunting, which undoubtedly became more rewarding during the 1847–97 period. McQuesten (1952: 3) tells us that it was when his party arrived at Fort Yukon in August 1873 that the Indians first saw a repeating rifle. Wilson, in Schwatka (1900: 340, 342, 343), however, states that the ablebodied Han men were each armed, presumably in 1883, with from one to three small-caliber, double-barreled shotguns, and a very few were provided with Henry rifles, but that there was difficulty in obtaining ammunition for the latter as the importation of cartridges was prohibited. In any event, the gun may have been a factor which decreased the attention to fishing. The substitution of fishnets made from foreign twine was an important labor-saving device, as was the much less significant steel fishhook.

This 1847–97 period also saw the introduction of such important commodities as matches and alcoholic drinks. The first real impact of the latter apparently came in the 1890s. Pike (1896: 221) tells us while writing at Fortymile in 1893: "Whisky had at times found its way into the camp, and the frightful concoction known as 'Hootchinoo,' distilled from molasses, has caused some trouble. But so far the sale of intoxicating liquor to Indians had been almost entirely prevented. The miners' meeting has pronounced that whisky is good and shall be allowed for the whites, but if any man sells it to the Indians after he has been warned he shall be punished."

This appreciation of liquor is emphasized in one of the best accounts of the town of Fortymile, which comes from the pen of Charlotte Selina Bompas, the wife of the bishop, in a letter of January 20, 1893.

> The miners make this, Forty Mile Creek, their headquarters during the winter. They have built themselves neat, comfortable cabins, some of them with kitchen gardens. Many of them are well-educated men, far ahead of the low average level of the mining camps. But others, again, are of a very different type, and these come from their mines flush of money, ready to spend it in any way that will furnish them with comforts, luxuries, and amusements. And two first-class traders are here, with well-equipped stores, containing every article that heart could fancy, from a flour-bag to a wedding ring (which latter article, alas, is perhaps the one least frequently asked for in the whole colony). Here is a good lending library and billiard-room. Here at least six saloons, several restaurants, and a theater. We can also boast of two doctors, two blacksmiths, one watch-maker, and one dressmaker, with the latest fashions from Duncan. And, worse than all these, there are several distilleries where rum or whisky is made and sold to the Indians, and they have learned to make it for themselves, and that other highly intoxicating spirit called "Hoochino." Thus our Indians, being brought into contact with the white man, fall in only too easily with his taste for luxury, love of gambling, coarse, vile language, and for the miserable and ruth-less degradation of women. [Archer 1929: 137–8]

Haskell (1898: 150) adds a few facts about the town in 1896: "At this time it [Fortymile] was the second place in size on the river, contained a sawmill, several blacksmith shops, restaurants, billiard halls, saloons and dance halls, of course, and a few bakeries. It also contained an opera house, and here, a little later, we found some of the women who had come over the [Chilkoot] pass with us singing the same old songs we had heard at San Francisco, and had heard once in awhile during the journey. They had a hard time of it, but they received 'big money' for the display of their talents. It is one of the peculiarities of mining regions that much of the gold goes to those who do not dig it."

The change in dress developed in a parallel fashion to that of food, but perhaps even more rapidly. Schmitter (1910: 4) tells us: "As far back as any of the present inhabitants [at Eagle] can remember, they have worn shirts made of calico which they say traders brought from New York." Wilson, in Schwatka (1900: 340, 343), writes of the Han at the mouth of the Fortymile, apparently as he saw or more likely was told about them in 1883: "White men's clothing has been pretty generally adopted by these Indians." Three pages later he writes of the Han at Charley Village: "White men's clothes are universally worn by these people." Considering the source, that Wilson was really distinguishing the degree of acculturation among the Han of these two localities, seems unlikely. At least by the end of the 1847–97 period, "fancy cottons and bright flannels" had to some degree replaced the caribou-skin clothing, and colorful Mackinaw coats were being worn by the younger men (Adney 1900a: 505).

Identification with white men through similar dress was a factor, but labor-saving and comfort must have been among the principal empirical causes for the attraction to the European clothing, while the decrease in the availability of caribou may also have affected the situation. Although the evidence is not clear, there seems to have been a gradual substitution of moccasins and of boots that tied below the knees for the older one-piece garment. Canvas came into use for the upper parts of the footwear and for parka-like overclothes, the parka itself being taken over from the Eskimo.

Hats were also adopted by the Indians and mittens were modified. I should likewise mention the introduction of the justifiably famous Hudson's Bay blanket which, apart from its usefulness as a covering, became for a period a unit of wealth.

One of the rare reversals was the decrease of interest in trade beads which surprised Schwatka (1885a: 260) at Eagle. "They evidently care very little for beads as ornaments, for I saw none of them [the Han] wearing that much coveted Indian adornment, while great quantities were scattered around by the trader's store, having been trampled into the ground. At no place on the river did I find such eagerness for beads as characterizes the American Indians of milder climes, but nowhere did I see such total disregard for them as was shown here." The store, about a mile below the Indian village at Eagle was deserted when Schwatka visited it in 1883. Beads in the monetary sense had become passé, no doubt because of their availability and cheap price, plus the impact of the new economy. Simply for decoration, the interest in beads apparently rose once again because they were easier to use than porcupine quills.

It was also during the 1847–97 period that the distinctive Han hairdress was discarded, as well as the equally exotic ornaments in the septum of the nose.

Information on the early changes in shelter patterns is rare. There is some evidence for the introduction of canvas, but I have found no satisfactory descriptive data on the subject (Schwatka 1885a: 200, 228, 247). The old-style log and skin structures, however, gradually gave way to Euro-American tents, log cabins, and houses of sawed boards. Menstrual lodges and the special ceremonial structures were no longer constructed. In some measure caches and smokehouses were retained, as well as the occasional brush camp so useful when one travels through the bush.

It is clear that the pattern of dog-driving introduced by the Europeans was taken over by the Han before the end of the 1847–97 period. More effective transport was a correlate of the new trapping and hunting economy. The tandem harness and the toboggan of the Hudson's Bay Company traders, plus the increase in the number of dogs in each team and the development of their capabilities as previously described, seem to have been the essence of the acquisition. I note, for example that Schwatka (1885a: 259) reports at Eagle in 1883: "A few Hudson Bay toboggan sledges were seen on scaffolds at and near the village; they seem to be the principal sledges of this part of the country." Schmitter (1910: 3, 10) also writes of toboggans and as though they were the common winter conveyance indigenous to the area, which they were not. Stuck (1916: 270–1) has a pertinent comment on dog teams which, although not directly referring to the Han, certainly must have included them. "When we left this encampment Isaac sent two of his young men to guide us, with a sled drawn by three or four small dogs, so gaily caparisoned with *tapis* and ribbons, tinsel, and pompons, that they might have been circus dogs. Here again is evidence of this tribe's affinity with the upper Yukon natives, and so with those of the Mackenzie. I never saw the *tapis*, a broad, bright ornamented cloth that lies upon the dog's back under his harness, on the Middle Yukon. It is characteristic of the Peel River Indians who come across by the Rampart House and La Pierre House."

Since the above statement pertains to natives near Lake Mansfield and the Tanana River, I assume that the customs described—so characteristic of the Arctic Drainage Athapaskans in the contact period—diffused by way of the Peel River Kutchin to the Han.

Here I can also take the opportunity to bring to the attention of ethnographers some pertinent information that might easily be overlooked. Stuck (1916: 397) writes:

The white man found the dog team in use amongst the natives all over the interior, but he taught the Indian how to drive dogs. The natives had never evolved a "leader." Some fleet stripling always ran ahead, and the dogs followed. The leader, guided by the voice, "geeing" and "hawing," stopping and advancing at the word of command, is a white man's innovation, though now universally adopted by the natives [of interior Alaska]. So is the dog collar. The "Siwash [i.e., Indian] harness" is simply a band that goes around the shoulders and over the breast. In the interior the universal "Siwash" hitch was tandem, and is yet, but as trails have widened and improved, more and more the tendency grows amongst white men [in Alaska] to hitch two abreast; and the most convenient rig is a lead line to which each dog is attached independently by a singletree, either two abreast, or, by adding a further length to the lead line, one behind the other, so that on a narrow trial the tandem rig may be quickly resorted to.

It must be pointed out, on the other hand, that Stuck (p. 392) has added to the confusion he mentions when he wants us to believe that the best term is *husky* for the admixture of Indian dogs with those imported by the fur traders and prospectors, for *husky* is a word surely bound to the Eskimo dog. I also wish to note Stuck's insistence (p. 395) that Alaskan sled dogs were never the offspring of a dog and a wolf, a view for which I have more sympathy, but not actual support.

Incidentally, there is evidence that shows the use of the words "gee" and "chaw" in dog-driving as early as the end of the century, while the Eskimo terms were also known (Haskell 1898: 172; Archer 1929: 164). Haskell (pp. 166–72), I might add, devotes four pages to dogs and dog-driving. Good work dogs were expensive and I take this opportunity to record that an average animal in the Canadian Northwest cost $25 in 1868 (Cody 1908: 69), while the value on the lower Yukon was apparently around $40 in 1879 (McQuesten 1952: 8). Season and demand varied the price, of course, and it is interesting that the Han Indians were loaning their dogs at Fortymile in 1896 for a dollar a day while miners coming up from Circle paid as much as $250 for an Indian dog (Cody 1908: 279). The missionaries complained that the Indians placed such high prices on things that it was hard to live among them, while the natives themselves squandered hundreds of dollars on needless food and dress, living in lavish luxury and extravagance during the gold rushes of the 1890s (Cody 1908: 271).

During the 1847–97 period, the birch-bark canoes began to disappear from the river, the bark first displaced by canvas, and then the narrow, pointed, whip-sawed plank craft known as the Yukon boat proved its superiority both in carrying capacity and in sturdiness. Even small scows must have been sometimes made by the Han at this period.

About European tools and implements, I can postulate that they increased in number, variety, and quality between 1847 and 1897. Murray (1910: 72), for example, states that the natives trading into Fort Yukon—and therefore including the Han—preferred the Hudson's Bay Company guns to those they had received from the Russians. Surely, the prospectors of the last quarter of the century brought even much better weapons into the country, and the Indians would certainly have acquired some of them. I know that Winchester repeating rifles were selling at Circle for $50 at least by 1896, and hence at other posts as well (Spurr 1900: 174).

The argument has been advanced more than once that muzzle-loading guns were hardly more efficient than bows and arrows (Slobodin 1963b: 31), but such substantiation as that given by Turner (1894: 279) with reference to killing deer in a human surround does not seem either wholly applicable or entirely convincing. To acquire skill in using the new weapons required time, and only a small percentage of the hunters became expert, but that was also probably true of shooting with bows and arrows. In any event, by the end of the nineteenth century, shotguns and rifles were generally available, of types with which the effectiveness of the bow and arrow could not be favorably compared. Incidentally, I was told at Moosehide in 1930 that after breech-loading guns came into use, empty cartridges were substituted over the ends of arrow shafts as a replacement for the aboriginal blunt-end arrows whittled from a single piece of wood.

I also recall that copper kettles were specifically mentioned as being introduced at the beginning of the 1847–97 period as a replacement for those of iron, which had the disadvantage of rusting (Murray 1910: 72). Furthermore, Jonathan Wood of Moosehide told me in 1932 that the distinctive knives with the handle beaten out into opposing spirals were made from old files only during the last half of the nineteenth century. Jones (1872: 322) describes such manufactures among the Kutchin at the same period.

The comments on tools can be concluded by noting that containers made of wood, horn, or woven basketry had largely disappeared by the end of the century, while one new container appeared. This was the special moose, or caribou, skin bag known as the poke, an innovation born of the sourdough's need to pocket the gold that he found in Han territory.

Indian raiding on outside groups for whatever reasons stopped abruptly in the 1847–97 period. The so-called peace of the fur traders does not seem really to have been so much directly imposed by them as directly achieved by the sudden enlargement of the Indians' conceptual world. One might go so far as to say that the impact of the Europeans distracted the natives sufficiently for them to discover a new commonality in being Indians with developing problems affecting their own survival. Since the Han were among the last to feel the direct force of the white man, and that from at least three directions, they showed even less than the little warlike resistance put up by some of the other Athapaskan groups such as the Tanaina. In any event, the white man had brought peace to the Indian tribes, thus doing for others what he did not have the ability to do for himself.

The white man also brought diseases which were even more destructive than warfare. Murray (1910: 51) speaks of what seems to be a sickness of epidemic proportions at the beginning of the 1847–97 period, while Schwatka (1885a: 292–3) states that Yukon was "a great thoroughfare for contagious disease" and noted that, as far as he knew, its course was always downstream.

It is interesting to find that in Schmitter's (1910: 19) opinion, the specific use of aboriginally known herbs was learned from the whites. Whether true or not, I recall the statement attributed to McQuesten that his life was threatened while he was at Fort Reliance by shamans whose services had been curtailed by his competition in supplying drugs (Schwatka 1885a: 245–6).

Whatever the Han may have had of herbal remedies, they were not effective against the diseases brought into the country by white men and, for that matter, the white man's superior medicine was not always able to curtail the epidemics either. The knowledge of primitive herbal remedies has exceptionally long-lasting qualities, however, and it would be interesting to know what an ethno-botanist could recover from the middle Yukon even now.

At this place in the discussion of changes during the 1847–97 period, I cannot resist quoting Josiah Spurr's classic description of Indians participating in a gold rush town in the summer of 1896:

> The evening of our arrival in Forty Mile Post we were attracted by observing a row of miners, who were lined up in front of the saloon engaged in watching the door of a large log cabin opposite rather dilapidated, with the windows broken in. On being questioned, they said there was going to be a dance, but when or how they did not seem to know: all seemed to take only a languid looker-on interest, speaking of the affair lightly and flippantly. Presently more men, however, joined the group and eyed the cabin expectantly. In spite of their disclaimers they evidently expected to take part, but where were the fair partners for the mazy waltz?

> The evening wore on until ten o'clock, when in the dusk a stolid Indian woman, with a baby in the blanket on her back, came cautiously around the corner, and with the peculiar long slouchy step of her kind, made for the cabin door, looking neither to the right nor to the left. She had no fan, nor yet an opera cloak; she was not even décolleté; she wore large moccasins on her feet—number twelve, I think, according to the white man's system of measurement—and she had a bright colored handkerchief on her head. She was followed by a dozen others, one far behind the other, each silent and unconcerned, and each with a baby upon her back. They sidled into the log cabin and sat down on the benches, where they also deposited their babies in a row: the little red people lay there very still, with wide eyes shut or staring, but never crying—Indian babies know that is all foolishness and doesn't do any good. The mothers sat awhile looking at the ground in some one spot and then slowly lifted their heads to look at the miners who had slouched into the cabin after them—men fresh from the diggings, spoiling for excitement of any kind. Then a man with a dilapidated fiddle struck up a swinging, sawing melody, and in the intoxication of the moment some of the most reckless of the miners grabbed an Indian woman and began furiously swinging her around in a sort of waltz, while the others crowded around and looked on.

> Little by little the dusk grew deeper, but candles were scarce and could not be afforded. The figures of the dancing couples grew more and more indistinct and their faces became lost to view, while the sawing of the fiddle grew more and more rapid, and the dancing more excited. There was no noise, however; scarcely a sound save the fiddle and the shuffling of the feet over the floor of rough hewn logs; for the Indian women were stolid as ever, and the miners

could not speak the language of their partners. Even the lookers-on said nothing, so that these silent dancing figures in the dusk made an almost weird effect.

One by one, however, the women dropped out, tired, picked up their babies and slouched off home, and the men slipped over to the saloon to have a drink before going to their cabins. Surely this squaw-dance, as they called it, was one of the most peculiar balls ever seen. [Spurr 1900: 116–9]

I can verify the behavior of the Indian women, as I have observed indentical behavior among the Athapaskans more than once.

The less visible the aspect of culture, the less we know about the effects of acculturation. It is recorded, however, that chiefs were appointed by the Hudson's Bay Company and supported in that position. The result of their so-doing on the Han is not clear, but analogies could be reasonably made from comparable data on the Crow River Kutchin (Balikci 1963: 48–9). The clan–sib system, social classes, the residence system, all began to disintegrate under the impact of the traders and other whites encroaching on Han country. The various early gold strikes with a sizable population of miners rushing from one creek to another, building towns and then evacuating them, shooting and fishing where convenience demanded, must have been something like having alien warring groups moving back and forth over one's territory.

One of the aspects of social culture about which we would also like to know the details in the nineteenth century was the potlatch. Probably the basic problem in comprehending this ceremony among the Athapaskans lies in gaining the culturally correct conception of property. Under aboriginal conditions, few mobile material objects had much continuing value, for between the losses and wear resulting from breakage and use, the effective life of most native manufactures was short. On the other hand, the majority of products were relatively easy to reproduce. There was no outstanding individual object with true monetary value, although one or two such as dentalia shells and red ocher may have approached it. This fact, however, does not keep one from recognizing materials that could be stockpiled for giving away—caribou skins and tailored clothing, lines of various kinds, red ocher, and dentalium shell beads, to mention the obvious ones. The Athapaskans have not been especially noted as a property-loving people, but that perhaps does not matter so much since ceremonial giving following a death, apart from payment of services rendered, probably had the acquisition of prestige as a primary component. The reason that the material aspects of the potlatch are reviewed here, I might add, is because they changed so much after 1847. Indeed the question could reasonably be raised as to how long before that day potlatching began among the Han. That it existed among the Kutchin, and consequently among the Han in the middle of the nineteenth century, is beyond dispute (Hardisty 1872: 317–8). On the other hand, Chandalar Kutchin informants told McKennan (1965: 64) in 1932 that although the potlatch was well known to them, they did not practice it, and the implication is more that they never had done so than that they had given it up.

I do not mean to suggest that potlatching was not an old aboriginal custom among some of the Athapaskans, but rather that the Han were close to the periphery of its functional range. Actually, the changing economy might have reinforced potlatch activity during the period of 1847–97. We simply do not know.

As in the previous period, birth customs were probably little affected by Europeans, except indirectly or in a rare case. Since the phonetics of the Athapaskan language was too complex for most aliens, the traders and particularly the missionaries gratuitously assigned European and especially Biblical names to the Indians. For a period, individuals enjoyed the advantage of double names, if it was an advantage. In some cases the names became blended. Again, some Indian names were translated, while others were Anglicized. This general pattern applied also to local geographical names. Obviously, the subject could provide an interesting paper, as well as detailed data that we now do not have.

In marriage customs, the most notable contribution of civilization was the introduction of the formalized system of the Anglo-American world, but with it came problems which seemed to have anticipated the disassociation of husbands and wives that characterized much of Western society in the twentieth century. In fact, the problems may prove greater for those who have given than for those who have received.

It must be emphasized that between 1847 and 1897 a great deal of admixing of the races took place. Much of this was not obvious except at the place and the hour, but there were still numerous cases of common-law and religiously sanctified marriages between white men and Indian women.

Charlotte Bompas (Archer 1929: 138) gives a neat picture of the situation at Fortymile between the miners and their girls: "Our American citizen would scorn to marry an Indian; indeed, by an iniquitous law of his country he is forbidden to do so; but the higher law of God he can set aside and ignore. The sweet, oval face and laughing eyes of our Indian girl please him; he knows that she can be made as deft with her hands, as tidy and orderly, as skilful with her needle as any white woman. She is sadly, deplorably vain, poor child, and a gay shawl or two, a pair of gold ear-rings, will sorely tempt her, as the bag of flour has tempted her father to wink at the transaction."

Symbolically, it is also worthwhile to recall that the distinguished Reverend Robert MacDonald, who was at Fort Yukon in 1863 and first reduced the Kutchin language to writing, was married to a girl whose native tongue it was (Stuck 1916: 22; Mathews 1968: 228). As might be expected, Indian accounts about the traders tell of their Indian wives and children, the founder of Fort Selkirk being no exception (McClellan, 1967: 59–61; Mathews, 1968: 90). Nothing will probably be so important in future studies of Han culture change as a consideration of the activities of the offspring of these mixed unions.

It would seem reasonable to assume that the attitude of the Han toward death itself must have been affected in some degree by the devastating epidemics that followed the coming of Europeans. Certainly, customs pertaining to the disposal of the dead were changed. Jonathan Wood, who was born in 1860, told me at Moosehide in 1932 that he only remembered hearing of cremation, but never saw a body burned. In any event, before the end of the 1847–97 period, the missionaries had imposed methods of disposal in accordance with Christian custom, practices which were soon to be fortified by the legal rules of the two countries that had taken jurisdiction over the Han and their territory.

Death and disaster have also the reputation of intensifying religious feeling among people, but whether or not the Han were thus affected, at least a nominal Christianity began to dominate the scene, with mission stations in Han territory first at Fortymile (1887) and at Eagle, Dawson, and Moosehide somewhat later. The influence of the shamans was still strong in 1883, however, as is borne out by the trouble they gave the trader McQuesten at Fort Reliance as noted earlier, and they were to survive into the twentieth century. In the long run, nevertheless, the contest between missionary and the shaman was too one-sided, and the rich, unritualized, and unwritten religious beliefs of the aboriginal Han were invalidated and cast aside because of the constant devotion of a paid priesthood bearing the Biblical message.

Changes: 1897–1947

Until 1897, the pattern of culture change was not unlike that which had affected most of the Athapaskans. Then for the Han came a shock. Since the previous decade they had become accustomed to hundreds of prospectors moving around the country, but this was as nothing compared to what happened the year after gold claims were staked on the Klondike. By 1897 when the next fifty-year period begins, people from all walks of life swept into the Han territory. Women of varying degrees of cultivation and virtue arrived along with the men. These gold-hungry adventurers came from up the river and down the river and from over the mountains. A few hundred Indians, the total population of the Han nation, were simply lost among tens of thousands of white immigrants whose diggings along every tributary of the Yukon, and along every side stream of the tributaries, literally changed the physical form of Han territory.

A city sprang up that for ten years could offer most of the wonders of civilization that were available at the beginning of the twentieth century. No other Athapaskans ever experienced the equal of it, and in some ways, no Europeans either. Although Han participation was limited in certain ways—we doubt, for example, that any Han woman took a bath in champagne, although a few may have been enticed into a tub—the influence of the more meaningful aspects of the new culture were inescapable.

To be more specific, within the period 1897–1947, except for salmon and large game which had been taken to by the Europeans, there was an almost complete displacement of the aboriginal foods by the ones sold in the stores. Schmitter (1910: 7) said of the Han: "These people have lately learned luxury to the extent that they think they are destitute when they have only animal food to eat, whereas I am told they never had anything but animal [native] food ten years ago."

Certainly one of the most remarkable innovations in the culture of the Yukon River Indians was the salmon wheel. This efficient construction, apparently invented about 1904 on the Tanana River by some unknown man of the gold rush, did for fishing what the power-driven washing machine did for laundering (cf. Stuck 1917: 113; illus. opp. 174; Gilbert and O'Malley 1921: 143; Mathews, 1968: illus. 244). Even though cleanliness be next to godliness, fish were more important to the Indians.

Wynne-Edwards (1947: 13–4) provides a fairly detailed description of one of three salmon wheels visible from the hill above Dawson in 1945.

A hollow-square raft is moored in a strong current a few yards out from the bank. Each side of the raft forms a catwalk, in the middle of which is a 3-foot upright post bearing one end of the 12-foot axle. The axle and its bearings are wooden, made from spruce trunks. Bolted radially to the axle are wooden frames covered with chicken-wire, each shaped in the form of a hollow scoop, about 10 feet square. Some wheels have three or four scoops, forming the blades of the wheel. The one we examined had a pair of paddle boards alternating with two opposite fish-scoops.

As the wheel is slowly rotated by the current, making two or three revolutions per minute, each frame in turn dips about 6 feet under water. The concave or hollow side is downstream; and in rising again to the surface it traps any fish which happens at that moment to swim against it. As it now swings up into the air, the fish slides inwards towards the axle, and is diverted to one side or the other by sloping gutters meeting at the center to fall into collecting boxes placed under the end of the axle on the catwalks.

Wynne-Edwards (1947: 14) also reported in 1945: "There seems little doubt that the Yukon salmon fishery has declined within living memory, almost certainly on account of operations lower down in Alaska." This decline probably affected the Han Indians relatively little in comparison to others such as the Crow River Kutchin.

Killing game animals was certainly easier with the repeating rifles of this period, at least when the game could be found, and moose were still being supplied to the Dawson market in quantities in 1904 (Sheldon 1919: 4). In Adney's (1900a: 505) opinion, the Indians' skill with the modern repeating rifle was remarkable.

It was said at Moosehide in 1932 that moose and caribou were still shared among the local group. Notes from Walter Benjamin at Eagle in the same summer contain the statement that geese could no longer be shot even in the spring when they used to fly low because "white men have scared them off." The Yukon had been becoming too populated.

Adney (1900a: 500–1) supplies a description of a meal eaten by the Klondike Indians in January 1898, although admittedly this was the winter of great shortages in Dawson. He writes: "We cooked a loaf of baking-powder bread in a frying pan. A scrap of bacon and a cup of tea completed our meal. The Indians were really near starvation. Isaac himself had the only sack of flour in the village. Each family had its own cooking outfit, consisting of a frying-pan, a tin milk-pan, a tin dish-pan, several tin cups and plates, and a small tin pail for boiling tea, and a larger one, holding two or three gallons, for making soup and boiling meat and washing the children's undergarments." If we add the unmentioned sugar, we have here a fair list of not only the basic European foods but the cooking utensils appropriate to the Anglo-Indian cuisine of the period.

For readers of a coming generation, I might add that a milk pan was a flat-bottomed tin plate with walls approaching the vertical, perhaps 5 inches high and 15 inches in diameter. It was the readily transportable successor to the lead-glazed earthenware milk pan, the production of which in New England ended around the middle of the nineteenth century. No longer used to skim cream from freshly cooled milk, it became a container for multiple purposes. A hungry Indian could devour all the pieces of meat a milk pan could hold, and some white men became notable competitors.

By the end of the first decade of the twentieth century, apparently the only articles of aboriginal clothing still in use were mittens and moccasins, and both of these may have been more or less changed. About the same time, the main types of shelter disappeared, to be completely replaced by log cabins and canvas tents. As an odd bit of culture change, I report being told by an informant at Moosehide in 1932 that he knew an old Indian who took sweat baths under a canvas-and-pole frame erected inside his house so as not to be bothered by the dogs and the children.

Apparently few, if any, birch-bark canoes were made in the 1897–1947 period. Again one thinks of the influences of the Dawson gold rush on native customs, but in such basic matters, probably the decease of the older men with the necessary skills had as much to do with the decline as anything else. Canoes with canvas covers probably continued to be made and, during the last half of the period, outboard engines became common on small river craft.

One specific point that Walter told us at Eagle should be recorded. He said that aboriginally the Han made snowshoes only with a rounded front (the classic Loucheux type) but that in 1932 they sometimes constructed them with frames pointed at the front, a style they had learned from the Peel River Kutchin. The latter had learned it from the Mackenzie River Athapaskans I presume.

Another note on transportation is provided by Schmitter (1910: 3), who was apparently writing about circumstances in 1906. He said: "Each man owns a team of about five dogs, employed in winter for pulling toboggans and sleds over the trails and in the summer for hauling boats up the river banks [or, more exactly, tracking along the river]." Adney (1900a), it might be observed, depicts Indians with two, three, four, or five dogs harnessed to toboggans.

I was surprised to discover that in 1904 there was a narrow-gauge railroad running from the mouth of Coal Creek twelve miles up to a mine which supplied coal to Dawson, a steamer and barges being regularly employed for the purpose, an upstream journey of about sixty miles (Sheldon, 1919: 5–6).

Before leaving matters connected with transportation, it should be mentioned that Dawson was one of the first settlements in the north to have an airfield, the latter having gone into operation in October 1934 (Lotz [c. 1964] 139). The effect on the Han was undoubtedly limited, but the air service did contribute to Dawson's becoming an active tourist center during much of the 1897–'1947 period.

Most of the aboriginal Han tools and implements were replaced by European items that proved more effective, but a few continued to be used periodically. Schmitter (1910: 5), for example, stated that moose skins not only still had their hair "scraped off with the end of a sharp bone spatula" but also, "as in primitive times, all sewing is still done with bone awls." No doubt these latter tools went the way of most others soon afterward. The statement does bring up the possibility, however, that there was some lag in the culture change among settlements at a considerable distance below Dawson and those closer to it.

While the tanning of skins remained to a limited degree, the technique of weaving basketry apparently disappeared early in the period, if it had not done so before. Simple aboriginal lines survived, but the more complex twisted ones were replaced by rope. By the end of the 1897–1947 period, it would be a surprise if there was a Han Indian left who could make an old-style basket fish trap of spruce or a dipnet for salmon, to say nothing of using the latter efficiently.

Simple snares, such as were originally made in order to catch rabbits, were replaced by the commercial variety, just as steel traps had finally supplanted deadfalls. Bows and arrows became merely the playthings of children, except perhaps for a few examples, homemade or imported, that represented a resuscitated art. Containers made of birch bark or woven skin lines, together with ornamental bags of moose or caribou skin (the two skins sometimes in combination) continued to be made in order to supply miners and tourists with Indian curios. Adequate descriptive data and few specimens have been found, however. There was certainly little of this type of material around Dawson or Eagle which would attract an ethnographer or museum curator in 1932. Apparently at that time the motivation to produce this kind of handiwork had declined along with the population and with the slowing down of the tourist trade as a result of the economic depression of the 1930s.

One should certainly not overlook the fact that during the 1897–1947 period the Han have had the privilege of fighting in two world wars, no doubt enjoying

it most when surviving to remember their fantastic experiences, so unlike the
group murders of aboriginal times.

Epidemics of diphtheria seem to have been particularly common in the early
1900s. Stuck (1916: 28) found an outbreak on the Chandalar River in December
1905 and said: "That disease had scourged the Yukon in the two preceding years.
Twenty-three children died at Fort Yukon in the summer of 1904, half a dozen
at Circle in the following winter, though that outbreak was grappled with from the
first; and all along the river the loss of life was terrible." It is not likely that the
Han could have escaped. There were other diseases. The Episcopal bishop,
William Bompas, who had moved to Moosehide from Fortymile, is recorded as
vaccinating the Indians there in July 1900, despite their strong protests (Archer
1929: 165).

As some aid to the people in these difficulties, we should note that three hospitals were established at Dawson by 1898, while perhaps more important for the
Indians was the hospital founded at Fort Yukon in 1915 (Stuck 1917: 104; Archer
1929: 159).

Han porcupine quill work would certainly have been appreciated in a more
sophisticated culture had it survived rather than having become degraded before
it disappeared, probably in the first half of the 1897–1947 period. Quill work
was in large measure associated with aboriginal items of dress, and consequently
was lost with the latter.

Dancing and singing were always important to the Han despite what might be
considered the inadequacies of their musical instruments. The incoming populace
introduced them to the potentialities of stringed instruments, including the piano.
Afterward, the phonograph became common and the radio almost ubiquitous.
The aboriginal tambourine drum stood little chance of holding out against such
an onslaught, to say nothing of the ancient Han songs. As for dancing, no group
of Indians probably ever suffered such concentrated terpsichorean influence as
was offered in the ten years following the founding of Dawson, although they had
enjoyed a good taste of it earlier.

It is uncertain which, if any, purely aboriginal games were still played by the
Han in the 1897–1947 period, but some that were simple and essentially for
children certainly survived. Along with modern schools came the Euro-American
game complex and, for the young people of the group, that was a real compensation.

It was during this period of 1897–1947 that the Han found themselves under
the control of not one new political system, but two. The Canadian Parliament
established the Yukon Territory as a new political unit in 1898 with provision "for
local government by a legislative council composed of the commissioner and six
persons to be appointed by the Governor [of Canada] in council" (Anon. 1916:
14). A detachment of the Northwest Mounted Police had arrived in 1894, and
the rule of this celebrated organization has often been referred to as a model for
law enforcement in the north (e.g., Stuck 1917: 57–9). As noted before, in the
Alaskan half of the territory, the Han had the benefits of a company of U.S.

soldiers and particularly Dr. Ferdinand Schmitter. The detailed effects of these developments are too complicated to be dealt with here, but it may add color to picture the situation as seen by the moral eyes of a liberal churchman of those early days (Stuck 1917: 56–7). Let us begin with what is said about Dawson:

> It seems altogether impossible that a tribe of Indians should live in the near neighbourhood of a considerable white town without suffering degradation. There are always white men eager to associate with them to debauch the women and make profit of the men; insensibly the native virtues are sapped, the simple native customs undergo sophistication into a grinning imitation of white customs; jaunty cast-off millinery displaces the decent handkerchief on the women's heads, cracked patent-leather shoes and even French heels displace the comfortable home-made moccasins on their feet; the men grow shiftless and casual, picking up odd jobs around town and disdaining the hunting and fishing by which they used to live.
>
> Each year a band of Indians from the Peel River (a tributary of the Mackenzie) make a long overland journey to Dawson with their furs, for purposes of trade, and their stalwart vigour of body and independence of manner no less than the gay bravery of their wilderness attire impress the citizens of Dawson very favourably, and much is made of the contrast which they present to the degenerates of Moosehide. Yet I have heard Bishop Stringer say that when first he knew the Moosehide Indians they were in every respect the peers of their Peel River brethren. It is as true in the Yukon Territory as it is in Alaska that he who would see the Indians at their best must see them remote from the settlements of the white man.

Then we can turn to his slightly earlier comment on the condition of the Han at Eagle (Stuck 1916: 285–6):

> A native village of eighty or ninety souls, with its church and school, lies three miles upstream from the town, so that the relative positions of village, town, and military post exactly duplicate those at Tanana. It must at once be stated, however, that this situation has not led to anything like the demoralisation amongst the natives at Eagle that thrusts itself into notice at the other place [Fort Gibbon near the mouth of the Tanana River]. Whether it were the longer training in Christian morals that lay behind these people, or better hap [luck] in the matter of post commanders (certainly there was never such scandalous irregularity and indifference at [Fort] Egbert as marked one administration at [Fort] Gibbon), or the vigilance during a number of consecutive years of an especially active deputy marshal and the wisdom and concern through an even longer period of a commissioner much above the common stamp, or all these causes combined, the natives at Eagle have not suffered from the proximity of soldiers and civilians in the same measure as the natives at Tanana. Drunkenness and debauchery there have been again and again [at Eagle], but they have been severely checked and restrained by both the civil and military authorities.

These are not an ethnographer's comments, as is shown by the classification of handkerchiefs as being decent in contrast to other types of head covering, but they do show by the comparisons with other groups and other settlements the relative impact of social and political developments within Han territory at the beginning of the 1897–1947 period.

It will also be worthwhile to quote an additional sentence about the Peel River Kutchin whose sojourn on the Yukon in the days of the great Klondike stampede made them later known as the "Dawson Boys." What they experienced, so must many of the Han. Slobodin (1963b: 30) makes some of the contacts specific. "The 'Dawson Boys' became familiar with bars, pool-halls, brothels, motion-pictures, drug stores, banks, pawn shops, and other specialized emporia." They also learned more English than most Indians in the area.

To continue by recording a detail of culture change, we were told by Richard Marten, a Peel River Indian living at Moosehide in 1932, that the last feast for the first king salmon had taken place among the Han in that area in 1926. He added that his own group never celebrated the arrival because they were accustomed to obtaining fish through the ice during the winter.

I should add that the old form of the potlatch disintegrated in the first half of the nineteenth century as a result of various pressures and the general dissolution of the Han social organization. The Indians could no longer afford to amass great quantities of gifts, and about the end of the nineteenth century the Canadian government seems to have forbidden potlatching, although it is not certain how much the Han were actually affected.

With respect to the life cycle, there is evidence that the establishment of hospitals and the assistance of Western doctors may have restored a favorable balance of births over deaths among the Indians of the Yukon (cf. Stuck 1917: 105). Schmitter (1910: 14), speaking of the isolation of girls at menarche said: "This custom is still in vogue, but the length of exile is usually cut down to a few months." Before the 1897–1947 period was over, we suspect that all separation of girls from their regular residence had ended, although some taboos at menstrual periods had not. Certainly burial according to Canadian and American custom was the only kind undertaken. As for religion, the same variations in Christian beliefs and practices were to be found among the Han as among the non-Indian population.

Changes: After 1947

Concerning this last period I have little to say in terms of specific differences in Han culture. About all that remained of the material culture of the Han was the snowshoe.

Unquestionably, the opening up of the Han area by the road-building program that in 1950 linked Eagle with the main roads to Fairbanks and Anchorage had significance. The next year a road westward from Dawson was joined with it. Then, in 1953, Dawson was connected with the Alaska Highway 335 miles to the south, which had been brought into existence as a result of World War II. Begun in March 1942, it had been completed the year following (Mathews, 1968: 277, 279). Thus it became possible to drive a truck or passenger car directly from Han territory to either Alaska or British Columbia. The resultant cheap transportation made steamboat traffic unprofitable, and all service by this means was discontinued on the Yukon in 1955 (Lotz [c. 1964]: 18–23). Perhaps snowmobiles can be expected to become popular in the future, although they can never supply the security of the dog and the toboggan, the latter having completely replaced the original Han sled.

Slobodin (1963a: 16), interestingly enough, writes of the 1960s that girls at menarche were still isolated at Eagle. "In Eagle at the present time a girl at first menstruation must remain for several weeks in a curtained-off part of the family cabin, and must observe certain tabus. As far as could be learned, menarche is no longer distinguished in any way among the Dawson Indians." This is certainly a notable instance of the retentive force of a meaningful Athapaskan custom at the former village, as well as another indication of the greater influence of white values at Dawson on the local Indians.

Most of the data on the Han during the last half of the twentieth century are still to be recorded and when, as it is hoped, such a study is undertaken by some anthropologist, the already available sources will also be analyzed. I might further speculate on present conditions among the Han from parallel cases, but instead let us look forward to someday having the descriptive data which will serve everyone much better. Here I shall do no more than give a reference to a few such useful papers as those by Gutsell (1953), Lotz [c. 1964], Tanner (1966), and Mathews (1968), the bibliographies of which will supply many additional sources.

The Han Attitude toward Change

In reflecting on the processes of cultural change, it seems possible to distinguish many of the traits that came to be adopted by the positive intent and desire of the Indian. Indeed, one might say that all of the alien traits that we can distinguish as existing among the Han in the period before 1847 belong in this category. It is notable that they comprise material objects to a large degree, although the behavior and value systems of the Indians were consequently impinged upon. I am, of course, speaking of such things as guns, metal implements and tools in general, beads, tobacco, and the various things for which the Han must have paid neighboring Indians dearly in the early part of the nineteenth century. These items seem to fall essentially into three classes: labor-saving devices, ornaments, and acquisitions for self-indulgence. In the following historic period, European food, clothing, medicines, liquor, and an endless number of other alien traits were likewise sought after and received in larger or lesser degree.

There were also aspects of culture that were thrust upon the Indians and which they found desirable only in a limited sense. First of all, there was the assumption of ownership and controls over the land and all that is appurtenant to it by the whites. From the Indian point of view, the Americans bought the Han country from the Russians who had never even seen it. That the British took another part of it by conquest involved a more traditional procedure. In either case, the alienation of their land had strange and unwelcome aspects to the Han, whose concept of ownership were based on a different set of rights and privileges. Even though it may have taken half a century for the Han to appreciate the fact, they had become over those years a conquered people in their own country. Despite the advantages, it is a condition seldom achieved by the choice of the recipients.

Then there was the contribution of religion. There have been statements by missionaries that the Indians at the time of contact were waiting for the gift of Christian salvation. This seems somewhat improbable. In any event the Indians were proselytized by a long series of churchmen, no doubt dedicated and sincere. Some Indians were pleased, while others, including the shamans, were embittered by this form of intrusion.

At the same time, there were the repressions of Indian social life involving the old patterns of love-making, betrothal and marriage, the disposal of the dead, and ceremonies such as the potlatch, results which were enforced by the combined power of the law and the church.

By the beginning of the twentieth century, the Han seem to have become almost numbed by the cultural upheaval, and new elements of culture could hardly be related to the old. Thus, probably the greatest number of traits in Han culture toward the end of the twentieth century belong to the civilized world and the attitude toward the advent of most of them has been neutral. Han culture is no longer Han, but a subculture of North American civilization.

Thus the history of the Han in the past hundred years has been the vitiation of the entire structure of the aboriginal society by the multiplicity of interactions caused by these changes, some sought after, some thrust upon them, and some quietly absorbed. That any meaningful revival of Han culture could take place, or would even be considered desirable by the people, is questionable. Some compensations and adjustments for losses sustained, however, might greatly reinforce the will of this small group to survive as a significant cultural minority.

With reference to the persistence of such small aboriginal enclaves and to the problems of acculturation as seen by the outsider, I take this opportunity to give a wider reception to an unusually sensitive statement written by George Pettitt (1950: 106) when thinking about these questions.

It is difficult for the average man to understand why his culture, which to him is obviously superior, is not quickly adopted by a minority group with a culture which to him is just as obviously inferior. When some individuals are able to leave the minority group and join the majority, it seems more reprehensible that the rest should not follow suit. Culture is man-made, the average citizen reasons, and it can be remade if there is a desire to do so. But this leaves out of account the depth to which the roots of a culture go, once it has matured, and the difficulty involved in clearing the ground for another planting. It also leaves out of account the sentiment attached to the gnarled trunk and spreading branches. Limbs may be cut off here and there and others bearing a different fruit may be grafted on, one at a time, but the entire tree can scarcely be cut down without first eliminating the people who live in its shade. Furthermore, even when the crown of the tree has been so changed by grafting that it looks like a new species, the owners thereof, for nostalgic reasons, will continue to tend the old limbs and even to cultivate new shoots out of the old root stock. The fruit of the old tree may seem sour and miserable to the stranger, but to the initiate there reside in it virtues which transcend the judgment of culture connoisseurs or culture dietitians. The fruit of a culture may leave the body starving but remain desirable because it nurtures the spirit. Doing traditional things in the traditional way brings satisfaction, when doing new things in a perhaps better way may leave just well-fed, well-clothed desolation. In some respects the craving for perpetuation of a culture to which one is accustomed is totally inexplicable on reasonable grounds; it may even have all the characteristics of a self-destructive addiction.

Special Problems

In attempting to organize and evaluate the cultural data on the Han, I am left with three problems or subjects for speculation which relate to each other and tend to merge into a whole. With the hope for greater clarity, I shall consider them one after another. The first concerns the relationship of the Han language to those of neighboring Athapaskans. The second problem involves the movements of Han Indians during the nineteenth century. The third and last problem centers around the shift in economy as a result of the fur trade.

Fortunately, I have been the recipient of assistance on the first problem by a personal communication from a colleague, Michael Krauss, who has been working on the Alaskan languages for some years. Among his contributions is additional and more precise confirmation that Han must be considered a homogenous language—to borrow a term from biology—not simply a dialectic variant of Kutchin or some other Athapaskan language. This conclusion had been predicted by the statements of early fur traders and, since their time, affirmed by linguists such as Sapir.

Having started with this assumption, I am now more immediately concerned with the relationship of the Han language to those of their neighbors such as the Kutchin, the Tutchone, the Nabesna (Upper Tanana), and the Tanana. Krauss has no doubt that Han is closer to Kutchin than to any other language. Hoijer (1963: 27) had given some evidence for this earlier. Krauss, in a letter, expresses the relationship between Kutchin, Han, and Tutchone in the following terms.

"Broadly, Kutchin has 1) lost many stem-final consonants, with 2) resultant development of tone and 3) diphthongization of stem-vowels, and resulting from 3) developed 4) a system of palatalization of stem-initial consonant series, and 5) merged several of the series in certain ways, differing partly by dialect.

"Han has done 1), 2), 3), and 4), but not 5).

"Tutchone has done only 1), 2), and only part of 3) and 4)."

Krauss also points out that Han shows certain traits in common with Nabesna (Upper Tanana) as well as with Tutchone. Finally, he is confident that Han is more closely related to Nabesna than to the linguistic groups on the middle or lower Tanana River, or on the Yukon adjacent to the mouth of the Tanana.

I would add that Arthur Wright, who supplied me with a vocabulary and some ethnographic data in the summer of 1937 at Nenana, made explicit that his dialect (a) centered at Tanana Village, and that it extended up the Tanana River only about half of the way to Nenana, and was distinct from another dialect (b) reaching from below Nenana up to about half of the way between Delta and Tanana Crossing, but not including the latter. He also stated, interestingly enough, that the speech of the villages above Nenana in this second group (b) varied slightly one from another.

With reference to Arthur Wright's failure to include the Tanana Crossing area with that of the river below it, I add a statement by McKennan (1959: 23) who writes: "between the Crossing and Healy River occur a whole series of rapids which today make navigation exceedingly dangerous and in earlier days practically prevented it."

In 1970, Michael Krauss gave me an identical dividing line between two linguistic groups which he calls "Inner Koyukon" (a′) and Tanana. This latter group, plus "Transitional Tanana" in which, however, he includes Tanana Crossing, is the equivalent of my (b) minus Tanana Crossing.

As valuable as this information certainly is, it actually gives us only focal points for comparison, and we are left with the problem of determining the linguistic— and hence, probably cultural—boundaries. Where exactly, for example, were the boundaries on the Yukon River between the Han speakers and the Tutchone to the south, or between the Han and the Kutchin to the north? Even more titillating is the question of the location of the linguistic boundary of Han in the direction of the Tanana. This leads to the second problem but, before engaging in a discussion of the complications it raises, I might record three of the difficulties which seem to have complicated the work of the linguists, especially when they have been forced to depend on data recorded by ethnographers. The first difficulty results from the mixing of aboriginal dialects as a result of long displacements of the speakers; the second is the acceptance of the location of the recording of linguistic data as the basis of geographic allocation rather than the provenience of the informant, while the third is inadequate transcription.

The first of these difficulties has frequently come to my attention among the Han. It is clear from Murray (1910: 53) that many of the Han and Kutchin were learning the other's language in the middle of the nineteenth century. Numerous representatives of the same two groups also were brought together for a long period by the attractions of Dawson.

In this connection, another statement by Krauss seems both pertinent and important. He writes that Han "is probably partially mutually intelligible with Kutchin (and there is probably lots of passive bilingualism with Kutchin by way of the Han), but [Han is] hardly at all intelligible (without learning) with Upper Tanana [Nabesna] and Tutchone."

At this point it will be possible to interpolate a note on terminology of a quite different linguistic order with the hope that explanation may eliminate the possibility of confusion. In 1936, I attempted a consistent and orderly presentation of the distribution of Athapaskan groups, applying names which met certain desiderata when possible. These were: (1) A name of three syllables or less, especially because of the limited space on most maps; (2) a name previously recognized for the group; and (3) a name easily pronounced (Osgood 1936b: 6). Thus I came to the choice of Nabesna for one group on the basis of Allen's (1887: 136) statement: "The natives of the Upper Tananá call that river Nabesná. For uniformity and by analogy to the term applied by Copper River natives to themselves, I have called them Nabesnatánas." The latter term which was adopted by the *Handbook* (1910, *2:* 4) was reduced by the elimination of the final two syllables which, with slight variations, mean "man" in many of the Athapaskan languages. Personally, I have no strong attachment to the name Nabesna, but I do think that modifying the term Tanana for a group of equivalent status has proved itself confusing. Therefore, with apologies to McKennan with whom I long have had polite exchanges on the subject, I shall continue to use Nabesna, rather than the incongruous Upper Tanana.

To turn to the second problem and the movements of the Han during the nineteenth century, I am primarily concerned with their appearance at and around Kechumstuk on the upper Fortymile River, a settlement that certainly mushroomed after the early gold strikes in that area. As an introduction I shall mention McKennan's (1959: 22–3) two paragraphs beginning: "To the north the journey from the upper Tanana to the Yukon is an easy one and there was considerable intercourse between the natives of the two areas." In these paragraphs, if I read them correctly, there are four opinions, outlined below.

1) The Indians at Tanana Crossing (hereafter called the Tanacross) are the same Indians who formerly lived at Lake Mansfield to the north.

2) There was always a traditional cleavage between the Nabesna and the Tanacross and they were often at war.

3) The Nabesna claim there is a closer linguistic relation between the Tanacross and the Ahtena of the Copper River than with themselves (Ahtena and Nabesna, incidentally, are not mutually intelligible languages).

4) The Tanacross had little or no contact with the Indians lower down on the Tanana because of the series of rapids.

In other words, we seem to be left with a small band of Indians who are not clearly related to any of the larger groups, and in an area that in the early nine-teenth century was one of potential movements on the part of the Han because of the attraction of Russian trading posts; and later in the nineteenth century it was one of considerable disruption both because of the advent of prospectors and the installation of the military telegraph line running from Valdez through Tanana Crossing directly to Eagle.

Having assumed that the entire drainage of the Fortymile River was in Han territory and that the Kechumstuk Indians were Han both for that and various other reasons, I was aroused by the possibility that the Tanacross also were an extension of the Han, after rereading a book by Hudson Stuck who journeyed by dog team from Tanana Crossing (Tanacross) to Eagle by the way of the Forty-mile River in March 1910. Somewhere near Lake Mansfield he encountered Indians of whom he states (1916: 261–2): "Already the chief difficulty we had to encounter presented itself. These people did not speak the language of the lower Tanana and middle Yukon—Arthur's language—at all. Their speech had more affinity with the upper Yukon language, and it dawned upon me that they were not of the migration that had pushed up the Tanana River from the Yukon, as all the natives as far as the Salchaket certainly did, were not of that tribe or that movement at all, but had come across country by the Ketchumstock from the neighborhood of Eagle—and were of the Porcupine and Peel River stock. This was certainly a surprise; I had deemed all the Tanana River Indians of the same extraction and tongue, but the stretch of bad water from the Salchaket to the Tanana Crossing was evidently the boundary of two peoples." This last point would be a confirmation of greater significance with relation to the linguistic data previously presented, did I not seem to remember that Stuck's "Arthur" was my informant Arthur Wright, an Indian gentleman of considerable sophistica-tion who had married a white missionary nurse.

To interpret and summarize what Stuck is saying, however, there seem to be two positive points, first, that the Indians on the Tanana River below Tanacross speak an Athapaskan language distinct from that of the Indians he encountered near Tanacross, and second, that the latter Indians had come from the country around Eagle, which would make me believe they were Han, not Kutchin as he seems to infer.

As to the second point, I am not so content since what "dawned upon" him sounds like the admission of a guess, although possibly a correct one, while his reference to "Porcupine and Peel River stock" suggests a general ignorance of tribal distributions.

The leader of the Indians that Stuck was referring to was an old man named Chief Isaac—apparently too old to be the father of Charlie Isaac of Dawson, but not too old to be his grandfather. He had been on the Yukon at one time, however, and others of the group had been to Kechumstuk (Stuck 1916: 270).

"The Tanana Crossing is a central spot for the Indians of this region," writes

Stuck (1916: 272). "Two days up the river was the village of the Tetlin [Nabesna] Indians. Two days into the mountain range were the Mentasta [Ahtena] Indians. Two days across towards the Yukon were the Ketchum-stock [Han?] Indians." I might add that the earliest reference to the Kechumstuk Indians I have found is that of Wells (1891: 412), who in 1890 was looking for them in the Fortymile country. He writes: "There was a disquieting report at the gulch that the Kitts-chunstalks had temporarily left their village, some forty miles away, and had gone on a fishing excursion to Tanana." There was obviously some fact in the rumor as there was no one to be found at Kechumstuk when he arrived, whereas he met two of the Indians near the Tanana shortly thereafter (Wells 1891: 412, 431).

From Tanacross, Stuck moved on to Lake Mansfield and the Fortymile River where he found fifteen Indians, and then into and across the Kechumstuk Flats following the telegraph line running to Eagle, an area he speaks of as one of the greatest of all caribou countries, with fragments of fences used in surrounds being passed all during the day (Stuck 1916: 276). I also recall that Allen (1887: 138) said, "A miner informed me that while prospecting between the Yukon and Tanana Rivers he found a 'game fence' 30 miles long."

Reaching Kechumstuk, Stuck (1916: 277–8) discovered all the natives ("there are some forty souls in this tribe") gone in the direction of Chicken Creek. He found them degraded by white contacts (the men cursed and the women chewed tobacco), but most of the adults had been baptized. Earlier, Stuck (p. 270) had reported that Kechumstuk had been visited by "our missionary at Eagle," a fact that suggests relationships between people in the same settlements.

After reviewing the available evidence, and particularly the significance of caribou movements, it reinforced my previous opinion that Kechumstuk, or sites in the immediate area, had originally been a Han winter hunting camp. With this assumption in mind, I wrote to McKennan asking if he considered the people at Kechumstuk to be Han. Helpful as usual, he immediately responded as follows:

> No, I do not consider the Ketchumstuk group to be Han, but rather another of the several bands inhabiting the upper Tanana Valley above the mouth of the Goodpaster River. The Mosquito Fork (on which Ketchumstuk is located) was the fall and winter caribou hunting territory of the band whose summer fishing camp was at Lake Mansfield (earlier at Dix Chada). Ketchumstuk is now abandoned and most of its former inhabitants now live at Tanacross.

The same nomadic subsistence pattern characterized the next downriver group who had summer camps at Healy and George Lakes and did their fall and winter caribou hunting on the Middle Fork of the North Fork of the Fortymile in the general area of the now abandoned settlement of Joseph. When the telegraph line came through stations were located at both Joseph and Ketchumstuk and as a result semi-permanent native settlements grew up at each station. The mining activity at Chicken also probably held some natives at Ketchumstuk and conceivably some Han stragglers may have joined this settlement also. However, my Ketchumstuk informants told me that the Han people only came up the Fortymile as far as Chicken, and they did this only occasionally.

As you may recall from my monograph this same subsistence pattern characterized my Upper Tanana bands—the Last Tetling–Tetling groups doing their fall hunting on the Dennison Fork of the Fortymile and the lower Nabesna band doing theirs on the upper Ladue River. Such is the geography of this area that it is much easier to get to these upper stretches from the Tanana then it is from the Yukon.

Thus I found my speculative canoe sinking with the bark ripped apart fore and aft. The case for Kechumstuk—apparently the approved spelling (Baker 1906: 357)—cannot be considered completely despoiled by this wetting, however, until the available evidence is presented. It can be marshaled as follows.

1) The area around the headwaters of the Fortymile River is known to be superb caribou hunting country with numerous old surround fences (Allen, 1887: 138; Stuck 1916: 276). If it is less accessible from the Yukon than from the Tanana, it was in no sense beyond the reach of people who, all agree, came up the Fortymile as far as Chicken. Additional confirmation on this point comes from Wells (1900: 515), a traveler of considerable experience in the north who in 1890 ascended the Fortymile to Lake Mansfield and crossed the Tanana. The latter, he writes, "is a river which can be easily reached from the Yukon from above or below Dawson by following up Sixty-Mile Creek or Forty-Mile Creek to the Tanana Divide, otherwise known as the Razorback. The ridge, which is easily ascended from the Yukon valley, is not over 2,500 feet in height, according to observations with a boiling-point thermometer. It is always possible to strike a good summer trail across the hills from Dawson to the head waters of the Tanana without following either of the streams mentioned. The country is rolling, but not mountainous."

2) A small group like the Tanacross could hardly have prevented the Han, who were noted for aggressiveness from hunting in the area. Furthermore, my informant Walter Benjamin of Eagle specifically mentions the Han bringing down caribou from the head of Fortymile River.

3) Since the earliest Russian trading posts were in areas to which Tanana Crossing is on a presumed trail, movement toward such posts for purposes of trade follows an established pattern of the Han. We are cognizant of the fact that the direction of the trade swung the other way after posts were established on the middle Yukon (cf. McKennan 1959: 28).

4) The mention by Schwatka (1885a: 247) in 1883 of numerous visitors at Nuklako, one of the principal Han villages on the Yukon, as being Tanana Indians (peculiarly pronounced *Ta-nah'-nee*) is significant. So many visitors from an *alien* tribe during the fishing season is a little incredible. Perhaps they were Han from the Tanana area.

5) When a missionary to the Han at Eagle visits Kechumstuk, it at least suggests a close relationship between the people involved (Stuck 1916: 270).

6) Schmitter (1910: 11–2) reports: "Joseph, the chief at Kechumstuk, has two boys which, it is said, were taken from the Tanana when they were infants, and, strange to say, such kidnapping appears not to be a serious offense." The "Joseph" of this sentence relates to a "They" in a previous one, and "They" are clearly the Han Indians in Schmitter's mind. The kidnapping of children strikes this Athapaskanist as strange. More likely the children were from a related group in the Tanana area. If so, admittedly, this assumption might be used for considering the chief at Kechumstuk not to be Han. Perhaps Joseph had a wife from somewhere close to, or on, the Tanana, for it is difficult to believe Schmitter was mistaken about Joseph himself.

7) Furthermore, Schmitter (p. 14) states that the Porcupine River Kutchin were not invited to a potlatch when the Eagle chief died (ca. 1906) because they were not related to the tribe. On the other hand, invitations were sent to the Moosehide, Charlie Creek, and Kechumstuk Indians. The implication is obvious.

8) Brooks (1900: 390) states on a journey to Eagle: "We saw nothing of the Indians of the Fortymile region. Their chief village is said to be Kechumstuk, which is on the Tanana trail, near the head of the South Fork of the Fortymile." It is difficult to correlate "Indians of the Fortymile region" with any but Han.

9) Chief Isaac, the well-known leader of the Klondike band of the Han, who died in 1933, was believed by his son Charlie Isaac to have been born in the Tanana area. Charlie Isaac believed that he himself was born in 1912 at Kechumstuk. He was raised at Fortymile and his father's brothers lived at Eagle (Slobodin 1963a: 21). If this family were not Han Indians, then the group whose aboriginal culture has been presented in this monograph must be redefined.

Part of the problem in reconstructing the situation is that over a century of time is involved. Actually, I still have not obtained much help from linguistic studies on this particular point since the Tanacross were at the extreme southern end of what Krauss refers to as "Transitional Tanana," a grouping clearly not Nabesna, however. Obviously, the difficulties previously mentioned with respect to linguistic work (p. 148) apply especially to this region of so many uncertainties. I do not wish to be insistent or antagonistic but, for the time being, I shall hold to the hypothesis that at least during the nineteenth century the upper reaches of the Fortymile River, and thus including Kechumstuk, were Han territory. As for the Lake Mansfield Indians being Han, that thought I shall allow to remain in the shadowy realm of speculation, and happily reaffirm or relinquish it with the presentation of more factual sunlight.

We come now to the third and last problem about which I have chosen to speculate. It centers, as I have said, around the shift in economy resulting from the fur trade into which the Han were enticed by the establishment of Russian and English companies. It is proper to admit, first of all, that I have already conceived of the life of the Han as quite different before 1847 than it became after that date.

The picture I have composed is drawn from a palette of experience that includes the variously tinted views of Athapaskans that have been gained along such rivers as the Peace, the Athabasca, the Mackenzie, the Copper, the Tanana, and particularly the Yukon. To these, the more atypical environments of Great Bear Lake and Cook Inlet must be added. I say this not to disavow prejudice with respect to specific subcultures, for I believe that deep prejudices lie concealed in every ethnographer, but rather to indicate that my prejudices are not narrowly based. I do not enjoy long periods of exposure to intense cold (and believe with most northerners that those who say that they do either have motivations for boasting or are weakened by short memories). I am, however, readily seduced by beautiful country. I have hunted and fished, and more of the latter than the former, but neither one nor the other when it could be avoided. I prefer a canoe to finding my way through pressure ridges of ice, and I would more quickly take to snowshoes and a toboggan than pack overland in the summer. I have some other mild prejudices such as those against mosquitoes and small gnats, but these prove so universal they need not be mentioned. Having thus presented my biases, I take up my brush and color a sketch of Han aboriginal subsistence patterns as I think they existed before 1847.

Everything I have learned about the Athapaskans, and particularly the data gathered together on the Han, leads me to the opinion that, like the people of the lower Yukon, they depended for food primarily on fishing, and in fishing primarily on salmon. I see them as having more or less permanent winter residences, together with nearby fish camps to which they spread out in summer in order to catch and dry their principal food. It is also clear that they hunted caribou on the migration routes of those animals primarily to obtain their skins from which to make clothing and other necessary things, and only secondarily for meat. Cooperative efforts were made at least once, if not twice in a year. Sporadic hunting parties also set out for caribou and other animals such as moose and mountain sheep when the men were motivated by mood or obvious opportunities. Apart from hunting trips, traveling around the country was limited to attending ceremonial functions to which one's band was invited, or even less frequently to conduct a raid in reprisal for the actions of unfriendly neighboring tribes.

Trying to view things as would an Athapaskan Indian under aboriginal conditions, I believe the above pattern of subsistence practices would emerge as the only sensible one if it were conceived from a knowledge of the Han territory alone. That territory is unique within the combined middle and upper Yukon regions as I have defined them (cf. p. 29). Below the Han, in the Yukon Flats, the conditions are made so unusual by the circuitous course of the river and its sloughs that it has been brought into question whether Indians ever lived in the immediate vicinity of Fort Yukon in aboriginal times (Schwatka 1885a: 280). Such a hypothesis may not have been founded on an adequate background of knowledge, but it serves my argument in setting off the much-admired stretch of the Yukon belonging to the Han. Above Han territory, the salmon decrease in quality and number, while the Tutchone country, even in its northern parts, has a character of its own. When we recall that the other Athapaskan neighbors of the Han did not actually live on the great river, and in some cases were even beyond the reaches of salmon on tributary streams, the point should have effectively been made that the environmental condition of the Han was something very special within the vast country east of the Tanana River.

In that situation, I assert that the Han had a fully adequate subsistence pattern based on salmon and that they would be unlike any other Athapaskans I have ever known to adopt a life of greater nomadism than was necessary during weather recorded to be of the coldest in which man has learned to survive.

Perhaps I should interpolate here a reference to Campbell's subsistence pattern in the north. It seems to have been an implicit part of his exceptional conquest of the environment that in every place he established a new post, his primary concern was to set up fisheries, and where there were not good ones, he had a poor opinion of the locality for settlement. I should add that these were mostly winter fisheries and in areas where either salmon were lacking or relatively limited in numbers. His activities in this respect are particularly obvious around Fort Selkirk where he stationed himself for the longest time (cf. Campbell, 1958: at Halkett, 34; at Frances Lake, 62, 71, 73, 75; at Pelly Banks, 87, 90; at Selkirk, 83–4, 85, 86, 87, 124). With even a limited background of experience in the north, one might deduce that the wisdom of Campbell's procedure was not only shared by the Indians but learned from them. It would not even be unreasonable to examine into the question as to whether the innumerable references to the Indians starving—apart from the prejudicial value system of the whites (cf. Osgood 1932: 37–8)—was not a correlate of the newly motivated mobility.

Now we approach nearer to the crux of the problem, which centers around the shift in the Indian economy. When the Han first discovered there was a very exceptional supply of foreign goods filtering into the country, what did they have to offer in exchange? If the new material was coming over the mountains, at the very beginning they may have offered dried salmon. The Athapaskans who lived primarily on fish were extremely fond of it, and those for whom meat was more common often valued it even more as a delicacy. In any event the shift in trade items to prime furs such as mink, marten, beaver, and fox must have quickly taken place. For a while, it is unlikely that the Han had to go very far to find them, since before they were so highly valued as a trade item, these animals flourished largely unappreciated in their natural habitats, to which Indian proximity was of very little consequence.

Probably the most active men who became involved in the opportunities for trade began to travel out toward its source. It seems almost certain, with all the Russian posts on Cook Inlet in the 1790s, that the flow of goods was reaching northeast to the Tanana River. Surely the Ahtena brought trade material into that region not long afterward (Allen 1877: 60–1). Such goods must have been a magnet for the Han, pulling them toward Lake Mansfield.

In the first half of the nineteenth century, trading posts were established on the lower Mackenzie—about 1815 at Fort Norman and perhaps even earlier at Fort Good Hope. Trade articles undoubtedly moved westward before contact was actually made with the Hudson's Bay Company traders in the 1840s. Shortly afterward the indications seem clear that the Han found their way to Bell's early post on the Porcupine, if not to Fort Macpherson itself. The details do not matter as much as the evidence that the Han were on the move.

Another fascinating bit of evidence of mobility is the precise statement of McQuesten (1952: 4) with reference to what was probably the wood crew of the steamer *Yukon* during the summer of 1874 when Fort Reliance was founded: "We had an old Chief called Catsah and ten of his men aboard—they were Trondiak [Klondike Han] Indians." I might add that during my own time in Alaska and the Yukon, it was still customary to carry Indians on the stern-wheel river steamers for the purpose of conveying four-foot lengths of wood aboard the vessel from the piles along the banks stacked up during the winter by the wood choppers. But how did eleven Han Indians obtain the jobs on the single steamer on the Yukon which had never been as far up as the Klondike? I shall have to guess, but before I do, I am fortunate to recall that Campbell (1958: 132, 137) wrote in his diary entry of July 21, 1852, while returning from his second trip to Fort Yukon and on receiving a message from Stewart at Fort Selkirk: "Sent Catza [sic] off with a note for him," and again in another entry on August 30, 1852, nine days after the sack of Fort Selkirk, "Catsah arrives with a note from Mr. Stewart." Most probably, the Han chief was in the employ of the Hudson's Bay Company and may well have been for some time. As for my guess, I suggest that Catsah had established his relationship with the company through Murray at Fort Yukon, that he was then recommended to Campbell by Hardisty in 1851, and that he served the traders off and on for the following twenty-odd years.

Like most of the Athapaskans, the Han became trappers, and that activity developed a new pattern of life, another kind of mobility. By the 1880s the repeating rifle must have been available with its inevitable invitation not only to deplete but to disturb the supply of game. The Athapaskans and much of the game depended to a large degree on their ears. Both were extremely disturbed by strange sounds and the effect of the piercing new noises may never be adequately assessed.

For a period of up to fifty years after the common use of the really effective gun began, it would seem that the enjoyment of caribou and moose meat increased until such important animals became more difficult to find, and the Indians shifted to a primary dependence on store food as did the white man, a circumstance no doubt greatly appreciated by the offspring of caribou and moose. Although still largely dependent upon salmon, the amount of fishing decreased.

The Klondike to the early prospectors was "known only as a great creek for Salmon" (Bruce 1899: 192), and the upper side of its confluence, later the river settlement of Lousetown which was across the Klondike from Dawson, has not infrequently been reported as an important Indian site. Slobodin (1963a: 5) states that in the summer, the largest concentration of Indians was at this fish camp. Therefore it is puzzling that on that famous day of August 1896 when, according to the seemingly well-documented story, Robert Henderson found George Carmack at the mouth of the Klondike and told him to look for gold on Rabbit Creek (later Bonanza), the only Indians ever mentioned are Carmack's two Tagish companions, Charlie and Jim. Was there an active Han fish camp there also? Certainly it was the middle of the fishing season. Unless we find evidence to the contrary, I suspect there were more Indians to be found around the dance halls of Fortymile; and why not? It would seem from the evidence that the extraordinary little cities, as they were called, which grew with incredible speed when fertilized by gold, had almost completely disoriented the normal activities of the Han. It is clear that the Han became moose hunters for the hungry men of the Klondike, and they had certainly played that role and others as well in earlier mining camps, places perhaps even more fascinating because of their novelty.

What has really concerned me is the change in the Han subsistence pattern and its effect on Han economy. My problem has been to determine not the fact but the degree of change, and I have probably raised more questions than I have resolved. Nevertheless, I am content that the evidence shows that between the fur traders and the miners, hunting perhaps became as significant as fishing in providing food in the period between 1847 and 1897, and that store food based on a money economy became most important after 1897, whereas before 1847, fishing had been the basis of the economy.

This being the case, I find the Han to be allied with the other major river groups —some of the Kutchin, the Koyukon, the Ahtena, the Tanana, and the Ingalik, together secondarily with the Tanaina on the coast—as primarily salmon-eating people with a basically sedentary economy. Around the Han was an almost enclosed ring of Indians—the Nabesna, the Tutchone, and some of the Kutchin— whose subsistence patterns were based as much, if not more, on hunting than on fishing, and whose pattern of life might be regarded as seminomadic. Again, however, it is a question as to how much the fur trade and complementary material culture were responsible for a change in the lifeways of the people of this partly broken ring.

Appendix A

Principal Sources by Times of Record and of Publication

Since it may be difficult for a reader to remember the relationship between the time of observation and the time of publication of data on which this monograph is based, it is hoped that this simplified table correlating these dates may be a convenience. Not all the sources have been included but most of those of which the writers were actually in Han territory or that of adjacent Athapaskan groups have been included. The authors are listed in the order of that contact, although for a few the exact extension of the time spent in the area is not certain. Under *Publication* is given the date of the most significant (and usually the first) publication from the point of view of this monograph. The authors supplying most of the ethnographic information on the Han are indicated by an asterisk.

Author	Contact	Publication
Campbell	1843, 1848–52	1958
Bell (via Richardson)	1844	1851
Murray*	1847–48	1910
Hardisty	1848–54+	1872
Jones	1860+ (?)	1872
Whymper	1867	1868
Dall	1867	1870
Raymond	1869	1900
McQuesten	1873–99 (?)	1952
Sim (via Wesbrook)	1881–85	1969
Schwatka*	1883	1885
Wilson (via Schwatka)	1883	1885
Ogilvie	1887	1913
Adney*	1897–98	1900
Schmitter*	1906+ (?)	1910
Osgood*	1932	1936
McKennan	1933	1959
Slobodin*	1961, 1962	1963
McClellan	1966	Notes

Appendix B

Tabulation of Han Culture Traits

The following list represents the occurrence of aboriginal culture traits and a few historic ones among the Han Indians on the basis of the data in this volume. Although limited in number, they provide a trait index to this study as well as facilitate comparisons with previous ones. Discussion of the trait may not be limited to the page given but continue into those following. Since a trait list was not consistently used during my brief period of work among the Han, few negative data have been supplied. The symbols used are given below:

X	Present	H	Historic borrowing
0	Absent	F	Animal killed for fur
R	Rare	( )	Information doubtful
T	Taboo	?	Applicability of data doubtful

The symbol for the absence of a trait, considered more exactly, means that informants do not know of the trait. The value of the negative statement does not equal that of a positive, since informants are limited in their knowledge as well as memory of their culture. The arrangement follows that of the Kutchin and Tanaina trait lists previously published.

Food
  Fish, etc.:

Salmon	X	98
Whitefish	X	105
Lake trout	0	106
Grayling	X	106
Jackfish (pike)	X	106
Loche (burbot)	X	106
Sucker	X	106

  Land animals:

Caribou	X	107
Moose	X	109
Black bear	X	110
Grizzly bear	X	110
Beaver	X	110
Muskrat	(0)	111
Lynx	X	111
Rabbit	X	111
Porcupine	X	111

Groundhog (marmot, woodchuck)........................ R   111
Ground squirrel..................................... X   111
Mountain sheep...................................... X   111
Mountain goat....................................... R   111
Fox... F   111
Otter... F   111
Mink.. F   111
Ermine.. F   111
Wolverine... F   111
Wolf.. T   111
Dog... T   111
Birds:
   Sea gull... 0   111
   Owl.. X   112
   Goose.. X   112
   Eagle.. 0   112
   Raven.. T   113
   Ducks.. X   112
   Grouse... X   112
   Ptarmigan.. X   112
   Swan... X   112
   Loon... X   112
Vegetable foods:
   Berry eating..................................... X   113
   Blueberry.. X   113
   Cranberry.. X   113
   Strawberry....................................... R   113
   Red raspberry.................................... R   113
   Gooseberry....................................... X   113
   Parsnip-like tuber............................... X   113
   Spruce fiber..................................... (0)   113
   Birch fiber...................................... X   113
   Cottonwood fiber................................. X   114
   Wild onions...................................... X   114
   Wild rhubarb..................................... X   114
   Wild roses....................................... 0   114
   Mushrooms.. 0   114
Chewing spruce gum.................................. X   114
Tobacco chewing..................................... H   114
Tobacco smoking..................................... H   114
Snuffing.. H   114
Fish primary food................................... X   115
Fish spearing....................................... X   69

Hunting:
    Bear spearing.. X   110
    Hunting with dogs................................... X   109
    Caribou surrounds................................... X   108
    Caribou speared..................................... X   109
    Semicircular moose tracking......................... X   109
    Giving away kill.................................... X   114
Smoke drying... X   106
Foetal animals eaten................................... X   48
Pit baking... X   114
Hot-stone boiling...................................... X   114
Fire drill... X   72
Strike-a-light... X   72
Dress
    Tailored clothing................................... X   90
    Caribou skin most important......................... X   90
    Gut clothing.. 0   90
    Fish-skin clothing.................................. 0   90
    Bird-skin clothing.................................. 0   90
    Woven rabbit-skin clothing.......................... X   92
    Rabbit-skin weaving................................. X   93, 98
    Open coat... H?   97
    Parka... X   91
    Blanket parka....................................... X?   91
    Shirt... X   91
    One-piece trousers and footwear..................... X   92
    Moccasins... X   94
    Grass duffel.. X   94
    Robe.. X   95
    Mittens... X   94
    Belt.. X   91
    Head band... X   95
    Skin hats... X   95
    Bark chair baby carrier............................. X   48
    Clothing decoration:
        Skin fringe..................................... X   95
        Feather... X   95
        Fur... X   95
        Porcupine quill................................. X   95
        Bead.. X   95
    Personal adornment:
        Tattooing (needle and sinew).................... X?   95
        Tattooing (puncture)............................ X?   95

Toboggans	H	82
Dog packing	X	82
Dogs hitched in tandem	0	82
Ability to swim	0?	61
Trade	X	66, 77
Manufactures and Implements:		
Techniques:		
Tanning	X	65
Woven basketry	X	66
Matting	X	66
Pottery	0	66
Lines:		
Babiche	X	66
Rawhide	X	66
Sinew	X	66
Willow bark	X	66
Whole willow	X	66
Spruce root	X	66
Braided	X	66
Twisted	X	66
Nets:		
Gill	X	66
Dipnet	X	67
Willow bark	X	66
Skin line	X	68
Simple trap fish weir	X	66
Basket trap fish weir	X	68
Simple detachable fish spear	X	69
Toggle-headed detachable fish spear	0	69
Fishhooks	X	105
Club (for fish)	X	69
Simple harpoon	X	69
Lance	X	69
Caribou snares	X	108
Moose snares	X	110
Bear spear	X	70
Bows and arrows:		
Bow with guard	X	70
Blunt bird arrows	X	71
2 rows of feathers	X	71
3 rows of feathers	X	71
Mediterranean arrow release	X	71
Bola	X?	64

Knives:
    Bone.. X   71
    Copper.. X   71
Scrapers:
    Bone.. X   66
    End scraper... X   72
Tooth awl.. X   72
Cut bone awl.. X   72
Stone adz... X   72
Stone hammer... X   72
Prehistoric iron implements................................. H   71
Pump-drill.. X   72
Containers:
    Sewn wood dishes.. 0   73
    Horn spoons... X   73
    Wood spoons... X   73
    Birch-bark baskets.. X   73
    Spruce-root baskets....................................... X   73
    Skin bags... X   74
    Babiche game bags... X   74
    Clay pots... 0   66
Snow shovel... X   74
War
    Causes:
        To gain women... X   64
        To gain property.. X?   63
        Revenge... X   64
    Weapons:
        Bow... X   70
        Knife... X   71
        Horn club... X   65
        Lance... X   69
    Bear skin armor... 0   63
    Slat armor.. 0   63
    War chiefs.. X   65
    Decapitation.. 0   63
Arts and Amusements:
    Cures:
        Spruce gum for snowblindness.............................. X?   58
        Sweat bathing... X   88
    Red paint most important.................................. X   58
    Paints:
        Red... X   58

Dyeing	X	59
Hair decoration	X	59, 62
Porcupine quill work	X	59
Drawing on snow	X	57
Musical instruments:		
Tambourine drum	X	55, 59
Plank drum	0	55
Willow whistle	X	59
Songs:		
Shaman's	X	37, 59
Love	X	59
Ceremonial	X	59
War	X	59
Games:		
Wrestling	X	59
Running races	X	60
Rope tug-of-war	X	60
Shinny	X	60
Tossing in moose skin	X	60
Hoop and pole	X	60
Ring and pin	0	60
Hand games	X	60
Blindman's buff	X	61
Swings	X	61
Snow-snake	X	61
Ball-in-air game	X	61
Social Organization		
Matrilineal sibs (Clans)	X	39
Exogamous moieties	(X)	40
Social classes	(0)	41
Slaves	0	41
Strong chieftainship	(X)	41
Inherited chieftainship (patrilineal)	0	42
Wealth primary prestige factor	X	41
Councils	X	42
2-family social unit	X	84
Blood brother partnership	0?	42
Communal eating	X	114
Individual ownership:		
Ownership marks	0	43
Patrilineal inheritance	0	43
Adoption	X	48
Blood revenge	X	43

Fire-man	X	39
Moon being	X?	38
Star being	X?	38
Amulets (Fetiches)	X	38
Shamanism	X	37, 58
Shamanism:		
Male and female shamans	X	38
Public performance	X	37
Power from animals	X	37, 58
Power through dreams	X	37
Masks	0	39

Bibliography

ADNEY, EDWIN TAPPAN
    1900a   Moose Hunting with the Tro-chu-tin. *Harpers New Monthly Magazine*, vol. 100, no. 598, pp. 494–507. New York.

ADNEY, EDWIN TAPPAN
    1900b   *The Klondike Stampede*, pp. xiii, 471. New York and London.

ADNEY, EDWIN TAPPAN
    1902   The Indian Hunter of the Far Northwest on the Trail to the Klondike. *Outing*, vol. 39, no. 6, pp. 623–33. New York.

ADNEY, EDWIN TAPPAN, AND HOWARD I. CHAPELLE
    1964   *The Bark Canoes and Skin Boats of North America*. Museum of Hist. and Technology, Bull. 230, pp. xiv, 242. Washington, D.C.

ALLEN, HENRY T.
    1887   *Report of an Expedition to the Copper, Tananá, and Koyukuk Rivers, in the Territory of Alaska in the Year 1885*, pp. 1–172. Washington, D.C.

ANONYMOUS
    1916   *The Yukon Territory: Its History and Resources*. Dept. of the Interior, Canada, pp. xi, 233. Ottawa.

ARCHER, F. A.
    1929   *A Heroine of the North: Memoirs of Charlotte Selina Bompas (1830–1917) Wife of the First Bishop of Selkirk (Yukon) with Extracts of Her Journal and Letters*, pp. 1–187. London.

BAKER, MARCUS
    1906   *Geographic Dictionary of Alaska*. Bull. 299, U.S. Geological Survey, Dept. of Interior, 2nd ed., pp. 1–690. Washington, D.C.

BALIKCI, ASEN
    1963   *Vunta Kutchin Social Change: A Study of the People of Old Crow, Yukon Territory*, pp. iv, 161. Ottawa.

BROOKS, ALFRED HULSE
    1900   A Reconnaissance from Pyramid Harbor to Eagle City, Alaska, Including a Description of the Copper Deposits of the Upper White and Tanana Rivers. *21st Annual Report of the U.S. Geol. Survey, 1899–1900*, pt. II, pp. 331–91. Washington, D.C.

BRUCE, MINER
    1899   *Alaska: Its History and Resources, Gold Fields, Routes and Scenery*, pp. x, 237. New York and London.

CAMPBELL, ROBERT (John W. Todd, Ed.)
    1958   *Two Journals of Robert Campbell (Chief Factor Hudson's Bay Company) 1808–1853. Early Journal 1808–1851; Later Journal [Diary] Sept. 1850 to Feb. 1853*, limited ed., pp. 1–151. Seattle.

CHERNENKO, M. B., G. A. AGRANAT, AND Y. E. BLOMKVIST (Eds.) (Trans. by Penelope Rainey)
    1967   *Lieutenant Zagoskin's Travels in Russian America, 1824–1844: The First Eth-*

nographic and Geographic Investigations in the Yukon and Kuskokwim Valleys of Alaska, pp. xiv, 358. Toronto.

CODY, HIRAM ALFRED
    1908   *An Apostle of the North: Memoirs of the Right Reverend William Carpenter Bompas, D.D.*, pp. xviii, 385. London.

COLBY, MERLE
    1941   *A Guide to Alaska: Last American Frontier*, pp. lxv, 427. New York.

DALL, WILLIAM H.
    1870a *Alaska and Its Resources*, pp. xii, 627. Boston.

DALL, WILLIAM H.
    1870b On the Distribution of Native Tribes of Alaska and the Adjacent Territory. *Proc., American Assoc. for the Advancement of Science*, vol. 18, pp. 263–73. Cambridge, Mass.

DALL, WILLIAM H.
    1877   *Tribes of the Extreme Northwest.* Contrib. to North American Ethnology, vol. 1, pt. 1, pp. 7–106. Washington, D.C.

DAWSON, G. M.
    1889   Report on an Exploration in the Yukon District, etc. *Annual Report, Geological Survey of Canada*, n. s. vol. 3, pt. 1 (1887–88), pp. 7B–277B. Montreal.

DRUCKER, PHILIP
    1965   *Cultures of the North Pacific Coast*, pp. xvi, 243. San Francisco.

EVERMANN, BARTON WARREN, AND EDMUND LEE GOLDSBOROUGH
    1907   The Fishes of Alaska. *Bull., Bureau of Fisheries*, Dept. of Commerce and Labor, vol. 26, pp. 219–360. Washington, D.C.

GILBERT, CHARLES H., AND HENRY O'MALLEY
    1921   Investigation of the Salmon Fisheries of the Yukon River. In Ward T. Bower, "Alaska Fishery and Fur-Seal Industries in 1920," Appendix VI to *Report of the U.S. Commissioner of Fisheries for 1921*, pp. 128–154. Washington, D.C.

GSOVSKI, VLADIMIR
    1950   *Russian Administration of Alaska and the Status of the Alaskan Natives.* 81st Congress, 2nd Session, Document no. 152, pp. v, 99. Washington, D.C.

GUTSELL, BARBARA
    1953   Dawson City. *Geographical Bulletin*, no. 3, Dept. of Mines and Technical Surveys, Canada. Ottawa.

Handbook
    1907, 1910 See Hodge

HARDISTY, WILLIAM L.
    1872   The Loucheux Indians. *Annual Report of the Smithsonian Institution for 1866*, pp. 311–20. Washington, D.C.

HASKELL, WILLIAM B.
    1898   *Two Years in the Klondike and Alaskan Gold-fields, etc.*, pp. xxxii, 558. Hartford, Conn.

HELM, JUNE, AND N. O. LURIE
    1966   *The Dogrib Hand Game.* National Museum of Canada, Bull. 205, pp. viii, 101. Ottawa.

HODGE, FREDERICK WEBB (Ed.)
    1907, 1910 *Handbook of American Indians North of Mexico.* Bureau of American Ethnology, Bull. 30, pp. xi, 972; iv, 1221. Washington, D.C.

HOIJER, HARRY
    1963   Studies in the Athapaskan Languages, *Univ. of California Pub. in Linguistics,* vol. 29, pp. 1–29. Berkeley and Los Angeles.

HONIGMANN, JOHN J.
    1949   *Culture and Ethos of Kaska Society.* Yale Univ. Pub. in Anthropology, no. 40, pp. 1–365. New Haven.

HONIGMANN, JOHN J.
    1954   *The Kaska Indians: An Ethnographic Reconstruction.* Yale Univ. Pub. in Anthropology, no. 51, pp. 1–163. New Haven.

JONES, STRACHAN
    1872   The Kutchin Tribes. *Annual Report of the Smithsonian Institution for 1866,* pp. 320–7. Washington, D.C.

KIRK, ROBERT C.
    1899   *Twelve Months in Klondike,* pp. xii, 273. London.

LOTZ, J. R.
    [ca.1964]   *The Dawson Area: A Regional Monograph.* Yukon Research Project Series, no. 2, Dept. of Northern Affairs and National Resources, Canada, pp. 1–209. Ottawa.

McCLELLAN, CATHARINE
    1967   "Through Native Eyes: Indian Accounts of Events in the History of the American Northwest." Ms., pp. 1–106.

McCLELLAN, CATHARINE, AND D. RAINIER
    1950   Ethnological Survey of Southern Yukon Territory, 1948. *Bull. of the National Museum of Canada,* no. 118, pp. 50–53. Ottawa.

McCONNELL, R. G.
    1891   Report on an Exploration in the Yukon and Mackenzie Basins, N.W.T. *Annual Report, Geol. and Natural History Survey of Canada,* n.s., vol. IV, 1888–89, pp. 10-163D. Montreal.

McKENNAN, ROBERT A.
    1959   *The Upper Tanana Indians.* Yale Univ. Pub. in Anthropology, no. 55, pp. 1–226. New Haven.

McKENNAN, ROBERT A.
    1965   *The Chandalar Kutchin,* pp. 1–156. Montreal.

McQUESTEN, LEROY N.
    1952   *Recollections of Leroy N. McQuesten: Life in the Yukon 1871–1885,* pp. 1–14. Dawson City, Y.T.

MASON, J. ALDEN
    1946   *Notes on the Indians of the Great Slave Lake Area.* Yale Univ. Pub. in Anthropology, no. 34, pp. 1–46. New Haven.

MATHEWS, RICHARD
    1968   *The Yukon,* pp. 1–313. New York.

MURRAY, ALEXANDER HUNTER
    1910   Journal of the Yukon 1847–48; Edited with Notes by L. J. Burpee, F.R.G.S. *Publication of the Canadian Archives,* no. 4, pp. 1–125. Ottawa.

OGILVIE, WILLIAM
    1913   *Early Days on the Yukon and the Story of Its Gold Finds,* pp. xii, 306. Ottawa.

OSGOOD, CORNELIUS
  1932 The Ethnography of the Great Bear Lake Indians. *Annual Report for 1931, National Museum of Canada*, Bull. 70, pp. 31–97. Ottawa.

OSGOOD, CORNELIUS
  1934 Kutchin Tribal Distribution and Synonymy. *American Anthropologist*, n.s., vol. 36, no. 2, pp. 168–79. Menasha, Wis.

OSGOOD, CORNELIUS
  1936a *Contributions to the Ethnography of the Kutchin.* Yale Univ. Pub. in Anthropology, no. 14, pp. 1–189. New Haven.

OSGOOD, CORNELIUS
  1936b *The Distribution of the Northern Athapaskan Indians.* Yale Univ. Pub. in Anthropology, no. 7, pp. 1–23. New Haven.

OSGOOD, CORNELIUS
  1937 *The Ethnography of the Tanaina.* Yale Univ. Pub. in Anthropology, no. 16, pp. 1–229. New Haven.

OSGOOD, CORNELIUS
  1940 *Ingalik Material Culture.* Yale Univ. Pub. in Anthropology, no. 22, pp. 1–500. New Haven.

OSGOOD, CORNELIUS
  1958 *Ingalik Social Culture.* Yale Univ. Pub. in Anthropology, no. 53, pp. 1–289. New Haven.

OSGOOD, CORNELIUS
  1959 *Ingalik Mental Culture.* Yale Univ. Pub. in Anthropology, no. 56, pp. 1–195. New Haven.

PETITOT, R. P. E.
  1876 *Dictionnaire de la Langue Dènè-Dindjié: Dialectes Montagnais ou chippewayan, Peaux de Lievre et Loucheux.* Bibliothèque de Linguistique et d'Ethnographie Americaines, vol. 2, pp. lxxxviii, 367. Paris.

PETROF, IVAN
  1900 The Population and Resources of Alaska, 1880. *Compilation of Narratives of Explorations in Alaska*, pp. 53–281. Washington, D.C.

PETTITT, GEORGE A.
  1950 *The Quileute of La Push, 1775–1945.* Anthropological Records, vol. 14, pp. vi, 120. Berkeley.

PIKE, WARBURTON
  1896 *Through the Subarctic Forest*, pp. xiv, 295. London and New York.

RAYMOND, CHARLES WALKER
  1870 Letter from Capt. C. W. Raymond, U.S.A., on the Yukon River and Tribes (1869). *Report on Indian Affairs for 1869,* pp. 591–4. Washington, D.C.

RAYMOND, CHARLES WALKER
  1873 The Yukon River Region, Alaska. *Journal of the American Geographic Society of N.Y.*, vol. 3, pp. 158–92. New York.

RAYMOND, CHARLES P.[?]
  1900 Reconnoissance [sic] of the Yukon River, 1869. *Compilation of Narratives of Exploration in Alaska*, pp. 17–41. Washington, D.C.

RICHARDSON, JOHN
1851   *Arctic Searching Expedition: A Journal of a Boat-Voyage through Rupert's Land and the Arctic Sea, in Search of Sir John Franklin*, 2 vols., pp. viii, 413; vii, 426. London.

ROGERS, EDWARD S.
1965   *An Athapaskan Type of Knife*. Anthropological Papers, National Museum of Canada, no. 9, pp. 1–16. Ottawa.

ROSTLUND, ERHARD
1952   *Freshwater Fish and Fishing in Native North America*. Univ. of California Pub. in Geography, vol. 9, pp. x, 313. Berkeley.

SCHMITTER, FERDINAND
1910   Upper Yukon Native Customs and Folk-lore. *Smithsonian Miscellaneous Collections*, vol. 56, no. 4, pp. 1–30. Washington, D.C.

SCHWATKA, FREDERICK
1885a   *Along Alaska's Great River*, pp. 1–360. New York.

SCHWATKA, FREDERICK
1885b   The Great River of Alaska. *Century Magazine*, vol. 30, pp. 739–51, 819–29. New York.

SCHWATKA, FREDERICK
1900   Report of a Military Reconnaissance Made in Alaska in 1883. *Compilation of Narratives of Exploration in Alaska*, pp. 283–362. Washington, D.C.

SHELDON, CHARLES
1919   *The Wilderness of the Upper Yukon: A Hunter's Explorations for Wild Sheep in Sub-Arctic Mountains*, pp. xxiii, 364, 2nd ed. New York.

SHERWOOD, MORGAN B.
1965   *Exploration of Alaska, 1865–1900*, pp. xiv, 207. New Haven and London.

SLOBODIN, RICHARD
1963a   "Notes on the Han," pp. 1–23. Ms.

SLOBODIN, RICHARD
1963b   "The Dawson Boys"—Peel River Indians and the Klondike Gold Rush. *Polar Notes*, no. 5, pp. 24–36. Hanover, N.H.

SPURR, JOSIAH EDWARD
1900   *Through the Yukon Gold Diggings*, pp. 1–276. Boston.

STUCK, HUDSON
1916   *Ten Thousand Miles with a Dog Sled: A Narrative of Winter Travel in Interior Alaska*, pp. xxii, 420, 2nd ed. (1st ed. 1914). New York.

STUCK, HUDSON
1917   *Voyages on the Yukon and Its Tributaries: A Narrative of Summer Travel in the Interior of Alaska*, pp. xvi, 397. New York.

TANNER, ADRIAN
1966   Trappers, Hunters and Fishermen: Wildlife Utilization in the Yukon Territory. *Yukon Research Project Series*, no. 5, pp. v, 79. Ottawa.

THOMPSON, H. A.
1962   Temperature Normals, Averages, and Extremes in the Yukon Territory and the Northwest Territories. *Arctic*, vol. 15, no. 4, pp. 308–12. Montreal.

TOMPKINS, STUART RAMSAY
1945   *Alaska: Promyshlennik and Sourdough*, pp. xiv, 350. Norman, Okla.

TURNER, LUCIER M.
  1894 Ethnology of the Ungava District, Hudson Bay Territory. *Eleventh Annual Report of the Bureau of Ethnology*, pp. 159–350. Washington, D.C.
WALDEN, ARTHUR TREADWELL
  1931 *A Dog-Puncher on the Yukon*, pp. 1–289. Cambridge, Mass.
WELLS, E. HAZARD
  1891 Leslie Alaska Expedition. *Frank Leslie's Illustrated Newspaper*, vol. 72, pp. 354–5, 378, 396, 412, 431, 448; vol. 73, pp. 10, 59, 75, 106. New York.
WELLS, E. HAZARD
  1900 Up and Down the Yukon. *Compilation of Narratives of Exploration in Alaska*, pp. 509–16. Washington, D.C.
WESBROOK, MARY E.
  1969 A Venture into Ethnohistory: The Journals of Rev. V. C. Sim, Pioneer Missionary on the Yukon. *Polar Notes*, no. 9, pp. 34–45. Hanover, N.H.
WHYMPER, FREDERICK
  1868 *Travel and Adventure in the Territory of Alaska, Formerly Russian America— Now Ceded to the United States—and in Various Other Parts of the North Pacific*, pp. xix, 331. London.
WHYMPER, FREDERICK
  1869 Russian America or "Alaska": The Natives of the Youkon River and Adjacent Country. *Ethnological Soc. of London, Trans.*, n.s., vol. 7, pp. 167–85. London.
WICKERSHAM, JAMES
  1927 *A Bibliography of Alaskan Literature 1724–1924*. Misc. Pub. of the Alaska Agricultural College and School of Mines, vol. 1, pp. xvii, 635. Cordova, Alaska.
WYNNE-EDWARDS, V. C., ET AL.
  1947 North West Canadian Fish Surveys in 1944–1945. *Fisheries Research Board of Canada*, Bull. 72, pp. 6–20, Ottawa.

Plates

Explanation of Plates

One drawing and two photographs that were preserved in the early publications of Tappan Adney have been reissued as rare views of Han Indian life (Plate 1). Plates 2 and 3 present eight of the sixteen specimens found which can be attributed to the Han Indians with reasonable certainty following a search of more than a score of museums. A few specimens recorded from the Han could not be located in the museums that received them. Two spoons and a bow with a guard at the National Museum of Canada have not been illustrated as well as four specimens in Yale's Peabody Museum which were almost certainly made in the second quarter of the twentieth century, having been collected in 1932. Various other specimens which may well be Han have not been included since a recorded provenience such as "upper Yukon" may refer to the Kutchin or Tutchone Indians. Further search would probably uncover additional Han specimens, but it seems unlikely that many well-documented ones exist.

The specimens illustrated are in the National Museum of Natural History, Smithsonian Institution, Washington, D.C. (SI), and in the National Museum of Canada, Ottawa (NMC), to which institutions I am indebted for photographs and catalogue data.

PLATE 1

HAN INDIAN CAMPS

Top. Indian camp scene depicting children playing the throwing-stick game (after Adney 1900a: 503) (cf. pp. 60 and 86).

Middle. Chief Isaac's salmon racks and birch-bark canoe (after Adney 1900b: 280) (cf. pp. 106 and 80).

Bottom. Indian camp on the Klondike River (after Adney 1900b: 451) (cf. p. 86).

PLATE 2

Canoe Model, Copper Knife, Spoons, and Shaman's Stones

A. Model of a man's birch-bark canoe with the prow decked with bark (length ca. 25 inches). Collected before 1880 by E. W. Nelson with the provenience given as Fort Reliance, Yukon Terr. (cf. p. 80) (SI: 38, 880).

B. Copper knife with handle enclosed in two pieces of wood and wrapped with rawhide (length 14½ inches). Collected before 1910 by F. Schmitter at Moosehide, near Dawson, Yukon Terr. (cf. p. 71) (SI: 255, 343).

C. Spoon or ladle of mountain-sheep horn with a shallow bowl and thin, backward-curving handle. The M-shaped designs extending outward from the handle are incised with small lines stained red. Near the end of the handle are encircling grooves stained red (length 54 cm; 21¼ inches). Collected before 1907 by E. E. Stockton at Dawson, Yukon Terr. (cf. p. 73) (NMC: VI-F-3 [VI-G-182]).

D. Spoon or ladle of mountain-sheep horn with a shallow bowl and backward-slanting handle which curves around to almost touch itself at the top. Edges of part of bowl and handle are incised with chevron designs and additional designs between them, all of which are stained red. Geometric designs are cut into the middle section of the handle (length 46 cm; 18½ inches). Collected before 1907 by E. E. Stockton at Dawson, Yukon Terr. (cf. p. 73) (NMC: VI-F-4 [VI-G-181]).

E. Shaman's war stones of bola-like construction made from two stones slightly over 2 inches in length or diameter and 3 ounces in weight. The stones have natural holes and are tied together with a double caribou skin string 17 inches long bound with porcupine quills in red, blue, and mostly white. Collected before 1910 from a shaman named Luke at the Indian village near Eagle, Alaska (cf. p. 64) (SI: 255, 333).

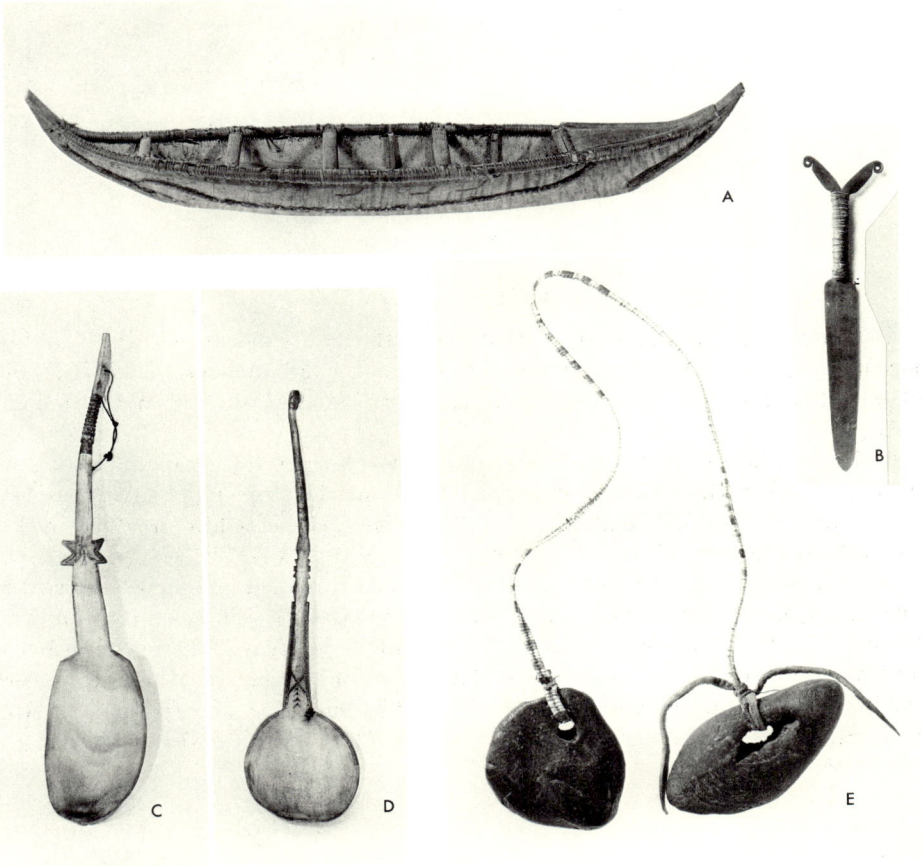

PLATE 3

A. Chief's collar of moose skin decorated with five strings of red, white, and blue porcupine quill work attached lengthwise (length 38 inches). Collected before 1910 by F. Schmitter at the Indian village near Eagle, Alaska (cf. p. 96) (SI: 255, 344).

B. Bag made of jaeger-leg skins and claws with a top strip and bottom of caribou (?) skin, the former edged with ermine fur. The top strip has a floral design in porcupine (?) quills (length 21 cm; 8¼ inches). Collected before 1907 by E. E. Stockton at Dawson, Yukon Terr. (cf. p. 74) (NMC: VI-F-I [VI-G-179]).

C. Beadwork bag formed of small glass beads threaded on sinew and woven to form a netlike mesh fastened to a top band of moose (?) skin laced through with a tanned skin line. The beads are strung by colors to create bands at the bottom, first white, then blue, yellow, and red. There is a top band of red, the beads between the bands being mixed colors (length 25 cm; 9⅞ inches). Collected before 1907 by E. E. Stockton at Dawson, Yukon Terr. (cf. p. 74) (NMC: VI-F-I [VI-G-179]).

A

B

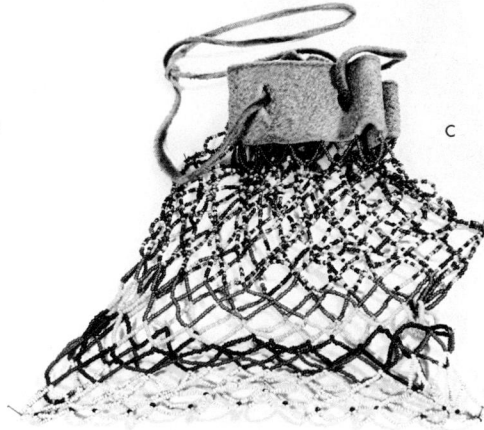

C

YALE UNIVERSITY PUBLICATIONS IN ANTHROPOLOGY

Numbers reprinted by Taplinger Publishing Company
29 East 10th Street, New York, N.Y. 10003

(Nos. 1–7 bound under one cover) Reprinted 1970. $4.00

1. *Population Changes among the Northern Plains Indians*. Wissler.
2. *Regional Diversity in the Elaboration of Sorcery in Polynesia*. Buck.
3. *Cultural Relations of the Gila River and Lower Colorado Tribes*. Spier.
4. *Hopi Hunting and Hunting Ritual*. Beaglehole.
5. *Navaho Warfare*. Hill.
6. *The Economy of a Modern Teton Dakota Community*. Mekeel.
7. *The Distribution of the Northern Athapaskan Indians*. Osgood.

(Nos. 8–13 bound under one cover) Reprinted 1970. $4.00

8. *Profane Literature of Buin, Solomon Islands*. Thurnwald.
9. *An Outline of Seneca Ceremonies at Coldspring Longhouse*. Fenton.
10. *The Shawnee Female Deity*. Voegelin.
11. *Human-Wolves among the Navaho*. Morgan.
12. *Musical Areas in Aboriginal North America*. Roberts.
13. *Rank and Potlatch among the Haida*. Murdock.
14. *Contributions to the Ethnology of the Kutchin*. Osgood. Reprinted 1970. $5.50.
16. *The Ethnography of the Tanaina*. Osgood. Reprinted 1967. $5.00.
20. *Kazak Social Structure*, Hudson. Reprinted 1964. $2.75.
21. *Prehistory in Haiti: A Study in Method*. Rouse. Reprinted 1964. $4.50.
22. *Ingalik Material Culture*. Osgood. Reprinted 1970. $12.50.
32. *A Comparative Study of Human Reproduction*. Reprinted 1964. $2.75.
51. *The Kaska Indians: An Ethnographic Reconstruction*. Honigmann. Reprinted 1964. $4.00.
54. *Kapauku Papuans and Their Law*. Pospisil. Reprinted 1964. $5.75.

(Nos. 57–64, Papers in Caribbean Anthropology, compiled by
S. W. Mintz, bound under one cover) Reprinted 1970. $8.00

57. *The Origins of the Jamaican Internal Marketing System*. Mintz and Hall.
58. *The Convince Cult in Jamaica*. Hogg.
59. *Jamaican Fishing: A Game Theory Analysis*. Davenport.
60. *The Marketing System in Peasant Haiti*. Underwood.
61. *The Entry of Man into the West Indies*. Rouse.
62. *The Spanish Olive Jar, an Introductory Study*. Goggin.
63. *Aboriginal Canoes in the West Indies*. McKusick.
64. *The Significance of Ethnological Similarities between Southeastern North America and the Antilles*. Sturtevant.
66. *Factors Affecting Human Fertility in Non-industrial Societies: A Cross-cultural Study*. Nag. Reprinted 1968. $6.50.

YALE UNIVERSITY PUBLICATIONS IN ANTHROPOLOGY

Numbers reprinted by the Shoe String Press
995 Sherman Ave., Hamden, Conn. 06514

19. *The Peyote Cult*. La Barre. Reprinted 1966. $7.50.
46. *Property, Kin, and Community on Truk*. Goodenough. Reprinted 1966. $6.00.

YALE UNIVERSITY PUBLICATIONS IN ANTHROPOLOGY

Numbers available through the Department of Anthropology
2114 Yale Station, Yale University, New Haven, Conn. 06520

Numbers 33–34 bound under one cover. $2.50.

33. *Ethnography and Acculturation of the Fort Nelson Slave.* Honigmann. 170 pp., 5 figs. 1946.
34. *Notes on the Indians of the Great Slave Area.* Mason. 46 pp., 4 pls., 4 figs. 1946.

Numbers 35–36 bound under one cover. $2.00.

35. *Excavations in the Cuenca Region, Ecuador.* Bennett. 84 pp., 17 figs. 1946.
36. *British Guiana Archeology to 1945.* Osgood. 65 pp., 13 figs. 1946.
37. *Prehistoric Ceramic Styles of Lowland South America, Their Distribution and History.* Howard. 95 pp., 15 pls., 15 figs. 1947. $1.50.

Numbers 38–39 bound under one cover. $3.00.

38. *Northwest Argentine Archeology.* Bennett, Bleiler, and Sommer. 160 pp., 12 pls., 26 figs. 1948.
39. *Lowland Argentine Archeology.* Howard and Willey. 42 pp., 8 pls. 1948.
43. *The Gallinazo Group, Viru Valley, Peru.* Bennett. 118 pp., 12 pls., 27 figs. 1950. $2.00.
70. *The Phonology and Morphology of Ulu Muar Malay.* Hendon. 176 pp. $3.50.
72. *Spanish Majolica in the New World: Types of the Sixteenth to Eighteenth Centuries.* Goggin. 240 pp., 18 pls., 27 figs. 1968. $7.00.
73. *Fengpitou, Tapenkeng, and the Prehistory of Taiwan.* Chang. 279 pp., 107 pls., 95 figs. $12.00.
74. *The Han Indians: A Compilation of Ethnographic and Historical Data on the Alaska–Yukon Boundary Area.* Osgood. 173 pp., 3 pls., 17 figs. 1971. $5.00.